BETRAYAL *of the* SPIRIT

BETRAYAL *of the* SPIRIT

My Life behind the Headlines
of the Hare Krishna
Movement

NORI J. MUSTER

Foreword by Larry D. Shinn

University of Illinois Press
Urbana *&* Chicago

This book is printed on acid-free paper.

Library of Congress Cataloging-in-Publication Data

Muster, Nori J. (Nori Jean), 1956–
Betrayal of the spirit : my life behind the headlines
of the Hare Krishna movement / Nori J. Muster ; foreword by
Larry D. Shinn.
p.   cm.
Includes bibliographical references (p.) and index.
ISBN 0-252-02263-7 (cloth : acid-free paper)
1. International Society for Krishna Consciousness.
2. Muster, Nori J. (Nori Jean), 1956– . 3. Hare Krishnas—
United States—Biography. I. Title.
BL1285.84.M87   1997
294.5'512—dc20
96-4451
CIP

You are the Supreme Lord, to be worshipped by every living being.
Thus I fall down to offer you my respects and ask Your mercy.
Please tolerate the wrongs that I may have done to You
and bear with me as a father with his son, or a friend
with his friend, or a lover with his beloved.
—from the Bhagavad Gita, 11.44

Contents

Illustrations follow page 104

Larry D. Shinn

Foreword

Betrayal of the Spirit is an honest and critical insider's view of the missionary Indian religious movement in the United States popularly called the Hare Krishnas and more formally named the International Society for Krishna Consciousness (ISKCON). It is also a thoughtful religious autobiography by a young woman who joined the Krishna movement in 1978 and assumed a position in the public relations office at the national headquarters in Los Angeles.

Betrayal of the Spirit, therefore, interweaves two narratives. The primary story line unfolds a well-researched account of what has happened to the Hare Krishnas in the United States since the 1960s. The second theme concerns the selective and personal account of a woman who struggles to find religious meaning inside a marginal religious movement. These commingled story lines provide behind-the-scenes glimpses into the inner workings of the public relations office in a sometimes besieged "cult" in the United States and also open a window on how religious meaning is constructed and then abandoned in the midst of such institutional conflict. The two narratives are intertwined with a deftness that provides an uncommonly well-written single story.

The significance of Nori Muster's book is that it represents a genre of religious literature that is too often lacking in our attempt to understand the religious traditions that surround us. As a spiritual reflection set in a religion's institutional context, it is an informed devotee's account of her experiences, which are interpreted from her enmeshed perspective. Muster provides important balance to a number of books that provide scholarly "outsider" explanations of various aspects of the Hare Krishnas, including *The American Children of Krishna: A Study of the Hare Krishna Movement* by Frances Jeanne

Daner (1976), *Hare Krishna in America* by E. Burke Rochford, Jr. (1986), and *The Dark Lord: Cult Images and the Hare Krishnas in America,* which I wrote and which was published in 1987. These studies attempt to understand the social and spiritual dimensions of ISKCON from the points of view of an anthropologist, a sociologist, and a religious studies scholar.

Nori Muster's book is not intended to be scholarly, and to a great extent that represents its strength. Muster does not lead the reader through sociological, psychological, or other such interpretive analyses to explain the movement or her involvement in it, but rather she offers an account of her memory and understanding of the movement and her journey of faith. She describes her role as a public relations officer within ISKCON and discusses not only the main crisis events of the movement but also the Krishna leadership's interpretative framework of denial and sometimes deception and her religious rejection of attempted cover-ups. Scholars and lay persons alike are given the opportunity to look over the shoulder of a strategically placed Hare Krishna devotee.

Muster's account shows that considerable personal and institutional denial took place among Hare Krishnas who were in positions of leadership and had the capacity to stop illegal economic activities or correct religious practices that were unethical by the Hare Krishnas' own standards. More circumspect leadership would have saved the group a half decade of public denial and internal conflict. In one sense Nori Muster's bid for journalistic independence was an attempt to reform the Hare Krishna movement from within. Her major concern was the leaders' deceptive communication style, an issue in the guru reform movement in the United States during the mid-1980s, as well as in the international reform movements that have taken place in Europe and India in the 1990s.

Nori Muster's book demonstrates that some of the public and social expressions of institutional reform often have personal religious origins. Certainly, that appears to be the case in this instance. *Betrayal of the Spirit* is an insider's account that is neither an exaggerated expose nor a personally self-justifying account. Muster's religious struggles reveal the dilemmas that nearly all persons of faith experience as they seek lives of meaning within religious institutions, whether conventional or marginal.

A variety of contexts should be kept in mind when reading *Betrayal of the Spirit.* First, much as a disillusioned spouse looks back on his or her marriage with both longing and regret, so, too, Nori Muster's story provides a selective remembering of her experiences within ISKCON. A quick perusal of chapter titles reads like a list of the major scandals and public relations fiascoes of the Hare Krishna movement in the United States. Therefore, many positive ISKCON news events are passed over for their more negative counterparts. It's not surprising that Nori Muster focuses upon the major critical events in the short life of the Hare Krishnas in the United States; her work in the public relations department often put her in the position of defending or explaining away these embarrassing events. Thus, a potential weakness of the book becomes its strength through an insider's view of how a marginal religious tradition under attack responds to its accusers and often distorts its fundamental purposes in doing so.

Betrayal of the Spirit is the single best source I have read of the crises and errors in judgment made by some Hare Krishnas in the United States that negatively affected the public's view of the whole movement. Although a critical account, it is also a faithful one. Nori Muster found herself in a position within ISKCON that few members have inside religious organizations. She was at the hub of the privileged information flow about activities of a far-flung worldwide movement that during the 1970s had more than fifty communities in the United States. Few inside ISKCON could have written this book, and many who are now devotees will learn much of ISKCON's troubled history by reading Muster's account.

A second context for reading this book acknowledges the differences between personal piety and institutional religion or, at its best, between spirituality and its social expression in religious institutions. In a fundamental sense, this is an autobiography of a person caught up in a rapidly changing religious institution rather than a spiritual autobiography marked by deep theological reflection and ethical struggle. Nori Muster does not provide much insight into the spiritual struggle she obviously underwent initially when she decided to join the Hare Krishna movement. Nor does she fully describe the religious practices, thoughts, and struggles that one would expect in a spiritual autobiography, such as Thomas Merton did in *The Seven Story Mountain*. Rather, the reader is provided with a brief glimpse of why Nori Muster entered the Hare Krishna movement and then is given a series of explanations for events that eroded her rational commitment to the movement.

Nori Muster hints at her continued appreciation of the spiritual path of the Hare Krishnas, a path that has provided a religious home to millions in India for more than four hundred years in its current form. She also introduces the social and institutional dimensions of her disaffection rather than her religious worldview, spirituality, and apostasy. I found the distinction between personal piety and institutional religiosity to be important in describing the various levels of commitment among the more than 150 Hare Krishna devotees I interviewed for *The Dark Lord*. It helps explain why some long-time members of ISKCON, who are aware of most of the information Nori Muster presents, choose to work within the institution and continue to find religious and spiritual satisfaction.

Muster, on the other hand, describes how she struggled with the viability of her faith in the cauldron of institutional conflict focused in the public relations office of ISKCON. Personal and institutional religiosity are never fully separable, and this is true for Nori Muster. Although there is considerable pathos in the story she tells, there is much more she could confide.

A third interpretative framework derives from the stereotypes of ISKCON in the United States. As I have described elsewhere, most lay people understand ISKCON to be a cult. Such an understanding will be confirmed by Nori Muster's presentation of the scandals that the public relations department had to describe and defend. Muster, however, clearly views ISKCON in a broader context.

ISKCON is a Hindu missionary movement brought to the United States in 1965 by a well-meaning and pious Indian businessman named A. C. Bhaktivedanta Swami Prabhupada. The Hare Krishna faith is a traditional Indian religion whose early sacred texts go back more than two thousand years; its present form was shaped in the sixteenth century by an Indian contemporary of Martin Luther. The language of the Krishnas' religious text is Sanskrit, and their dress, food, and social conventions are distinctively Indian.

The shaven-headed Hare Krishnas who dance on the streets of Bombay or Calcutta in orange robes blend into the Indian religious landscape, whereas those same devotees in the streets of New York, Chicago, and Los Angeles are cultural anomalies. Thus, the Hare Krishnas have always lived at the margin of U.S. society and have had no real audience or financial support as do conventional religions. This marginal existence has often led to excesses of behavior that are common in missionary movements around the world. It also allows misappropriation of the religious movement by new converts who have rejected their own religious upbringing, and sometimes their families and culture as well.

As one reads Nori Muster's presentation of events, one can see how this Hindu religious tradition, adopted by those often at the margin of U.S. society, struggled to give root to its spiritual calling in the midst of social and institutional conflict. Nori Muster's story shows how the enthusiastic and charismatic beginnings of the movement gave way to what Max Weber calls "rationalization" as the institutionalization of ISKCON began to take shape. This transition was not complete when the founder of the movement died in 1977. His death led to a period of institutional dislocation that was just beginning at the time Nori Muster joined ISKCON in 1978 and reached its peak in the mid-1980s as six of the eleven appointed successors to the founding guru fell, one by one, from their lofty spiritual and organizational positions. The period Nori Muster describes, therefore, is predominantly the time of ISKCON's institutional reformation in the aftermath of the death of the founder.

After Nori Muster left the movement, reforms continued not only in the United States but also in India and throughout the world. It is not surprising that the Hare Krishnas who experienced major institutional setbacks began to develop mature spiritual and institutional reforms in response to these crises. The third, and broader, context of this volume, therefore, acknowledges the maturation of faith that religious institutions experience over periods of time. Although the Hare Krishna movement in the United States will never be much more than a marginal Indian transplant, it has succeeded in developing strong communities in some cities, as well as in Europe, Asia, and Africa and at the dominant holy sites of India. It is important, therefore, to understand that Nori Muster writes about ISKCON in the United States during the 1980s, not the Hare Krishna movement throughout the world during the 1990s. These are rather different stories.

Betrayal of the Spirit is a delightfully written narrative tapestry that presents a controversial and marginal religious movement in the United States as outsiders—and sometimes insiders—seldom see it. It is ironic that public images of cults take for granted mind control, brainwashing, or some loss of rationality by those who join such movements as the Hare Krishnas. What one finds in the pages of this book instead is a constant reminder that even a devoted follower such as Muster had to defend her new faith constantly, continually raising deep questions that ultimately led to her rejection of the institutional form of that faith. Not all faith struggles take place at the level of theological or ethical reflection. Some, as in the case of Nori Muster, take place at the juncture of institutional religious faith and the world in which it strives to succeed. Muster took her new faith at face value and constantly scrutinized the decisions of the leaders of the movement in terms of the proclamations of ISKCON. This is hardly the behavior of a person debilitated by "thought control," and yet that is exactly how she must have appeared to her friends, and certainly to the anticultists outside the movement during the ten years she was a member.

Muster's experience of faith, doubt, and disaffection has been repeated many times among the Hare Krishna devotees I have interviewed. Each of their stories is different, but all contain the same thread of personal control over individual destiny that is surprising to those who would claim the Hare Krishna and other "cults" diminish their members' critical and rational capacities. Although few of these stories have been told beyond second-person accounts in scholarly books, Nori Muster's narrative provides a clear window into the heart and mind of a young woman attracted to the Hare Krishna movement and who then finds her faith slowly eroding before the inconsistencies and hypocrisies of her public relations work. Because the fear of cults continues to run high in the United States, this book should do a lot to allay concerns about mind control. It portrays a thoughtful young woman who questions her faith, and the movement of which she is a part, throughout her ten years of service.

Betrayal of the Spirit is an indictment of every religious institution that fails to live up to the lofty promises it makes to its members. In *Ascent of the Mountain, Flight of the Dove,* Michael Novak reminds us: "Thus the profound religious struggle . . . is between the human spirit and *all* institutions, between the human spirit and its natural habitat. Institutions are the normal, natural expressions of the human spirit. But that spirit is self-transcending. It is never satisfied with its own finite expressions."

Nori Muster expected much of her new Hare Krishna faith because it promised much. From her vantage point in ISKCON's public relations office, the very spiritual truths and austere living that the Hare Krishnas preached indicted the movement's leaders each time a young guru fell or she was encouraged to bend the truth. Although Muster's may sound like the story of a foreign faith, it also has a familiar ring to all religious adherents as Novak suggests. It is a story worth pondering.

❀

Preface

I met Hare Krishna devotees at a critical time, just when their founder died in 1977. In *The Dark Lord,* Larry Shinn describes this crisis as the "transmission of charisma," a dilemma of passing on authority in an organization that had depended heavily on Srila Prabhupada for leadership. I was a senior in college at the time and moved into the Los Angeles temple the day after graduation. As a devotee of ISKCON, the International Society for Krishna Consciousness, I wore a sari, studied the philosophy, and chanted every day. During the course of my work for the public relations department, I learned about many troubling organizational issues. This book focuses on my experiences in Southern California, and my journals of those experiences fill many notebooks.

Some readers have complained that the title sounds harsh, considering that most Krishna followers are gentle people who observe the principles of celibacy, sobriety, and vegetarianism. Millions have found peace through chanting Hare Krishna, and I believe A. C. Bhaktivedanta Swami Prabhupada brought genuine spirit to the West. The word *betrayal* refers to the attitudes and events that betrayed the spirit. Spirit cannot be harmed, but *Betrayal of the Spirit* is a story I needed to tell.

After the idea for the book came to me in 1987, I began writing at the UCLA Extension Writer's Program. By the end of 1989 I had five hundred pages of notes and memories. I'm grateful to my teachers and friends who read the material and encouraged me to write more. In blending my remembrances with news accounts and basic information about ISKCON, I found it effective to describe some of the events and present others as scenes. The dialogues in this book are my portrayals of exchanges that actually took place. These scenes are written in a descriptive style usually associated with fiction. However, there are no made-up events or characters in *Betrayal of the Spirit.*

I would like to thank the people who took part in the evolution of the manuscript: Dave Schiller/Uddhava, Larry Shinn, Mary Giles, Arnie Weiss, Burke Rochford, John Hubner, Steve Gelberg/Subhananda, Mukunda Goswami/Michael Grant, Anuttama/Geoffrey Walker, Rishabdev/Roy Richards, Madhava Puri, Anaghastra, and Srimad Bhagavatam McKee. I also thank Elizabeth Dulany and the University of Illinois Press for lovingly guiding the book to publication. Thanks also to my family and close relations, lifelong godsisters, and friends who stayed by me.

People in This Volume

The Eleven Gurus

Name	Responsibilities
Bhagavan	Western and Southern Europe, Israel, the United Kingdom, South Africa, and Mauritius (after 1982)
Bhavananda	Australia, New Zealand, parts of India and the United States
Hamsadutta	The Northwestern United States, Hawaii, the Philippines, parts of Asia, Sri Lanka
Harikesh	Scandinavia, Eastern Europe, and the former Soviet Union
Hridayananda	Florida, parts of South America
Jayapataka	The Southeastern United States, Bengal, parts of India, and South America
Jayatirtha	The United Kingdom, Chicago, South Africa, Ireland (before 1982)
Kirtanananda	New Vrindaban (W.Va.), Ohio, co-Governing Body commissioner of Bombay
Ramesvara	Southern California, Colorado, Hawaii, and Japan (after 1984)
Satsvarupa	The Northeastern and mid-Atlantic United States, Ireland (after 1982)
Tamal Krishna	Texas, Oklahoma, Fiji, parts of India, Hong Kong, the People's Republic of China, and the Philippines (after 1983)

The Public Relations Department

Mukunda	Governing Body commissioner, minister of public affairs, *ISKCON World Review* executive editor
Nandini	Public relations secretary, *ISKCON World Review* associate editor
Uddhava	*ISKCON World Review* managing editor
Bhutatma	Public affairs writer, treasurer, general manager
Bill Muster	Media consultant
Arnie Weiss	Media consultant

Also in the P.R. department: Drutakarma, Maharudra, Yasoda-mayi, Navasi, Satarupa, Bharata, Anuttama, and others

The Bhaktivedanta Book Trust (BBT)

Ramesvara Swami	Guru; Governing Body commissioner, BBT trustee, North American BBT president
Mahendra	BBT accountant
Koumadaki	BBT secretary
Radha-vallabha	BBT press general manager (before 1979)
Rajendranath	BBT press general manager (after 1980)
Subhananda	BBT staff writer
Jadurani	BBT artist
Narayana	BBT legal office paralegal

Others

Agnidev	Laguna Beach temple president (1977–87)
Badri-narayan	San Diego temple president, Governing Body commissioner for the Western U.S. Zone (after 1987)
Hari-vilas	Governing Body commissioner for the Bay Area (after 1987)
Panchadravida	Guru appointed in 1982
Ravindra Svarupa	Philadelphia temple president, Governing Body Commission chair (1987)
Sulochan	Outspoken guru reform advocate (murdered in 1986)

BETRAYAL *of the* SPIRIT

1

ISKCON: The Krishnas' International Society

The Hare Krishnas' Western world headquarters is on a residential street in West Los Angeles called Watseka Avenue, just off Venice Boulevard near Culver City. Every weekend the temple holds a gathering, the "Sunday Love Feast," for the congregation. It was a warm summer evening in 1978. I was twenty-two and had been a Hare Krishna for about a month. Dozens of people milled on the sidewalk and more cruised Watseka Avenue for parking places. A loudspeaker atop the temple gift store broadcast the rhythmic, fast notes of an Indian raga over the congregation. I walked up the block, beginning at the church on the corner, past the green, yellow, white, brown, and brick red apartment houses and bungalows. ISKCON owned buildings on both sides of the magnolia-lined street.

Beyond the Krishna community, Watseka Avenue was quiet. Non-devotee neighbors generally ignored the temple. I waited in the shadows at the last Hare Krishna apartment for two old friends, Pam and Diana, who said they would visit. Then in the darkness I spotted a blue Mercedes-Benz with diminutive, blond Pam behind the wheel. I'd known her since 1970. The other woman was Diana, a friend since junior high. The last time I'd seen her was the previous summer, when she invited me to her acting class in Hollywood. Diana's classmate, the yet unknown Arnold Schwarzenegger, imitated a roaring lion at the instructor's request. His performance was one I'll never forget.

I flagged down the Mercedes and directed my friends into the driveway, saying, "Park back here."

I met them under the building, and Diana hugged me and looked me over. "Is that a sari?" she asked. The traditional garment was a single piece of cloth draped all around, covering my head.

"I knew you would like it," I said, noting her soft brown curls falling over her black velvet vintage dress and black leather vest. Pam was barefoot, wearing cut-off jeans and a skimpy halter top, and she looked like an underfed model.

"Let's go to the temple," I suggested, hoping to show them the Radha-Krishna deities I worshipped. My friends were vegetarian and they both liked music and art, so I felt sure they would appreciate the temple. As I led them down the crowded sidewalk, the music blared louder, many hearty conversations adding to the clamor. The services had ended, and people poured from the temple to locate their shoes and go off to look around.

"Do you want to see inside?" I asked my friends.

"Not if I have to take my cowboy boots off," Diana said. "You don't know what a hassle that can be."

"I just want to sit down somewhere," Pam said, turning away from the crowd.

I didn't want to force my new enthusiasm on my guests, so I led them back to the building where they had parked. My office upstairs was a convenient, quiet place to talk. We went up the steps in a narrow hallway, and I loosened a key from the chain around my neck to let us in.

"Does someone live here?" Pam asked, glancing inside one of the rooms as she followed me to the kitchen.

"No one's here," I said, turning on the lights. We stopped at my desk, which was wedged into the hall. House plants hung everywhere and sat on all the tiled counter tops. My boss liked to keep them around for atmosphere.

Pam and Diana sat in comfortable conference room chairs, while I sat on the edge of my desk. "How do you like it? This is where I work," I said.

"I don't get what you do here," Diana said.

"This place is creepy," Pam said. "You don't belong here." Her usually dreamy eyes had become serious and compassionate. "Did they make you give them your money? What about your car?"

"I use my car for my service," I said, my heart suddenly pounding, "and money is material. They didn't make me give it to them—I wanted to because they use it to serve Krishna."

Diana and Pam looked at each other. "Oh sure," Pam said.

"Come on, what's happening Nori?" Diana asked.

"You seem so different," Pam said.

"People are worried," Diana added. "Think about how your old friends feel."

"We're going to get something to eat," Pam said. "Can you come with us? Will they let you out for one night?"

"But they're serving dinner at the temple," I said, feeling dizzied by their onslaught.

"That food smelled awful," Pam said.

"Please come with us," Diana said.

Both of them looked at me, and there was a silence.

"But this is my home now," I said, gripping my desk. "I'm here because I want to be. I like to start the day by seeing Krishna, and I like to meditate. I don't take drugs anymore, and I have a good job. This is my life now."

They gazed at me while I talked on.

"Haven't you ever wondered what it's all about, or why we're here? I always wanted to know if life had a purpose. Now I know that I'm a soul, that I'm meant to serve God. I don't have to search anymore because I've found it." I caught my breath and waited, hoping they might approve.

"It's stuffy in here," Pam said after an uncomfortable silence. She turned to Diana and said, "Let's go."

I sighed and hopped down from the desk. As I followed them back to the carport I tried to explain myself again, but they didn't want to listen. I walked alongside as Pam backed the Mercedes out of the driveway. The top was down, so when we reached the sidewalk she stopped and took my hand.

"Call me," she said. "I hate to see you fuck up your life in a place like this."

"You don't want to be a Hare Krishna. Think about it," Diana added.

Pam sat there, the radio blaring louder than the ritual music from the temple, and then she squealed out of the driveway and roared off into the darkness of Watseka. I watched until the taillights faded. I hoped my friends would come back someday, but feared I'd lost them forever.

"I can't believe a nice girl like you has friends like that," someone behind me said.

I turned quickly to see who was speaking. It was the temple president, who had been standing nearby. I was sure he totally misunderstood me. A lot of devotees thought I was naive and innocent when I joined, but it was just the sari that made me look that way. I'd been on my own for eight years, since my parents' divorce. When my mother moved to Phoenix, Arizona, to marry my stepfather in 1970, my brother moved with the family. Even though I was only fourteen, I refused.

I couldn't live with my father that year because he traveled continuously for business. As president of Greene Line Steamers of Cincinnati, he and vice-president Betty Blake had to defend the *Delta Queen* steamboat against congressional Safety at Sea legislation that would have put it out of business. They executed an ingenious P.R. campaign to "Save the *Delta Queen*" and win a congressional exemption from the legislation. Thousands greeted the Mississippi paddle wheeler when it passed through river towns, its calliope playing. The *Delta Queen* made headlines throughout the year because it seemed the boat was doomed to retirement. My dad and Betty were always in the news, especially in the river towns. An estimated quarter of a million Americans signed petitions and wrote to legislators, and the boat won a last-minute reprieve, signed into law December 31 by Richard Nixon. The campaign kept my father too busy to pay attention to me.

Rather than live with either parent, I moved in with a family in the San Fernando Valley that was also going through a divorce. The children smoked pot, took harder drugs, and used the house for parties whenever their mother went away. I don't know if it was the case all over Southern California or just in my parents' circle of friends, but by the time I joined my blended family in Phoenix three months later it seemed as if every adult in the world was getting a divorce. I was glad to be living with my family again but regretted that it didn't include my father.

The 1960s and early 1970s were times of social change and experimentation. Writers Allen Ginsberg and Alan Watts and Harvard researchers such as Timothy Leary believed that LSD could open doors to religious experiences. Some people thought their experiments should have stayed in the laboratory, but hundreds of thousands of others tried LSD. At age fifteen I was one of them. The drug opened my mind to questions about the nature of reality, especially the possibility that I had lived before. Unfortunately, I had no one with whom I could talk, and I became confused. For the next six years I pushed the questions out of my mind with antispiritual drugs such as alcohol, cocaine, codeine, and prescription tranquilizers.

When I was twenty, in my junior year of college, a renewed spiritual longing surfaced. Just when my history professor had us read St. Augustine and parts of the Bible, I became fascinated with religion and spiritual identity. Along with my school books, I began reading metaphysical and Eastern philosophies. Then an internal alarm clock went off, telling me to give up drugs, become vegetarian, and practice celibacy to progress on the spiritual path. I left Humboldt State University for the University of California, Santa Barbara, where I believed my destiny would find me.

At first I had trouble making friends because it seemed all the students used alcohol or drugs. Then I met Phillip, a mystic Christian who worked at the Starlight Bookstore. I took a class there and ended up spending time with Phil, discussing God and the purpose of life. He suggested that I look into Krishna consciousness because my beliefs sounded similar to theirs. He met some Hare Krishnas a few weeks later and asked them to open a "preaching center," a missionary outpost, near the UCSB campus. Soon they did.

I had seen the saffron-robed men chanting on Hollywood Boulevard and in Trafalgar Square in London and had bought an occasional *Back to Godhead* magazine at the airport. Their books were in the UCSB library, and I read one passage that said that just by seeing a pure devotee one could experience "ecstatic symptoms" such as standing of the hair, shivering, laughing, and rolling on the ground. I wanted to find out whether that was true. I couldn't wait to meet a devotee face to face.

When the preaching center was about to open with a Sunday feast, Phillip asked me to go early and make the Hare Krishna visitors feel welcome. Their place was half-way between my apartment and campus, so I walked to the address and knocked. A man with white Indian clothes and a shaven head answered. He had a steady, strong gaze and a contented smile. "Yes?" he said.

Maybe it was my imagination, but I felt an inner excitement, a recognition, a deja vu that filled me with expectation. He told me his name was Radha-vallabha, but I could call him Radha. Then he asked me to wait in the living room while he finished preparing the food. The apartment was almost completely bare except for a makeshift altar draped with cloth, a bookshelf with Hare Krishna books, and a wicker basket of tambourines and brass cymbals. Although it was ordinary and empty, light filled the apartment along with the smells of food, incense, and fresh flowers, and harmonious music played on a portable cassette player. I listened to the gentle conversation and joking of the men in the kitchen as they worked.

Several cars full of Hare Krishna men and women pulled up, then Phillip and his friends from the bookstore arrived. Suddenly the bare apartment was alive with conversation and laughter. Radha-vallabha sat down in the living room and started playing brass cymbals, chanting Hare Krishna. Everyone joined in, singing responsively. I had heard the mantra in the musical *Hair,* in George Harrison's song "My Sweet Lord," and on another album called *The Radha-Krsna Temple,* so I happily chanted along. After the meditation came food and a philosophical talk.

The women in my hatha-yoga class had warned me that Hare Krishnas were chauvinistic, so during the question-and-answer period I made sure to ask how women were viewed within the group. Radha-vallabha, who gave the lecture, enthusiastically explained that because men and women were eternal spirit souls, sparks of God's energy, they were completely equal. I believed that too, so I was glad his explanation was so simple. After the lecture he told me that he was the general manager of the Bhaktivedanta Book Trust (BBT), the organization's publishing arm. Everyone I met that night

worked for the BBT Press as proofreaders, Sanskrit experts, production managers, secretaries, typesetters, or graphic artists. They told me it was a multimillion-dollar enterprise and gave me one of their paperbacks, a lecture by
their guru.

The devotees got out a movie projector and showed a film about the
worldwide International Society for Krishna Consciousness (known by its
acronym of ISKCON) organization's temples, schools, and rural communities. Their guru Prabhupada had become a fixture of the hippie scene in New
York in 1966, and from there ISKCON spread all over the world with more
than 108 branches. Prabhupada, a descendant in a line of gurus in India, carried on an ancient tradition of Krishna worship and already had disciples in
his homeland. After the movie I talked to Radha-vallabha and Phillip for
another hour. Radha-vallabha said he'd been wanting to open a preaching
center for some months, but it took that extra nudge from Phillip to make
him do it. We all agreed that the center would be successful because of the
university nearby.

Walking home that night, I thought about the devotees and decided that
they were great. They seemed serious about their spiritual practices and happy in their alternative life-style. They told me they followed four regulative
principles: no meat-eating, no intoxication, no illicit sex, and no gambling,
which meant they were the friends I was hoping to meet. I was also interested in the BBT. Their publications were completely professional, with color
illustrations of oil paintings produced by devotees at the BBT art department
in Los Angeles.

Radha-vallabha and his friends drove up every weekend for the Sunday
feast through the fall. I didn't know why, but they stopped coming in November. I thought it could be a lack of interest from the college students, but
then I read in the newspaper that their guru Prabhupada had died.

Whenever I walked to class I stopped at the preaching center to knock on
the door and peer in the window before continuing on my way. Fall became
winter, and the first quarter was almost over. Then one day while riding the
bus to school I saw some Hare Krishna men in front of a market. After class
I went to the preaching center and knocked.

"Hare Krishna," said the man who came to the door. "Who are you?" I
didn't recognize him, either. His eyes were dark and penetrating. He wore
saffron robes and had short black hair and glasses.

"My name is Nori. I used to come here for the Sunday feast."

"I'm Subhananda. But today is Wednesday. Why have you come today?"

"I want to learn more about Krishna consciousness," I said.

He invited me in. There were several men in the apartment, but Subhananda and I sat in the living room undisturbed. He told me his service was to write for the BBT and that he had written the introductions to some of Prabhupada's books. He also assisted college professors who wanted to study the organization. He said his guru had given him an order to write a book on the psychological aspects of devotion, and he planned to stay in Santa Barbara to write.

"I want to ask you something," I said, taking a deep breath. "I read in the *Los Angeles Times* that your guru died. Is that true?"

Subhananda's smile faded. "My friends and I have just come from India. We were with Srila Prabhupada when he left his body."

Prabhupada was eighty-one and had been frail from many months of illness. Death had come on November 14, 1977, so recently that it had only been a matter of days. Subhananda read from his journal notes about Prabhupada's passing: "For several minutes there was complete pandemonium. Devotees lay on the ground sobbing or, blinded by tears, wandered aimlessly, wailing and crying unashamedly, falling into walls and into each other. The sadness was monumental, but there was also exultation. We'd witnessed, after all, a cosmic drama. To the loving eye of a disciple, Prabhupada had left his mortal body in a blaze of glory: a triumphant warrior exiting the battlefield, a sage departing to distant lands."

Subhananda read to me for a long time. Within his candid manner I felt his deep sadness and believed that what he had witnessed and written about was a rare, mystical event. The great soul Prabhupada had left his body in Krishna's birthplace, Vrindavana, transcending this material world of darkness and duality.

When Subhananda's friends moved on, he stayed to write his book, and I went to see him every day. In our after-school sessions he read to me from the BBT books and taught me to chant mantras. These practices were the basis of an ancient religion called Vaishnavism, the religion Prabhupada knew from childhood. Vaishnava refers to Vishnu worship, and the religion is based on mantra meditation. Some of the BBT books were translations of Sanskrit mantras that were meant to be chanted. The *maha-mantra,* or "great mantra," was "Hare Krishna, Hare Krishna, Krishna Krishna, Hare Hare, Hare Rama, Hare Rama, Rama Rama, Hare Hare," and it could be sung in *kirtan* to many different tunes. Subhananda taught me to play along on cymbals, tapping them together in a one-two-three beat.

He also taught me to chant *japa*, repeating the *maha-mantra* using beads like a rosary. Radha-vallabha had given me a string of wooden *japa* beads and a cloth bag in which to keep them that could hang around my neck. Chanting the whole string of 108 beads takes about eight minutes and is called "one round." Initiated devotees vow to chant sixteen rounds, or about two hours' worth daily. I started doing one round a day, and Subhananda encouraged me to increase gradually. *Japa* was a particularly meaningful meditation for me. After reciting the mantra a few times, the beginning and end join together to form a continuous loop: Hare Krishna, Hare Krishna, Krishna Krishna, Hare Hare, Hare Rama, Hare Rama, Rama Rama, Hare Hare. Hare Krishna, Hare Krishna, Krishna Krishna—and so on. In a state of deep contemplation, the mantra becomes a direct link to God. Subhananda taught me that mystical communion was the essence of *bhakti-yoga*, the yoga of loving surrender.

To teach me the solitary meditation, Subhananda had me chant in unison with him, each of us moving our fingers along our beads at the same pace. He called this a *japa* lesson. We usually chanted a round together every day.

"You must chant with utmost concentration," Subhananda said one afternoon.

"Aren't I?"

"You were. But I saw you looking distracted. Try again."

Again we chanted. This time I strained to listen to the mantras, concentrating on each syllable.

"Oh, now you look like you're doing it right," Subhananda interrupted with a teasing voice.

I kept chanting.

"My guru's guru used to say, 'The mind is difficult to control.'"

I stopped chanting and looked at him, wishing he would be quiet.

Subhananda continued, "He used to say, 'The mind is very difficult to control, so in the morning you must beat it with a shoe and at night beat it with a broomstick.'"

"Very interesting," I said, and resumed chanting.

We chanted for a few minutes, then Subhananda said, "I see your mind is wandering again."

"Sorry."

"No, Nori, don't be sorry. The mind is very difficult to control," he said, looking stern. He chanted another mantra, then got up and left the room. When he came back he had a twenty-four-inch mailing tube partially hidden behind his back.

"What's that?" I asked, catching the glimmer in his eyes.

"Someone sent me a poster in the mail. Whenever I see your mind wander I'm going to use this to bring it back. Ready? Chant."

"I can't chant," I said.

"Just chant. I'll watch. If I see your mind wander, I'll use this to bring it back to the mantra."

"How can I possibly chant with you holding that over my head?"

"You'll find a way," Subhananda warned. He teased me by rearing the tube back, as if to threaten me.

"Let me concentrate. I'll get into it."

"My guru's guru said—and I think this is a good way to train you to chant attentively—you have to beat the mind. You'll thank me later."

Unable to stand his taunts, I wrestled the tube away from him and tapped him on the head with it.

He tried to get it back, shouting, "See, it works for me!"

We struggled for control of the mailing tube, forgetting our meditation. Our *japa* lessons often ended with laughter.

As the weeks passed, I learned that Subhananda met devotees at a time when he was searching for spirituality, in part via psychedelic experiences. The devotees in Denver answered many of his questions with references to Prabhupada's books, and he joined their temple, giving up LSD to follow the regulative principles. In 1967 Prabhupada had a talk with Allen Ginsberg about the effects of LSD. Ginsberg thought LSD to have mystical properties, but Prabhupada declared it a "material chemical" and recommended chanting Hare Krishna as the path to enlightenment. Prabhupada's writings provided answers to my questions about the mysteries of God and LSD. I visited the preaching center daily to meditate with Subhananda and listen to him read and explain the philosophy.

2

Unexpected Requirements

During the winter quarter another group of devotees passed through Santa Barbara and asked me to start a *bhakti-yoga* club on campus. Having an official club meant that we could chant and give out BBT literature in front of the student union. I did the paperwork and got my sociology professor and a few students from my psychology class to sign as club sponsors. After the traveling devotees went on their way, Subhananda and I enjoyed our afternoons "preaching" on campus. We brought a string instrument called a tamboura and brass cymbals, spread a rug on the concrete, displayed a Bhagavad Gita, and chanted. When students came over, Subhananda told them about the books that he helped to publish and answered their questions. If no one came by, we simply chanted.

Besides reading, chanting, and preaching, I found myself learning two languages because devotees quoted Sanskrit and Bengali right and left. Everyone had names that meant something in Sanskrit. Subhananda told me his meant auspicious (*subha*) bliss (*ananda*). He taught me dozens of words, phrases, and mantras that joined straight English in both verbal and written communication. "*Jaya, prabhu.* I need some *lakshmi* because I got in *maya* and lost my *chaddar*" (Spiritual victory, esteemed master. I need money because I became materially illusioned and lost my shawl) might be spoken by one devotee to another, and perhaps to a temple treasurer. Anyone could be called *prabhu* (master). It was the humble thing to do.

In another lesson Subhananda told me about the morning program. It started promptly at 4:30 A.M. and lasted until 8:30; four solid hours of worship, meditation, and philosophy. For Subhananda, the morning program was the best part of the day, and he wanted me to appreciate it, too. He taught me how to bow down and offer obeisances, gestures of great respect. Bowing rituals during the morning program could last several minutes at a stretch, including a blessing ceremony called the "jaya om prayers." Obeisances were offered upon entering or leaving the temple, during ceremonies, upon seeing one's guru or the temple deity, and sometimes upon greeting friends. Practicing bowing to each other in the preaching center started as a joke, but he wanted me to learn the etiquette before visiting the Los Angeles temple.

Subhananda explained that ISKCON was based on Vedic culture, an ancient civilization that thrived in India before recorded history. Vedic society was god-centered and agrarian, in perfect harmony with the balance of nature. People worshiped Vishnu (Krishna) and served him in one of four categories: *brahmana* (teacher), *vaishya* (merchant), *kshatriya* (warrior), or *sudra* (laborer). The caste system is a remnant of this ancient culture. Vedic society was blessed when it had benevolent monarchs who were religious and just. The BBT books tell stories of Vedic kings who ruled with loving and generous hearts. *Brahmanas* were advisors who guided society through education and ceremonial rites. People who joined ISKCON were raised to the level of *brahmanas* through initiation, Subhananda explained. Part of the Hare Krishna mission was to recreate the dharma of the Vedic social system, called *varna-ashrama-dharma*. Prabhupada had said that anyone could live a peaceful and productive life with four acres of land and a cow. Rural communities, such as ISKCON's dairy farm in Pennsylvania, were part of the effort to recreate *varna-ashrama-dharma*.

In terms of pure anthropology, I found Vedic culture fascinating. Unfortunately, women remained on the sidelines of the ISKCON utopia. Unless spoken to, they were not to look at men or talk to them. They had no voice whatsoever in social affairs. Subhananda said this was to protect the chastity of the men dressed in saffron, who were practicing celibacy. At the temple, women had to cover their heads with a shawl and their legs with a long skirt or, preferably, wear a sari. Men wore saffron garments of renunciation and shaved their heads as monks. The rules were there for a reason, Subhananda told me. He suggested that even though I was not the type to tempt a celibate man purposely, it would be better if I willingly observed the rules. I accepted his scanty rationalizations about celibacy and renunciation, but they only made sense to me after I read more about the topic in a book by a woman guru from India. She explained that women devotees (including gurus) should be cautious around celibate men to respect their renunciation by having minimal interaction. This made me sad because I gradually realized that Subhananda and I would not be allowed to "associate," be friends, in the temple because of his saffron robes.

Another unexpected twist was that if I wanted to advance on the spiritual path of Krishna consciousness I would have to move into the Los Angeles temple. I didn't want to join anything. I wanted more education, either a master's degree in sociology or paralegal training. Subhananda explained that what I needed most was a guru, because the guru plants a *bhakti-lata-bija* (seed of devotional service) in the heart at the time of initiation. The disciple cultivates the seed, giving it enough light and water in the form of hearing and chanting about Krishna. After the creeper sprouts, the individual must protect it and weed out the delusions of the material world, which could strangle the young plant. Subhananda told me that because of the hazards I could face alone, it would be best to live in a temple with others following the same path.

The really bad news was that I could not have Prabhupada as my guru, at least not my initiating guru. Eleven disciples had become gurus to carry on the tradition, and the guru for Los Angeles was a young man from New York who met Prabhupada in 1970. His name was Ramesvara. I questioned whether an American male from my generation, who had dropped out of college to join ISKCON, could be a pure devotee guru. Still, I kept my mind open because he had been named as a successor to the real guru.

While visiting Subhananda one day I told him of a recurring dream I'd been having: A girl asks one of her professors, "Who is God?" and the professor says, "I don't know." Next she asks her parents, "Who is God?" and they say they don't know. Then she asks a minister, "Who is God?" and he doesn't know either.

Subhananda thought for a moment then said, "The girl wants to know who God is, but it's simple: Krishna is God."

I'd struggled so hard in my life. I'd slipped from the path so often, but now this saffron-clad Hare Krishna man, who had become my best friend, was giving me the answer. It seemed possible that Krishna could be God. I had always wanted God to be a beautiful, loving friend. My parents gave me no conflicting images of God because they were agnostic. It all added up. I had been looking for something specific and couldn't deny that a tangible spiritual presence had entered my life.

Subhananda interrupted my thoughts, saying, "You have so many things to worry about. You always complain about your homework, your professors, your car. You weren't meant to be burdened by all these things. You only have five months left of school. After you graduate, I want you to move into the L.A. temple. What do you say?"

I just stared at him.

"Is that okay?" he said. "All you'll have to worry about is chanting, dancing, and making flower garlands for Krishna. Doesn't that sound great?"

"Give me a minute," I said. I wasn't a subservient woman, and I didn't want an American guru. In addition to more education, I also wanted a career.

"Life could be so simple," he continued, "just serving Krishna. Wouldn't that be great?"

A heavy sigh was my only answer. Subhananda left the room, and I sat there a long time. His voice ran back and forth in my mind as I walked through block after block of student apartments. Once at home I tried reading a book but couldn't concentrate. My situation seemed so monumental: I was at a crossroads where I could choose between a material career and the mystic path. It was as if Subhananda held open a secret door to the spiritual world. Could I turn it down? He was inviting me in, and I had to consider his offer seriously. I decided to calm myself by doing hatha-yoga exercises.

I had quit using cigarettes, alcohol, tranquilizers, and all dangerous drugs but still used marijuana occasionally. I smoked some; it was very potent. When I sat down and stretched, a sense of calm came over me. I held my ankles and rested my head on my knees. As I sat there, a vision of Shangri-la formed in my mind. Among the caves and ancient stone buildings were sages with brown skin, matted hair, and simple, saronglike garments; they were meditating. I asked them, "Who is God?" and they revealed the object of their meditation: a lustrous dark being with black, flowing hair. The figure was dressed in glowing silk cloth, golden bangles, and flower garlands and playing a golden flute. Celestial beings, angels, and demigods offered flower petals and prayers to the vision. Tears of joy came to my eyes because I realized I had an eternal relationship with this god, Krishna.

When my vision faded I made up my mind to begin following the path of strict vegetarianism, celibacy, and sobriety, including prohibitions against tobacco, alcohol, and drugs of all kinds, even caffeinated soft drinks, tea, and chocolate. After my decision, I reached for the Fritz Perls book I'd been looking at earlier. It was the perfect thing to read because Perls, the German gestalt therapist, praised the process of meditation and the spiritual quest. I felt as if he was speaking directly to me.

In one section he instructed a woman to release her anger by shouting and beating a pillow. It may sound crazy, but I put the book down, punched my pillow into a ball, and struck my bed over and over. With each blow I yelled,

"I don't have to do what you say!" "You can't make me become a nun!" and "I don't want an American guru!" The phrases became angry mantras that I chanted over and over as I swung the pillow. At last, I fell down laughing, drained of all fear. I decided to immerse myself in Hare Krishna culture, study Prabhupada's writings, and chant every day. The devotees I met were nice people, and they were my friends. It seemed my destiny to pursue Krishna consciousness. My anger and resistance were gone. Just then the telephone rang.

"Subhananda, hi," I said, gently tossing the pillow aside.

"You feel okay?" he asked.

"Oh, I'm fine now," I said.

"Well, have you thought about moving into the temple?" he asked.

"Oh yes," I said casually. "It's just what I need to do."

In the days that followed I learned that my women's studies seminar required a major term paper. I'd been lucky to get into a limited enrollment class with Christina Safilos-Rothschild, a visiting feminist professor. She approved my idea of writing about the role of women in ISKCON. Subhananda lined up interviews for me at the Los Angeles temple, and we made plans to drive there in my car.

The temple was in a part of town that I knew, not far from the UCLA campus. Apart from the pink church on the corner, it was an ordinary city block lined with apartment buildings. I parked under a shady magnolia tree and stood near my car while Subhananda went inside one of the buildings to find someone. In the still afternoon I could make out the sound of bells jingling in the pink church building. From the opposite end of the block came the sound of children singing. Then I saw them: A dozen boys, all with shaved heads and ponytails and dressed in orange robes, were marching in two lines and chanting in Sanskrit. I leaned against my Datsun, watching the teacher lead them across the street toward the pink building. They stopped at the steps to take off their shoes then disappeared behind tall wooden doors.

Just then I noticed Subhananda with a woman dressed in a sari.

"This is Koumadaki," he said. "She'll take care of you." He took his suitcase from my car and said he would see me later.

Koumadaki and I gathered up my things and walked to her apartment. A Canadian expatriate in her thirties, she was secretary to the guru, Ramesvara. Her apartment was immaculate and bare, like the preaching center. She gave me a key, and we chatted for a few minutes before she went back to work.

After she left, I realized I'd met a professional woman who had taken a little too long a break from her busy office.

I wandered alone into the courtyard, where a beautiful dark-skinned woman had several saris on display for sale. She said she knew Koumadaki. I bought one and asked her back to the apartment to help me put it on. It was six yards of silk that wrapped around like a holy veil, covering me from head to toe.

Now dressed in a sari, I went to the temple. The children had gone, and the room was as silent as a museum. To the side of the altar was a massive golden seat, like a throne, with a gold-framed painting of Prabhupada on its red velvet cushions. Vedic custom provided a sitting place, or *vyasasana*, for the guru, so I assumed Prabhupada must have sat here when he was alive. I stood before the *vyasasana* and meditated on his picture, thinking about his death just three months earlier. I felt grateful that he had come to America, because he brought knowledge of Krishna. After paying my respects, I walked around, examining the framed oil paintings and the notices pinned on a bulletin board. The floors were black, pink, and white marble, and a painted design of lotus flowers and dancing cows adorned the walls. Green onyx columns rose along the sides, and life-sized Hindu demigods seemed to stand watch on narrow shelves above. Overhead murals made a Krishna version of the Sistine Chapel. The devotees had a Vedic temple, and it was the focal point of their community.

The room gradually filled with men, some talking, some humming the *maha-mantra* on their beads, others tuning drums. They were young Americans, but dressed in dhotis, wrap-around pants of a single piece of cloth, and *kurtas,* loose, collarless shirts. Most of the men had shaved heads, with a ponytail called a *sikha.* One of them politely asked me to stand at the back, women's place as Subhananda had already explained.

At exactly 6:30 the doors opened to reveal three brass altars. The marble figures on the central altar were Radha and Krishna, dressed in hand-beaded gowns and draped with jewelry and garlands of pink roses. I thought they were beautiful and wanted to get a closer look. The altar to the left had wooden deities of Lord Chaitanya and Lord Nityananda, incarnations of Krishna and his brother, Balarama. The third altar had Jagannath deities, carved wooden figures with cartoonlike, colorful eyes and exaggerated smiles. They represent Krishna with his brother and sister as they are worshiped in the Indian state of Orissa.

One of the men started chanting a Bengali song I didn't recognize. At first I felt sorry for myself for having to stand at the back, because I had a poor view of the altar. More men crowded into the temple, making it even harder to see.

The chanting grew faster and changed to familiar lyrics, so I sang along. The men danced back and forth across the room. A group of women also began to dance, pulling me by the hand into their circle. I'd never experienced *kirtan* with this much dancing, and I appreciated the women's genuine joy and friendliness. We jumped up and down on the marble floor, laughing and singing Hare Krishna as loudly as we could. Chanting filled my mind with loving surrender, and I forgot I was at the back. When I danced I felt Krishna holding my hands, taking me higher. The *kirtan* lasted half an hour. At the end everyone paid obeisances as a man recited Sanskrit verses for several minutes, the exotic syllables and rhymes cascading over me like cooling water.

After the service, I joined a crowd of devotees who were waiting to go to Hollywood in a yellow school bus. When the bus's doors opened, Subhananda and the other men went to the front, but the women opened the rear gate to climb in, handing up babies and strollers. It seemed an awkward way to board a bus. I didn't like it at all, but no one else seemed to mind. Once everyone was seated the bus jerked forward, and one of the men started a soothing, calm, almost melancholic *kirtan*. I sat next to a woman who quietly fingered her beads, holding her baby her arms, in an obvious struggle to finish her daily chanting.

The bus lumbered east on Venice, then turned north on La Brea and onto Highland Avenue. We drove past my father's office on Santa Monica Boulevard, where I had worked as a receptionist in previous summers. I knew the area well. When we crossed Hollywood Boulevard the bus driver pulled over and let everyone out. I watched the ready-made street parade of flowing orange robes and flowered saris emerge from the bus. The leaders started a familiar beat on their drums, then cymbals and voices joined in. The chanting party started down the sidewalk into a Friday array of neon nightlife.

I noticed that the women patiently waited for the men to go first before joining in at the rear. I found myself walking next to a tall blond woman with a thin silver ring in her nose. Her turquoise sari shimmered in the street lights, making her look like a goddess. If I slowed down, she slowed down too. I felt like she was following me, so I looked at her and giggled.

"We have to walk in two lines," the woman said. "The police don't like it if we take up the whole sidewalk."

"Good idea," I said. We were quiet for a while, and then I asked my partner, "Why do the women always walk in the back? I'm doing a report for school."

"Submission is the ornament of a woman."

"Ornament?" I had never heard it put that way.

"We have the greatest liberation," she continued, "because we're going back to Godhead. Women's libbers will never get out of the material world because they don't know what real liberation is."

I considered her words but couldn't help thinking that total submission was a mistake. I've always found that if I speak up for myself I feel more satisfied. I also thought that making generalizations about feminists was ridiculous because some were probably quite spiritual.

"Anyway, Krishna takes care of us women," she said. We quickened our pace to keep up with the rest of the chanters.

I must have walked this sidewalk a hundred times, I thought as my feet passed over the inlaid metal stars. Despite its fame, I knew Hollywood was a dangerous place where street people outnumbered starry-eyed tourists. Our chanting parade stopped in front of the Chinese Theater, where tour buses lined the curb and people walked around the historic patio looking at stars' handprints and autographs in the cement. My family had taken me to movies at the Chinese Theater when I was growing up. During the 1950s, my father had been a Capitol Records marketing executive, promoting such artists as Frank Sinatra, Nat King Cole, and Duke Ellington. Going to Hollywood was like coming home. A devotee handed me a dozen *Back to Godheads*, glossy color magazines with a picture of Krishna on the cover, and told me to give them away free.

As I hoped, the chanting party continued walking up the block, stopping in front of the Garden Court Apartment Hotel, where Rudolph Valentino, Marilyn Monroe, and James Dean had once lived. There was a dance school in the basement where actresses such as Debbie Reynolds and Jane Fonda had studied. The building was fifty-nine years old, the dance school was still in the basement, and the people who worked in the stately lobby were old enough to remember the early days.

During the summer before college I had stayed there with a musician friend who was trying to get a recording contract. He had his demo tape and photos of his band. We sat in our third-floor room, smoking cigarettes and dreaming of stardom, looking out on a revolving gas station sign, a liquor store, and a Chinese restaurant. He often talked about how popular his band was at the clubs back in Chicago.

Hare Krishna. I stared at the third-floor window that had once been ours, realizing that Subhananda was right, everything is temporary. Love, especially, I decided. The musician and I lost touch after two years, but I had thought that he would become famous and I would know him forever. Instead, I couldn't even say if he had loved me or not. The devotees said real love was

with God, and I believed them. Here I was, my arms full of *Back to Godhead*
magazines, a sober, celibate, vegetarian standing in front of this old landmark.
I felt liberated because I had found love that would last forever. No matter
about the devotees' peculiar customs. I had come for the chanting, the philosophy, and the connection with God. Hollywood was beautiful that night.

When I got home, I unlocked Koumadaki's door and peered in. It was only
10:30, but all the lights were out. I wondered why. There were people sleeping in the room, so I crept silently into my sleeping bag, which someone had
laid out for me with a pillow.

The next thing I knew, Koumadaki was shaking me awake. "It's 4:15, time
to get up! We're going to be late." It was still dark. Shrill music blasted from
a loudspeaker on the wall.

"What in the world is going on?" I said, sitting up and rubbing my eyes.
Subhananda had prepared me, but it was a stirring realization that the morning program happened every morning, even on Saturdays. I got up, show-
ered, and put on a long skirt and shawl.

As we walked through the courtyard, I noticed lights on in most of the
apartments. People streamed from all directions to the temple, robed figures
in the chilly predawn mist. Koumadaki instructed me to leave my shoes outside on the concrete steps and follow her. I felt the cold marble floor on my
forehead, hands, and knees as I offered obeisances. She led me up to the balcony, where she said we would have a better view of the deities. Upstairs were
fifty women, some sitting with toddlers in blankets, others pacing back and
forth chanting *japa*. The room buzzed with a roaring *japa* sound, a concentration of intense energy. I took out my beads and started on my daily vow.

Downstairs, eighty men chanted on their beads, some quite loudly, beating a circular path around the room. I noticed Subhananda in the sea of bald
heads. Each devotee had a mark on their forehead called *tilak,* a U-shaped
symbol representing God's presence within the material body. Several times
a day devotees apply the sacred clay markings, which easily wear off. ISKCON
taught that it was bad luck to enter the temple without *tilak,* so Koumadaki
had marked my forehead before leaving the apartment.

At exactly 4:30 the lights went down, and the altar doors folded open with
clacking sounds. Everyone offered obeisances, so I did, too. The room was
dark except for the lights illuminating the altar. Three priests blew conch
shells to signal the beginning of the ceremony, then a man picked up a drum
and started chanting. The priests offered incense to the deities in slow cir-

cular motions, in a Hindu ceremony called *arotik*. As the ceremony progressed, the priests offered oil lamps, flowers, and scented oils to the deities, then volunteers carried the articles to the rest of the congregation as *prasadam*, blessings. Devotees touched the lamp flame as it went by, then touched their forehead. I also passed my hand through the flame and touched my head. It felt sacred. I didn't know the words to the songs but wanted to soak up the flowing, vibrant energy.

People kept slipping in, so by 5 A.M. there were three hundred adults and a hundred children singing in the temple. Everyone focused on the spotlighted deities, now being fanned with silver-handled yak-tail whisks. When the *arotik* ended everyone bowed, and the priests blew the conch shells again. The overhead lights came on, and, as another song began, the priests closed the altar doors. This was followed by more bowing. The crowd thinned after that, and those who were left resumed the cacophonous *japa* chanting. I sat by the balcony window, watching the sun come up over Venice Boulevard. From seven to eight o'clock there was a lecture, then more singing, dancing, and bowing.

On Sunday morning, after my second day of this schedule, Koumadaki took me to meet someone she described as "Prabhupada's first disciple." As we walked down the block, I noticed children having fun with a ball. I wondered what they were like. Some had been raised on Hare Krishna; they'd never been to public schools. We went up a flight of stairs in one of the buildings, through a hall and into a room, where a man dressed in saffron robes greeted us. He had broad shoulders, large, dark eyes, and a slight gap in his teeth that showed when he smiled. I figured that he was in his thirties.

"Please have a seat," he said, pointing to some comfortable chairs facing his desk. "I'm Mukunda. How do you like the temple?"

I barely had time to answer when Subhananda appeared from seemingly nowhere. "Mukunda has been working on a TV script," he said, taking a chair.

"They called for permission to film at the temple," Mukunda said. "The script was full of misconceptions, but they took a lot of my suggestions. I think it turned out okay."

It was an episode of *Lou Grant*, a drama about the editors at a busy Los Angeles newspaper office. Mukunda explained the plot: One of Lou Grant's colleagues has a son who becomes a Hare Krishna. The parents visit the L.A. temple to see their newly converted son, who is headstrong about his beliefs and alienated from his family. While at the temple, the distraught father meets deprogrammers who say they can get the boy out. As the show progresses, the deprogrammers are revealed as thugs who will kidnap the boy and deprogram him with forceful, violent methods. They choose Lou Grant's house to do the deprogramming, but Lou convinces his colleague that deprogramming is bad because everyone should be allowed to follow their own path. Father and son go for a walk in the rain while Lou Grant throws the deprogrammers out his back door.

We talked about the issue of freedom of choice and then there was a silence.

"I have $2,000," I said candidly. "My father gave it to me to invest, but I'm not sure what to do with it." I wanted to test my new friends because someone at school had told me that Hare Krishnas always ask for donations.

Another silence, then Mukunda said, "Why don't you use it to go to India? ISKCON has a new temple in Bombay. I went there for the grand opening."

He explained that he had flown from Bombay to New Delhi three times to contact *Newsweek* reporters and make sure they covered the story. He went on explaining how the media operated in that distant country. There had been a delay, but the article, "Krishna-by-the-Sea," had just come out on the stands at the end of January.

We talked a while longer, then when Koumadaki and Subhananda had to go back to work, Mukunda invited me for a tour of the community. We walked down Watseka Avenue, stopping to see the artists' studios, the photo lab, and the BBT Press, where I recognized devotees I had met in Santa Barbara. Now they were in their natural environment, preparing their guru's manuscripts for publication. One man showed me the processing machine. Columns of type hung drying on a clothesline nearby. In another room graphic artists stooped over light tables while women at typesetting machines clicked away.

We continued the tour in Mukunda's 1965 Mustang, a donation from a well-wishing Indian family, to see the BBT headquarters, a twenty-five-thousand-square-foot industrial building in Culver City. First, Mukunda took me through the ground-floor warehouse where thousands of cartons of books and magazines were arranged in mazelike aisles. Outside the roll-up steel doors and loading dock was a full-sized truck bearing the BBT logo. This was where the books started on their way to the nation's airports, parking lots, and street corners.

Mukunda and I walked through the rest of the building, including the Spiritual Sky incense factory and executive offices, the ISKCON television studios, the legal department, and the BBT mail order department, where workers fulfilled orders for books, incense, musical instruments, clothing, and other Hare Krishna paraphernalia. At each stop Mukunda introduced me as a student from UCSB who would join the temple after graduation. The men and women I met were sophisticated, friendly, and busy. Some wore Western clothes and hairstyles, some wore Hare Krishna robes and hairstyles, but most dressed in a casual combination of both.

After that, Mukunda took me to a stained glass studio on Venice Boulevard where some devotees ran their own business. From there we had to hurry back to Watseka Avenue to view the First American Transcendental Exhibition (FATE) before it got crowded. The exhibition, built into a room next to the temple, featured clay figures set in dioramas. Devotee artists had traveled to Bengal to learn the art form, and computer-controlled sound, lighting, and robotics had been engineered practically single-handedly by an L.A. devotee. The exhibition started with a diorama of Prabhupada in Vrindavana, India, translating Sanskrit scriptures during the 1950s. Another diorama, "Changing Bodies," portrayed the transformation of the body within one lifetime, from infancy to death, using an array of statues.

Mukunda said that when Associated Press photographer Eddie Adams had recently toured the museum, he asked to photograph the Changing Bodies figures in Topanga Canyon. Devotees hauled the exhibit in a pickup truck, and Adams captured humanity's mortality at sunrise against the ageless backdrop of the Santa Monica Mountains. The exercise provided an eye-catching Sunday color photo feature that also appeared in the Associated Press's yearbook *1977 in Pictures.*

After seeing the FATE museum, I said goodbye to Mukunda and ran back to Koumadaki's apartment to tell her about my day. Sitting on straw mats in her living room, we sipped herbal tea and talked until it was time to go to the Sunday feast. A crowd was already gathering at the temple, including dozens of Hindu families. They were dark, sober, and mysterious, and I noticed that they stood reverently facing the deities during the *kirtan.* They didn't jump and dance, nor did they sing the *maha-mantra* as loudly as ISKCON devotees.

After a lecture on the Bhagavad Gita, everyone sat in rows on the marble floor to wait for the feast. In the commotion to get seated, Koumadaki and I ran into Subhananda, and we all sat together. I asked him why the Hindus didn't dance. He said they liked to worship in a more subdued way, especially through *darshan,* the viewing of the deities. Hardly any Hindus gave up their jobs and homes to move into a temple, he said, but that was okay because they were "householders," and rules for householders were less strict. Subhananda said that Prabhupada wanted the full-time devotees to uphold the most orthodox Vedic customs and monastic life-style in order to build a foundation for a Vedic social system that would last ten thousand years.

Subhananda and Koumadaki explained that some Hindus revered the ISKCON devotees, whereas others considered them novices and neophytes.

Koumadaki added that her boss, the guru Ramesvara, made sure Hindu visitors were well cared for on Sundays. Evidence of the spiritual alliance overflowed on the temple steps in the form of the intermingled shoes of the exuberant ISKCON converts and the more reserved Hindu visitors.

I drove back to Santa Barbara that night and felt lighthearted as I walked to campus the next morning. I'd been attending other spiritual group meetings, but Phillip was right. I felt affinity with the Hare Krishna philosophy and sensed it could answer my yearning for enlightenment.

When Subhananda returned later in the week I went to see him. He was pleased that my first experience at the temple had been positive. The telephone interrupted our conversation. It was Mukunda, who said, "This is Mukunda, remember me? I'm looking for someone to work in the P.R. office. Would you like the job after graduation?"

I said yes without hesitation. Working for Mukunda would be the perfect opportunity to combine a material career with spiritual life, or "dovetail in Krishna consciousness" as the devotees liked to say. My last reason to join the material world had just been blown away. I would have a career in public relations, like my father, and serve Krishna within ISKCON.

As the end of the quarter approached, I prepared to write my "Women in ISKCON" paper. I reviewed the interviews I had recorded with two BBT artists and a BBT photographer. All three women had assured me that Krishna-conscious life was all I dreamed it could be. I'd seen women working in offices, side-by-side with men, and of course there was Koumadaki, who was the perfect role model. My paper concluded that a woman in ISKCON was free to become whatever she wanted.

Instead of doing objective research, I had been looking for evidence that ISKCON would treat me well if I joined. Dr. Safilos-Rothschild wasn't impressed and gave my paper a C. Crushed, I went to see her in her office, where she told me that I didn't get it: Women were considered inferior in Indian culture and likewise in ISKCON. She offered to reconsider my grade if I reexamined my premise. I reworked the paper, but when my report card came she had given me a B- for the course. I had persuasive evidence that most ISKCON women played the subservient role, but I wanted to believe it wasn't true.

3

Going Solo into ISKCON

Subhananda and I were studying together one day when he announced that he would leave Santa Barbara soon to spend a year preaching at the Denver temple.

"I'm sorry to have to leave you, but in spiritual life, everyone ultimately has to fly their own plane," he said. "It's called going solo."

I accepted his philosophical remarks but felt sorry I would lose my friend. In exchange for a year of service, the Denver temple president had offered to send Subhananda to the Mayapur Festival, an annual gathering in India. The pilgrimage marks the appearance of Lord Sri Chaitanya Mahaprabhu, the medieval saint and avatar of Krishna. Subhananda read aloud from Chaitanya's biography and spoke about Chaitanya every day until I understood his need to go.

Chaitanya rejected the caste-conscious brahmins and their dogmatic rules. He preached that anyone of any caste could chant Hare Krishna and attain enlightenment. He and his followers chanted throughout Bengal, immersed in love of God and ignoring the rigid, contemporary religious leaders. Chaitanya later traveled on pilgrimage in southern India, chanting, performing miracles, meeting with scholars, and attracting thousands of followers. He proclaimed that love of Krishna would one day spill over India's borders and the world would acknowledge him as a great religious figure. He predicted a golden age, a ten-thousand-year reprieve from the darkness of the Age of Kali.

Chaitanya's disciples recorded his teachings, and several wrote biographies. His movement branched out until it almost disappeared, but the books provided the basis for a late-nineteenth-century Chaitanya revival. In the early part of the twentieth century, Prabhupada's guru, Bhaktisiddhanta Sarasvati Thakur, founded the Gaudiya-math, a confederation of Vaishnava temples that revered Chaitanya. Although it never succeeded internationally, the Gaudiya-math was influential in India.

ISKCON was the Gaudiya-math's American offspring, started by a single former Gaudiya-math member, Prabhupada. Like their Gaudiya-math predecessors, ISKCON devotees practiced the *arotik* ceremony, studied the scriptures of the Bhagavad Gita and Srimad-Bhagavatam, wore dhotis and saris, chanted in public, and had networks of temple-based communities that published and distributed literature. In 1935 Bhaktisiddhanta predicted that the Gaudiya-math would split into factions and deteriorate after his death. His exact words were, "There will be fire in the Gaudiya-math." He told Prabhupada that instead of fighting over the real estate it would be better to sell the marble from the temple floors and use the money to print books.

Like the Gaudiya-math, ISKCON had a governing board of directors. ISKCON's was called the Governing Body Commission (GBC), and it held its annual meeting to coincide with the Mayapur festival. It was the official time to go over political matters and make resolutions for the coming year for all of ISKCON. GBC meetings were held behind closed doors, but news of the discussions spread by word of mouth to everyone who came for the festival. Subhananda liked to keep abreast of political matters, which was another reason he was determined to go.

I was in the middle of winter finals when it came time for Subhananda to leave for Denver, still, I drove him to the airport and waited with him. The Santa Barbara airport was a one-room building with only a few gates. I could see the airplanes moving around on the runways. It was raining, and Subhananda's flight was delayed.

"Remember one thing," Subhananda told me. "Krishna is God, and Lord Chaitanya is Krishna."

I fidgeted in the plastic chair, distracted by occasional P.A. announcements and people rushing back and forth.

"You're up to eight rounds a day now," he said. "If you increase by just two rounds a week, by Lord Chaitanya's appearance day you'll be chanting sixteen rounds, just like me. Can you do that?"

I promised him I would. The P.A. announced that his plane was boarding.

"Wait," I said, wishing I could keep him from leaving. "You've been reading to me every day from the Srimad-Bhagavatam, but I want to read the whole thing, like you said to do."

"That's a good idea," he said, repeating a lesson he had given a dozen times already. "If you begin with the First Canto, you'll understand Krishna by the time you read his transcendental pastimes in the Tenth Canto. After that, read Chaitanya's biography."

"Please accept my humble obeisances." I put my palms together in *pranams,* a gesture of respect, and looked at him. It was a signal to bow down and offer obeisances before parting.

"Are you kidding? I'm not going to bow on this crummy floor. Look at that floor, Nori."

He smiled, as if wanting to say more or possibly give me a friendly hug, but as a celibate Hare Krishna male he didn't allow himself to do that. Instead, he teased me as I held back my tears.

"You know how many people walk across this floor every day?" he continued. "Do you know what's on their shoes? Let's just say goodbye."

I laughed gently and tried to hide my face behind my bangs as Subhananda and I bowed our heads to offer our obeisances while sitting in our seats. As he walked to his gate, he turned to wave one last time. My spiritual friend was gone.

I drove to the L.A. temple nearly every weekend during spring quarter. Mukunda borrowed an IBM Selectric II typewriter from the BBT so I could do my schoolwork. Back then, the Selectric was a cutting-edge word processor and much better than the one I had at school. I appreciated the extra care Mukunda took for me and looked forward to working for him full-time.

My new boss had dedicated his whole adult life to serving Prabhupada. Mukunda had met his guru in New York in 1966 and, abandoning his prospects as a studio musician, helped open the first temple, a storefront near Greenwich Village. He also became president of the first ISKCON corporation. Once things were well established, Mukunda, then married, asked Prabhupada's blessings to take an extended trip to India. Prabhupada told him it was all right but asked him to start a temple on the West Coast before leaving the country. Mukunda agreed to try, so he and his wife went to San Francisco on the advice of a friend, who also decided to come along. There they met Allen Ginsberg, who already knew Prabhupada from New York. The devotees opened a storefront in Haight Ashbury that served hot breakfast to anyone who showed up. Ginsberg helped plan a reception for Prabhupada at the San Francisco airport, with a hundred flower-bearing hippies chanting Hare Krishna.

Mukunda and his friends arranged a two-hour performance for Prabhupada to chant with sitar and drum accompaniment at the Avalon Ballroom,
along with the best San Francisco rock bands: the Grateful Dead, Jefferson
Airplane, Moby Grape, and Big Brother and the Holding Company with Janis Joplin. Multicolored lights swirled across images of Krishna and Rama,
and despite rules against intoxication, hippies spiked the punch with LSD.
Timothy Leary was there and pronounced it a "beautiful night."

Although he didn't approve of drugs, Prabhupada was pleased with the
reception given the Hare Krishna mantra. Charles R. Brooks has said that "the
swami became a cult hero to most of the hippie community, whether or not
they appreciated the details of his philosophy and the life-style restrictions
that he suggested." Another temple opened in Berkeley, and Krishna consciousness took root in the alternative culture of the Bay Area. Temples soon
opened in Los Angeles, Toronto, and forty more cities.

In 1968 Prabhupada sent Mukunda, his wife, and two other couples to start
Krishna consciousness in London. After a period of doubt and struggle, they
met the Beatles, and John Lennon invited Prabhupada and his entourage to
stay at his Tittenhurst estate for several weeks. Meanwhile, George Harrison
helped Mukunda lease a house on Bury Street in London for the first temple. Harrison then asked Mukunda to make a recording at Apple Records.
Mukunda worked out musical arrangements and brought devotee musicians
to the studio. *The Radha Krsna Temple* came out in 1971, and one of the tracks,
"Hare Krishna Mantra," became a hit in seven European countries. Devotees went on tour and appeared four times on the British music show *Top of
the Pops,* and in Mukunda's words "went from street people to celebrity status. Overnight." Krishna consciousness blossomed, and people all over Europe heard the *maha-mantra.* In 1973 George Harrison donated a twenty-
three acre estate on the outskirts of London, which ISKCON named
Bhaktivedanta Manor. Meanwhile, devotees opened new centers in Germany, Amsterdam, and other European countries. Prabhupada traveled to
Moscow and even initiated a man there.

Mukunda's wife left ISKCON and returned to the United States, but Mukunda stayed to manage the British temples until 1976. That year the Governing
Body Commission passed its first resolution about P.R., possibly in response
to several public relations problems that were already smoldering. For one
thing, *The New York Times* began covering airport solicitation in 1975. The GBC
resolution asked that "ISKCON create a public relations bureau to counter
unfavorable, unfair publicity in the media," naming Mukunda for England and
other men for the United States, Germany, India, and France.

When Prabhupada visited England in 1976, Mukunda asked his blessings to move to Los Angeles to write. Once in L.A., Mukunda started conducting near full-time public relations. He had majored in music in college and had no formal public relations training, but relied on instinct. The prevailing ISKCON wisdom was that the mantra sold itself, so there was little need for a P.R. effort of the kind employed by mundane commercial enterprises. Mukunda went against the grain when he started to use "material" (i.e., professional) P.R. methods such as news releases, telephone calls, and personal visits to reporters. When Mukunda opened his office in L.A., it marked the beginning of ISKCON's organized attempt to communicate directly with the men and women of the media. I was glad to join the effort because I believed that helping Mukunda would be a meaningful way to serve Krishna.

Mukunda was a busy person with little time for filing. He had news clippings stuffed in every drawer and cabinet of his tiny office apartment. When I offered to set up a filing system, he wholeheartedly accepted. Searching through the chaos, I found some articles that were favorable, like a review from the *Herald Examiner* when the well-loved singer Lata Mangeshkar performed at the L.A. temple. An *L.A. Times* report, "Two Hundred Scholars Support Hare Krishna," spoke of a petition for ISKCON's religious liberty. I found another folder about a farm in West Virginia called New Vrindaban, the biggest Krishna commune in the United States.

Besides the good publicity, I also discovered many unfavorable articles, including some about a drug smuggling ring in Laguna Beach, California, that involved a murder by ex-Mafia gangsters. I made a file for the subject, sure that Mukunda had dealt with it in the best way possible. There seemed to be a lot of news stories from Laguna. In one of the kitchen cabinets I found an *L.A. Times* piece about a family that was suing ISKCON for brainwashing their daughter. The girl had joined at age fifteen in Laguna Beach and had been hidden from her parents for a year. Digging a little deeper, I found articles about other people who were either suing or being sued by ISKCON.

The bad publicity didn't set off any alarms, but it wasn't because I had been brainwashed. I had grown up around the P.R. business, watching my father run a variety of publicity campaigns. Among other things, when he worked for Ampex in the early 1960s he and another man marketed prerecorded magnetic tape in order to increase reel-to-reel recorder sales; in the 1970s he and a partner published and promoted the *World Traveler's Almanac* for Rand McNally, and he successfully lobbied the telephone company in California to let people buy their own telephones (he was selling them). Each campaign had its different challenges and setbacks.

His Save the *Delta Queen* campaign was almost defeated in 1970 when an ambivalent U.S. senator accused Greene Line Steamers of polluting the waterways. A reporter, inspired to seek truth, followed the riverboat in a small craft one night. *Delta Queen* cocktail napkins floating in the wake proved to the reporter that deckhands were dumping garbage overboard. My father had a lot of explaining to do to legislators and the media about the embarrassing incident. For better or worse, his example taught me that P.R. means selling yourself out occasionally to defend your self-interest. I naturally gave ISKCON the benefit of the doubt.

Working on the P.R. files was a quick course in ISKCON history. I found a scrapbook from the Public Relations Center, Inc., a firm in Chicago that the devotees had hired in 1975 to publicize Prabhupada's visit there. The scrapbook started with a press invitation to the Chicago Sheraton Hotel, where Prabhupada was prepared to host a press conference. Reporters from the *Chicago Tribune, Sun-Times, Daily News,* and a local television and radio station attended. Instead of the advertised topic, "America's manifold problems of crime, economic difficulties, moral and political degradation, and racial strife," Prabhupada found himself defending an outdated Bengali belief that women are less intelligent than men because their brains are smaller.

Reporter Peggy Constantine began her *Chicago Sun-Times* article, "Forgive me if this story is not well-written. I am a woman. My brain weighs less than a man's and I am not equal in intelligence."

On the air, the local Channel Five News reporter Royal Kennedy (a woman) asked Prabhupada, "If women were subordinate to men it would solve all of our problems?"

Prabhupada, surrounded by male disciples, answered, "Yes. Man wants that women should be subordinate—then he's ready to take charge. Man's mentality, women's mentality—different. So, if the woman agrees to the man and is subordinate, then the family will be peaceful."

Cut to the reporter summing up: "The Swami's ideas about women are based on research done in 1918. I asked him how he could depend on medical statistics over fifty years old. 'They're perfectly reliable,' he said, 'because women's brains have not grown in fifty years.'" Back at the anchor desk, Floyd Kalber said, "An interesting footnote to all this: the swami's story was assigned in our newsroom today by a woman, it was photographed by a woman, it was reported by a woman, and a female producer selected it for this show tonight. That's the news, good night."

I got a shiver reading the scrapbook, sensing the challenges that could lie ahead as a P.R. secretary. ISKCON seemed a clumsy, eccentric organization, prone to making the wrong impression on reporters. Even a professional P.R. company couldn't get the right spin out of its own press conference. I excused Prabhupada's old-fashioned attitudes about women because I was a faithful new follower. The party line in ISKCON was that because Prabhupada knew Krishna, he knew everything else as well. I was swept along. Although I could overlook Prabhupada's comments, I was concerned at the way his puckish white male followers perpetuated the small-brain theory with headstrong conviction. If Prabhupada said it, it must be true. Despite all evidence to the contrary, women were less intelligent because their brains were smaller. Many accepted the notion as literal truth; others took it as analogy. ISKCON members also taught that women's "lower birth" is because in past life they were men who thought of their wives or sweethearts at the time of death instead of thinking of God.

The demeaning stories were a clue to how chauvinistic the organization was, but I didn't see things that way at the time. Despite my parents' atheism, they had passed on their German work ethic and Lutheran self-righteousness to me. I wanted to build a successful career in ISKCON just to prove that a woman could do it. I was already committed and wasn't about to let anyone tell me that being a woman made me inferior.

Easter weekend I visited L.A. to find that Ramesvara, the Governing Body Commission representative and guru, had just returned from the annual Mayapur meeting. On Monday morning devotees gathered to hear him explain what the organization's governing commissioners would do now that Prabhupada was gone. Everyone from the community, as well as devotees living away from Watseka Avenue, crowded into the temple.

I sat in the balcony, peering down through the wrought iron railing and waiting for Ramesvara's entrance. We sang, and when Ramesvara arrived a lull came in the *kirtan* as everyone bowed. The *kirtan* resumed, and someone pulled the microphone to the platform when Ramesvara sat down. He had jet-black hair and piercing, busy eyes. Although I didn't dislike him, I was disappointed at how ordinary the young guru looked. If dressed in different clothes he could have passed for a businessman.

"Hare Krishna," Ramesvara said, tapping the mike with his index finger. He clashed his cymbals together and led another ten-minute *kirtan*. After the chanting he drew the microphone closer and said, "Hare Krishna" again.

"Hare Krishna," the devotees responded.

"This was the first time the Governing Body Commission has met since Prabhupada's passing. It was the first official GBC meeting." He spoke in a heavy New York accent:

> The mood was very, very grave. All of us could feel the weight of responsibility. All the GBC men felt Krishna's and Prabhupada's guidance in the holy land of Mayapur. The GBC members, Prabhupada's designated heirs, have endorsed a policy to explain how the process of initiation will go on in Prabhupada's absence. You may ask what is the qualification of those empowered by Srila Prabhupada to act as gurus? Let me answer with a story: Once during the war, there was a patriotic advertisement that showed a picture of a military uniform. It said, "Just take this uniform and the dress will show you what you have to do." Eleven senior disciples have been given the sacred charge to become gurus, and now they must learn to execute the duties of that post. Krishna will help and guide them from within the heart.

With that introduction, Ramesvara began reading "The Process for Carrying Out Srila Prabhupada's Desires for Future Initiations":

> In May 1977 His Divine Grace A.C. Bhaktivedanta Swami Prabhupada felt that his days in this material world were almost at an end. He traveled to Vrindavana and asked that his leading disciples come and join him. . . . The GBC members met together in Vrindavana and prepared a few last questions to put before Srila Prabhupada. One very important question was how disciples would be initiated into the *param-para* [spiritual line] after the departure of His Divine Grace. When asked this question, Srila Prabhupada replied that he would name some persons who could initiate disciples after his disappearance. Then one day in June he gave his secretary the names of eleven disciples who would be the initiating disciples.

The paper listed them: Bhagavan, Bhavananda, Hamsadutta, Harikesh, Hridayananda, Jayapataka, Jayatirtha, Kirtanananda, Ramesvara, Satsvarupa, and Tamal Krishna.

The Governing Body Commission decreed that the eleven gurus would be treated with the same respect formerly paid to Prabhupada. Disciples would place their gurus' pictures on the altars when they worshiped, and each temple would provide its guru a *vyasasana*, an elevated seat, so disciples could offer *arotik* to their guru along with worshiping Prabhupada. The essay further instructed Sanskrit experts to write mantras of praise for the new gurus' worship.

"The Process for Carrying Out Srila Prabhupada's Desires" specified that new gurus initiate only within their own zones to prevent "delicate situations" of rivalry from developing. Because L.A. was in Ramesvara's zone, he was to become the "transparent via medium" through which Prabhupada's spiritual power would touch me. I already felt a connection through other disciples of Prabhupada, such as Mukunda, Koumadaki, and Subhananda, but they were not gurus. According to the essay, the gurus themselves would determine if and when others could join their ranks. They called it "empowering" new gurus. The essay counseled older devotees to keep their thoughts about the matter "in the mental world" so that new disciples' "faith is not disturbed."

I believed that Ramesvara would make a fine guru. The transition of power seemed to go smoothly, but Prabhupada's death and the resulting zonal guru system were devastating turns of fate. Behind-the-scenes politics were concealed from newcomers like me. I could hardly imagine that the Governing Body Commission's position paper amounted to a bloodless coup, but it did. The gurus claimed the mantle of power and called themselves the "collective body" of Prabhupada. There were severe consequences for any Prabhupada disciple who disrespected the zonal guru system. A scholarly devotee in India had written to one of the gurus to express philosophical points that made him doubt the validity of the system, and then he was silenced and forced out of the organization. His assignment of translating the remaining volumes of Srimad-Bhagavatam passed to one of the gurus. They made an example of him, and the incident chilled the atmosphere for anyone else who wanted to speak out. All ISKCON temples became the gurus' territory. Many people were unhappy with the arrangement that began at the 1978 GBC meeting, but no one could do anything about it.

The spring quarter passed quickly, with school and visiting the L.A. temple on weekends. I usually stayed with Koumadaki, and we became friends. I told her I wanted to wear a sari to my graduation, so she loaned me a beautiful black and gold silk one. She was there for the ceremony, along with my family and another friend from L.A. In the afternoon I took everyone to the preaching center to meet devotees at the Sunday feast. Dad supported my involvement because he was glad to see me change certain aspects of my lifestyle, and he knew it made me happy. He told the rest of the family to let me make my own decisions. After all, I was twenty-two.

The day after graduation I packed my belongings in my car and drove from school to the L.A. temple for the last time. The engine overheated on the freeway, steam blew from the radiator when I parked under the building, and the car wouldn't start when I tried the ignition. I believed Krishna was telling me I had come to stay.

Up until then I had never lived under very strict rules. As a child I was allowed plenty of freedom. My parents were students of Dr. Spock, Parent Effectiveness Training, and followers of the hippie movement. My life at college had also been very casual, but when I moved into the ashram I gave up my freedom. The temple president had set up an apartment for new women devotees, where I moved in with several others. An older, more experienced devotee stayed with us to act as house mother and teach us the rules. I thought Subhananda had already taught me everything, but I soon found out there were thousands of nuances of ashram life I had yet to understand. For example, I had to work out a written "schedule" with my "authority" that would account for every minute of the day. The ashram mother taught us elaborate rules for sleeping, washing, eating, dressing, and just about everything to do with the body. What's more, everyone followed the rituals in a uniform way, just as they would have at a strict parochial boarding school. I tired of it in a few days but then decided I'd better make the best of it because living in the ashram was a big part of being a devotee.

One authority figure suggested that I give up hatha-yoga because exercising the temporary material body was a waste of time. I learned to beware of the many things that could lead to lust, such as eating too much before bed. Lust was the enemy that could send one's soul to hell. Despite the restrictions, men and women mixed all the time—and not just for preaching. To promote chastity, lecturers at the temple constantly reminded us that sexuality was forbidden except in marriage for the purpose of procreation. Natural feelings of attraction were personified as the goddess of illusion, Maya Devi, and women were agents of Maya's charms.

Ashram rituals of cleansing were many because cleanliness, being next to godliness, could drive away Maya. The right hand was considered clean (*suchi*) and the left hand dirty (*muchi*); therefore devotees ate only with their right hands. They taught us to roll our sleeping bags, stack them neatly in the closet, and then wash the floor. After we ate, we washed the floor. To help keep the floors surgically clean at all times, there was a bucket of soapy water and a rag in each room. Walls, counters, baseboards, door handles, telephone receivers, and bathrooms were cleaned on a near daily basis. Cleaning rags were *suchi* or *muchi*. Once a *suchi* rag touched something *muchi*, like a floor, it became *muchi* and could never again clean a *suchi* counter. It was useless to argue that electric washing machines and detergent cleaned all the rags pretty well.

Cleanliness can become an obsession for reasons other than killing germs. For Westerners, all this washing, along with daily reminders about the evils of lust and material desire, reinforced bodily shame. Rather than sort out what was necessary in America, ISKCON disciples were eager and unquestioning students who accepted everything their authority figures told them to do. Once a routine became established, it was cast in stone, especially if it was introduced with the words "Prabhupada said." The American devotees prided themselves on their compulsivity and eagerly taught converts "the standards."

In the context of ashram life, comfortable furniture was considered an unnecessary expense and spiritual impurity. We had a regulation ashram: bare linoleum floors, a simple altar, and no furniture. The bedroom was also completely empty except for the sleeping bags stored in the closet. There was no privacy and no place to keep my belongings. I couldn't adjust instantly. Being naive, on the first day I spread my antique rug on the bedroom floor, hung my clothes in the closet, and set my plants on the windowsills and counters. Throughout college, the rug and plants had been the common denominator for all the places I had lived. The ashram leader wouldn't allow the *muchi* rug. It was old, so I reluctantly threw it in the trash. Another woman whom I trusted advised me to throw away the personal things I kept in a trunk at my father's house: my photographs, poems, journals, and paintings. I gave my books, records, clothes, and other possessions to some devotees for a yard sale, stoically discarding every shred of my material history.

After working full-time in the P.R. office for a week, ashram authorities complained to Ramesvara that I wasn't getting proper training. The temple president then rearranged my schedule and told Mukunda I could only work a few hours a day because I would attend special classes in the mornings and go out every afternoon for street chanting. Technically, the office was independent of the L.A. temple but to minimize friction Mukunda asked me to go along with the arrangement.

The required classes were strict study sessions for memorizing the Bengali songs of the morning program as well as learning to recite the Sanskrit verses of the Bhagavad Gita and Srimad-Bhagavatam. I loved studying but didn't expect the rigid, boot-camp atmosphere. My plants got sick in the sterile environment. I put them in front of a sunny window but came home one evening to find them piled up on a counter after someone had washed the floor. The little friends that I'd watered, talked to, and repotted through four years of college had all died.

4

My Zonal Guru

One summer morning the alarm clock failed to go off, and everyone in our ashram woke up late. We had a good excuse, but I hated being late to anything, even the dentist. The ashram mother reinforced my compulsivity by reminding me that the whole day would be less spiritual on account of missing the conch shell at 4:30 A.M. I could picture the temple room lights dimming and the altar doors opening. The morning prayers were beginning as I waited in line with my towel. By the time I got to the temple room the service was almost over. I went upstairs in the darkness and worked my way to the front of the balcony to catch a glimpse of the deity. Staring into Krishna's loving face, I knew there was no offense. The altar doors closed, and everyone paid obeisances.

When I sat up and peered through the railing again, Ramesvara stood and took the mike. I bowed down again to my future guru. Other aspiring disciples bowed as well. He said he would read the *"sankirtan* scores." The word *sankirtan* literally means "congregational chanting," but Ramesvara told us that selling a book was just like having a *kirtan* because of the chance that the person taking the book would someday chant. Bhaktisiddhanta, the founder of the Gaudiya-math, started this notion during the 1920s, when his disciples distributed books all over India. Christian sects have been doing the same with Bibles for hundreds of years, so it's a well-worn concept. Ramesvara stressed "Lord Chaitanya's *sankirtan* movement" constantly to pressure temple residents to sell books at the airport.

Ramesvara had a core of full-time booksellers called *"sankirtan* devotees," but he could draw twice as many volunteers from the community to make a marathon. He lectured so convincingly that "everyone" go out to preach that even when I was still a college student I went to the airport one day. Some of my new associates at the temple were taken aback and spent hours helping me digest the experience. Some devotees resisted marathons, either because they had too much to do or because they found the experience humiliating. Once a week, Ramesvara honored those who were willing to do it by reading their scores aloud in the temple. "Scores" included money collected and numbers of books given out. To make it seem less materialistic, Ramesvara called the dollar scores "*lakshmi* points." Lakshmi is Lord Vishnu's consort, the goddess of abundance and good fortune. To Ramesvara, *sankirtan* meant that Krishna (in the form of the book) attracts Lakshmi (in the form of the money). In his thinking, this exchange was fundamental to Krishna worship.

"I've calculated the scores from this weekend's marathon," Ramesvara would say, standing with his back to the closed altar doors. "I'd like to read the women's scores first, since they have once again beaten the men in this transcendental competition."

The winners, the women around me in the balcony, would echo "*jaya*," meaning "victory."

Ramesvara, chuckling, would tease them again that they always managed to outdo the men in airport collections. He would unfold a sheet of paper and recite each *sankirtan* woman's score. Like at a high school pep rally, women cheered for their friends who did well. There were thirty full-time *sankirtan* women in the temple (about 10 percent of the community) and fewer than thirty *sankirtan* men, but their combined incomes paid mortgages, bought food and flowers, fueled a fleet of vehicles, and printed more books. "Empowered" book distributors could collect as much as $1,000 a day when the airport was busy.

I wasn't great at *sankirtan* but had to do it occasionally. One time I got "in the fire" at the airport, which meant that selling books became easy. I met several people who wanted a Bhagavad Gita, including one young man who was on his way to India to look for truth. Selling books felt spiritual, as if Krishna was sending receptive customers. Selling the guru's books could be a spiritual experience, and for some it was consistently spiritual, but not for everyone at all times. It could also be discouraging when every traveler said no.

What devotees called "pure book distribution" was a rarified state. They didn't call it "impure" book distribution, but it certainly was impure when collecting donations outweighed the importance of distributing the books. The difference was subtle, but the shift in consciousness significant. Instead of giving, it became taking. Devotees who were self-conscious about their activities found it easier to ask anonymously for the donation. Wigs and

Western clothing helped, but giving away a book meant giving away one's identity. Despite Ramesvara's lectures about the goodness of their activities and the benevolence of Prabhupada's books, some devotees were reluctant to give them away. The BBT solved this problem by taking the money collected on *sankirtan* as "credit" and allocating books to be given away free at more friendly venues such as college campuses.

Traveling *sankirtan,* devotees selling books cross-country, also ran the spectrum of book-focused to money-focused. The Radha-Damodar traveling party, named for the deities they carried, had fanned out across North America, collecting money part time and giving out books and magazines on campuses part time. They were notorious among temple presidents for pirating away hearty male converts looking for adventure. At its peak in the mid-1970s the Radha-Damodar party had six former Greyhound buses, each converted into a traveling temple with deities, libraries of Prabhupada's books, and meditation areas.

Women also did traveling *sankirtan,* but the ones I knew generally stayed at the temple to work Los Angeles International Airport, conveniently just fifteen minutes from the temple. Some women agonized over their quotas. For others, talking to people and selling things came naturally. There was also an element of deception in some of the transactions; it was called the "change up." In the change-up routine a *sankirtan* woman might pin a paper flower on a man's lapel and say, "Hi, sir, I'm giving a flower to all the cutest guys in the airport." Then she might say, "Can you please give a donation to print educational books for college students? Everyone's helping out today." If the man opened his wallet to reveal large bills, the devotee might say, "Oh, sir, I've been collecting all day and I have so many dollar bills I feel like a walking salad bowl. I could change a hundred."

If the man pulled out the bill, the devotee added it to her collection and then started counting back change, slowly. "Five, six, seven, eight, nine. Sir, could you give the rest in charity? It will come back to you a thousandfold." At the L.A. temple, change-up techniques were exchanged in the ashram and demonstrated to all *sankirtan* devotees in a presentation in the temple room. The technique slipped out to other temples, as well.

Even though the L.A. women's team brought in $20,000 a week, they had no real power. Women didn't make decisions for the organization or hold any rank. They could even be mistreated unless a male sympathizer acted as an advocate. Ramesvara was that man for the *sankirtan* women in his zone. It's probably an exaggeration to say that all of them were in love with him, but I knew at least a few who were. He loved them, too, and loved to preach to them.

Ramesvara had been Prabhupada's right-hand man in the publishing business. Under Ramesvara, Prabhupada's translations were printed and sold by the millions. To keep book distributors "fired up," he wrote his *BBT Newsletter,* listing scores from a hundred temples around the world. He called *sankirtan* a transcendental competition and told his distributors that their scores would prove who worked the hardest to serve Krishna. Some worked a little too hard, because *sankirtan* was the basis of bad publicity and some 150 lawsuits, starting in 1975. Part of the problem was that when Ramesvara preached he called suffering souls "karmis," people practicing karma rather than yoga. The word sounds condescending, but most devotees used it. In many situations, at many critical junctures, such snide attitudes toward the outside world defeated the mood of compassion taught by Prabhupada, Krishna, Buddha, and great world teachers from all traditions.

As I became acclimated to temple life, I realized that much of the politics revolved around the allotment of apartment units for offices and residences. Some buildings, and within each building, certain units, were considered better than others. Once admitted to the community, seniority and power determined who got what. The *sankirtan* women were given a great new setup in the fall of 1978, so to save money and free up a spare apartment the temple president moved us new women devotees into the *sankirtan* ashram.

The ashram was large, actually two apartments joined together by installing a doorway. One of the living rooms was a temple and the other was a dining room where we ate our meals sitting on the floor. They gave me a locker and a place to put my bowl on the kitchen shelf. I shared a room with six women; seven more filled the other bedroom, and others bedded down in the living rooms.

The *sankirtan* ashram was strict as a convent, and the leaders were like mother superiors. They removed the bathroom mirrors so we wouldn't commit the sin of vanity by looking at ourselves too much. This was extreme; most ashrams were not as fanatical. Considering their apparent prudishness, it's surprising that only months before the women lived with a male leader, and a different one slept with him each night. This scandalous form of management took place in several U.S. temples, but it did not come from Prabhupada, nor did he know about it. The GBC passed resolutions to ban it in 1977 and 1978. The 1977 resolution said, "Regarding [women's] *sankirtan* parties— Resolved: The philosophy that the man *sankirtan* leader is the eternal husband and protector of the woman in a women's party is rejected. The phi-

losophy of the man *sankirtan* leader as the representative of the spiritual
master—and not the husband—should be preached instead."

Ramesvara was willing to acknowledge the problem in Los Angeles and
put a stop to it. The new *sankirtan* ashram was an experiment. In ISKCON
it was controversial to have women manage anything, but Ramesvara wanted to try it, and it worked. Books kept going out and money kept coming in,
just as it had under the male leader. I was glad Ramesvara let women manage something important, and despite certain drawbacks the situation was
good for me. New devotee training was over, so I could work in the P.R office
from nine to five, five days a week or more.

My first big assignment was to coordinate a summer media campaign for the
Festival of the Chariots, ISKCON's annual parade and festival at Venice Beach.
While Mukunda managed the fundraising drive among former, fringe members, and people at the temple worked to put on the festival, I contacted the
L.A. media with news releases and telephone calls. Reporters were curious
because every major intersection between Venice Beach and downtown L.A.
had thirty-foot banners announcing the festival. Few outside the temple knew
what "Festival of the Chariots" meant. The Sanskrit name is Ratha-yatra.
Ratha means "chariot" or "carriage," and *yatra* means "pilgrimage." It symbolizes Krishna's return to Kurukshetra to reunite with his childhood friends.
Deities of Krishna, Krishna's sister and brother (Jagannath, Subhadra, and
Balarama), are taken on procession down the boardwalk then honored at a
festival of pilgrims, devotees, and tourists. The original Ratha-yatra in Puri,
India, has been celebrated for thousands of years and was a favorite pastime
of Lord Chaitanya in the 1500s.

In 1967, Haight Ashbury devotees staged ISKCON's first Ratha-yatra on
a flatbed truck. In 1970, a disciple named Nara Narayan studied pictures of
the Orissan festival and designed authentic Ratha carts for ISKCON. After a
devotee named Jayananda had a vision of the parade on the Venice boardwalk, a carpenter-devotee (who had been with him at the time) built the carts.
Jayananda had organized many Ratha-yatra festivals, but when he came to
L.A. he was dying of leukemia. Although he could not work due to his cancer, his vision inspired the Los Angeles community to make their Ratha-yatra
festival the greatest one in the United States. Jayananda died peacefully in his
apartment in the courtyard of the green building just weeks before the event.

Prabhupada cannonized Jayananda as the first disciple to achieve perfection by serving Krishna up to the hour of death. Mukunda had known Jay-

ananda for a decade and had been with him to the end. He often spoke of his friend and praised his sacrifice. He wanted to follow in Jayananda's footsteps and always reminded me to pray to Jayananda if there was a setback in the festival preparations.

Because this was only the second annual Ratha-yatra, Mukunda wanted to make the media aware of the event. He planned a press conference at the temple on the day before the festival. He knew it would take an unusual publicity stunt to draw reporters, and then it came to him what that stunt should be. A paralegal at the BBT legal office owned an elephant that he rented out to movie producers and fairs. The elephant was booked for Ratha-yatra that weekend. Mukunda thought that if he could get the elephant to the temple, he could hold a great press conference. My father encouraged him and helped him write press invitations.

On the morning of the press conference temple workers set up tents and tables, householder women prepared refreshments, volunteer office workers photocopied our press materials, and some experienced friends handled the elephant. The first journalists to arrive were from L.A.'s Spanish-language TV station, then a network affiliate van with transmission equipment pulled up. A reporter climbed out and asked, "Where's the elephant?"

Mukunda took the camera crews to see artisans painting the wooden festival carriages in the corner parking lot, cooks loading a forty-foot refrigerated trailer with barrels of eggless potato salad in front of the kitchen, theater troupes rehearsing plays in the temple room, and seamstresses sewing canvas tents for the festival site.

Several newspaper reporters arrived while Mukunda was gone, so I invited them to take press materials while we waited for the elephant. Just then my dad walked up. He and I mingled with the reporters, sampling food and talking. At noon everyone moved to the backyard, where the trainers helped the television reporter onto the elephant's back. Once the camera started rolling, someone handed her a mike, and she said, "Don't dare miss the festival tomorrow. The Hare Krishnas will have three elephants just like this one and they'll be giving rides." After everyone left, one of the reporters used Dad's camera to take a photo of us with the elephant. The beast raised its trunk and screeched just as he snapped the picture.

The press conference was the kind of media coup my father knew well. In 1970, during the Save the *Delta Queen* campaign, Betty Blake had collected seventy thousand signatures on a roll of newsprint and then taken it to Washington, D.C. When she unfurled the petition on the steps of the Capitol Building, more than a few members of Congress and media representatives were there. As a youngster, P.R. people had been my role models, and I truly respected my dad's and Betty Blake's efforts. The *Delta Queen* was the under-dog, a piece of Americana that would have faded from the scene unless they saved it. Hare Krishna was similarly authentic, an ancient strain of Hinduism, transplanted in the West. I believed the *Delta Queen* was a worthy cause and so was ISKCON. My dad must have agreed because he told me that he appreciated Mukunda's elephant press conference.

The next morning the carts looked ethereal, poised in front of the Pacific Ocean like miniature riverboats with wheels. I helped decorate the railings with flower garlands and watched some men hoist thirty-foot-high red, yellow, and blue canopies that billowed like sails in the breeze. At 11:30, the Jagannatha deities arrived in a limousine, and priests raised them onto the carts. The parade started at noon, with three elephants leading a vibrant river of people down the boardwalk for an hour. Devotees chanted the whole route, pulling the carts with heavy ropes while drivers on the carts managed braking and steering.

When the parade arrived at the festival site, a roaring *kirtan* was underway, with electric guitars, bass, and drums. Hundreds of Southern Californians danced, enjoying the music, the sunshine, and the blue sky. There were other stages around the festival site, as well as booths that sold everything from books and saris to slices of watermelon. There were plenty of people; some must have seen our prefestival publicity, while others joined in because they happened to be at the beach that day.

I spent hours walking around with press kits, looking for reporters. In late afternoon I joined Mukunda in the media booth to watch the news on his portable television. The reporters didn't stop by our booth, but they had been to the festival: the Ratha-yatra parade was right there on the local news. It was the first time that something I promoted made it onto television. I felt that the publicity had done itself, it was so easy. In the following days, I picked up copies of half a dozen local papers that covered the parade and festival, and I carefully pasted the articles into a scrapbook. Mukunda was pleased. He told me I could look forward to doing the Ratha-yatra publicity every summer.

After living in the temple for almost two months, I had hardly spoken to Ramesvara, my future guru. Once he stopped me on the street to ask me to do something, but we'd never had a talk about spiritual truth, such as one might expect to have with a guru. Usually the only time I saw him was at the morning program when he read the *sankirtan* scores or led a *kirtan*. According to the Governing Body Commission's instructions, we worshiped him during the second half of the program when everyone gathered at 7 A.M. to greet the deities and offer *guru-puja,* or guru worship, to Prabhupada. If Ramesvara were there, he would sit on his own *vyasasana,* next to Prabhupada, to receive a fresh flower garland and *arotik* worship, just like Prabhupada. The men (including his peers) offered flowers and bowed at Ramesvara's feet, then the women lined up to offer flowers. (In temple ceremonies women demonstrate submissiveness by queuing up behind the men.) We also sang a Bengali song in praise of our guru, Ramesvara.

Sometimes Ramesvara gave "Bhagavatam class," an hour-long part of the morning program based on a Sanskrit reading from the Srimad-Bhagavatam. After reciting the Sanskrit verse, English translation, and commentary, the lecturer speaks on a related topic for the balance of the time. It was a tradition of the Six Goswamis of Vrindavana, sixteenth-century disciples of Chaitanya, but in ISKCON, besides philosophical discussion, ambitious speakers used the class to transmit their charisma, assert their authority, and gain popularity. The fact that women weren't allowed to give Bhagavatam class reinforced their second-class status. It was key to keeping women nameless and faceless at the temple. Ramesvara once said that if a woman devotee was truly chaste none of the men would be able to make the connection between her voice and her face.

Each preacher added his own character to the Bhagavatam class. Subhananda's lectures were humorous, Mukunda's were metaphysical, and Ramesvara's were evangelical. Ramesvara usually included something about the evils of lust. He preached that sex would bind the spirit soul to the material world, even sex between married partners. According to the scriptures, the only exception was for procreation, before which married partners were supposed to chant fifty rounds of *japa* (six hours' worth) for purification. Ramesvara frequently reviewed this concept in his lectures. Homosexuality was another irksome issue for Ramesvara, as it was for many ISKCON men. Some apparently homophobic Bhagavatam speakers could cite scriptural references and offer moralistic arguments ad nauseam. More often than not, the Bhagavatam class became a forum for criticizing and condemning the rest of society.

Ramesvara was a forceful, fiery person. He pressed so hard when signing his name that it left a mark in the table below. His housekeeper told me that he could demolish five toothbrushes a month. When an authority figure like that says something over and over, it sinks in. Most disciples obeyed Ramesvara without question and expected everyone else to do the same by remaining celibate and going on *sankirtan.* Despite many nonspiritual traits, Ramesvara was the leader, and because the GBC backed the system the only alternative for dissidents was to leave—either the zone or the movement. Many left both. For those who stayed, Ramesvara was beyond scrutiny.

Subhananda told me to wait until I was absolutely sure of my faith before taking initiation but gave no hint that the foregone conclusion could be a mistake. He just told me of his own decision to become initiated by Prabhupada, emphasizing the seriousness of the commitment. When I learned of an initiation scheduled for Janmastami, Krishna's appearance day in late August, I wrote to tell Ramesvara that I would like to become his disciple someday but not yet. Mukunda was out of town, and Subhananda had gone back to Denver. A few days after I wrote the letter, Koumadaki came to my office door.

"Ramesvara got your letter. He wants me to find out why you're not ready to be initiated. He said it would be good for you, so you would feel more a part of the community." She was out of breath from running up the stairs.

"He wants me?" I said. "But I've only lived here a few months. Don't I have to wait at least six months?" I was flattered.

"He wants you. Do you want to get initiated or not? I have to tell him." Koumadaki looked like she was in a hurry. As Ramesvara's secretary she usually was.

"Tell him okay. Wait, what about Mukunda?"

"We'll call him. Got to go, bye." Koumadaki sped off, the heels of her sandals striking a staccato down the stairs.

That was all there was to the decision. I had faith it would work out well. The initiation ceremony, called *diksha,* was an ancient ritual to invoke the disciple's link with a succession of gurus called the *param-para* lineage. Every Hindu sect can trace its lineage back thousands of years; ISKCON printed its spiritual ancestry in the frontmatter of *Bhagavad-gita as It Is.* Some Hindus dispute the authenticity of ISKCON's lineage, but all I cared about was being linked with Prabhupada. I had settled into believing that his disciple Ramesvara would provide the connection.

The initiation ceremony takes about two hours. One of the rites is to pass the *maha-mantra* from one generation to the next. To symbolize the transference, the guru chants one round on a new string of *japa* beads. During the ceremony, he gives the beads to the disciple, who vows to chant sixteen rounds and follow the four regulative principles. The guru also bestows a spiritual name meant to guide the disciple's mission. He gave me the name Nandini, meaning "Servant of the Ganges River Who Gives Pleasure to All."

Being in P.R., I figured my mission was to make everyone happy. Not an easy proposition in ISKCON or elsewhere. "Nori" had been my former identity, but now I had to leave it behind. Ramesvara lectured often about giving up our past, sinful lives, and that day I was ready to do it.

After the name-giving ceremony, the second half of the ritual is an *agni-hotra,* literally, "fire ceremony." A priest chants mantras and pours ladles of ghee into a sacrificial fire while initiates recite mantras and throw grains in the fire. Karma is said to be like a seed or a grain that will later fructify into activity. Throwing grains in the ceremonial fire symbolizes burning off one's karma in the fire of knowledge and devotion. Part of the relationship between gurus and disciples in ISKCON is the transfer of karma from the disciple to the guru. Prabhupada said a guru could suffer a bad dream or physical illness for sinful acts a disciple might commit after taking vows. Therefore, following the four regulative principles was even more important after initiation. Cleansed of karma by the fire sacrifice, the initiate who maintains the vows has a clear path, and the initiating guru becomes the disciple's earthly link to God. The disciple humbly serves the guru in the hope of understanding and pleasing God.

I believed in the ritual and felt blessed to take part in it because my family hadn't practiced religious ceremonies when I was growing up. We only went to church a few times a year, and we celebrated Christmas with a tree and presents but little religious sentiment. Temple life offered a full calendar of ceremonies, festivals, and holy days. On these special days, Bhagavatam reciters told stories related to the meaning of the day. With each cycle of holy days in the year, the stories were retold so that everyone could enter into the mythology. I loved the stories of avatars and saints that I had learned so far.

Many people took first initiation and received a spiritual name but then dropped out of ISKCON. For those who stayed, the option of taking "second initiation," usually given a year later, offered a deeper sense of commitment. Second initiates received a silent mantra—a *gayatri*—to chant three times daily and could take on the work of a *brahmana,* or teacher. As *brahmanas,* men could give class, offer the morning *arotik* ceremony, or lead the morning *kirtan.* These were all prestigious positions, and men who could lead these functions were revered for their dedication. These leaders usually progressed up the ISKCON organizational ladder once they were recognized.

Women could cook or care for the deities once they were *brahmanas.* They were respected for these services, partly because they were staying within their role of submissiveness. Everyone respected the priests, called *pujaris* (male and female), because they were directly serving the deity of Krishna.

There was one more level of initiation, available only to men. This was the *sannyas* order, an initiation ceremony that included vows of lifelong celibacy. In India, a man renounced home toward the end of life, leaving his wife a widow under the care of their adult sons. He travels to the holy sites as a pilgrim, dependent on God for sustenance.

Sannyasis had been Prabhupada's constant companions during the final years. Most of them were honest, devoted followers. Unfortunately, more than a few had taken the lifelong vows prematurely. Many had trouble with their celibacy or chanting vows and fell from their positions. ISKCON strayed from the traditional understanding of the *sannyas* order in another important way. The institution covertly allowed men to leave home without providing for their families. When a man became a *sannyasi,* his widow was left dependent on the organization. Some left ISKCON to pursue life as single mothers, whereas others stayed. There was so much abuse of the *sannyas* order that the GBC suspended all *sannyas* initiations from 1978 to 1982, with only a few exceptions.

In its Western incarnation, the religion had developed a stern institutional patriarchy. Devotees in the temples answered to the temple presidents, who were like middle managers, and to the *sannyasis,* who were like cardinals of the Governing Body Commission. The GBC was the executive level, insulated with ministers and secretaries. Within the GBC, only eleven men were gurus; some were also BBT trustees. The more zonal territory a guru controlled, the more powerful his influence. These men had worked hard for their positions, just like executives in any corporation.

The Boardwalk and Park Place of the Governing Body Commission were in the West, and there was a subgroup called the North American GBC, which was a powerful lobby. It was responsible for most of the wealth, because historically the North American BBT, headquartered in Los Angeles, had always been the opulent book publishing entity that tied together the worldwide organization.

The amount of honor bestowed upon leaders made it a status symbol to be a *sannyasi.* Temple presidents were obliged to let a visiting *sannyasi* lead *kirtan* and recite the morning Bhagavatam versus. *Sannyasis* used the title "his holiness" before their names, like the pope of the Roman Catholic Church, followed with "swami" or "goswami," titles of great respect in the Vaishnava tradition.

Prabhupada had designated his own title, "founder-*acharya*" (founder and spiritual preceptor) of ISKCON. He never meant to relinquish the role, but as soon as he was gone, several gurus printed stationery identifying themselves as an *acharya* of ISKCON. Disciples had honored Prabhupada with the title "His Divine Grace Srila Prabhupada." The new gurus used the title by

GBC decree. They also adopted terms of honor. Satsvarupa became "Guru-pada," Bhavananda became "Vishnu-pada," and Kirtanananda became "Bhakti-pada." No one dared use the name Prabhu-pada, which translates as "The Master at Whose Feet All Others Bow," because that would have been too obvious. Guru titles were commonly as many as seven words long, as in "His Divine Grace Srila Kirtanananda Swami Bhakti-pada." Names given in this book have been shortened to their simplest form.

Instead of living as pilgrims, ISKCON *sannyasis* and gurus arranged exclusive dinners, flew around the world on expense accounts, and enjoyed the best accommodations that temples could provide. People bowed to them every day, and they had "servants" to do their errands and housekeeping. Some let their meditational practices go by the wayside as they became stars, charismatic figures on the ISKCON skyline. This led to the phenomenon of "guru groupies" and "*sannyasi* groupies" who were fans of particular leaders. Some of the men welcomed charismatic followers, perhaps to assure themselves that their spiritual practices mattered less.

It was easy to develop a reputation in ISKCON because it was a small world. There were about five thousand full-time members living in the temples in those days, about the population of a small college. Everyone either knew each other or could at least name a few mutual friends. Looking through a stack of *Back to Godhead* magazines was like looking through old yearbooks. Los Angeles was a cosmopolitan place because it was the Western World Headquarters. There were hundreds of residents, and international gurus and *sannyasis* visited constantly. Prabhupada had named it New Dvaraka, after the bustling capital where Krishna once ruled as king. Old Dvaraka sunk into the Arabian Sea thousands of years ago, where divers have identified its remains. The joke was that Los Angeles would someday sink into the sea during an earthquake, hence the name. New Dvaraka was widely known as Ramesvara's domain, base of operations for the publishing enterprise.

Those devotees who were not fortunate enough to live in the upper rungs of ISKCON were expected to at least play by the rules and support the system. *Brahmacharis* were students, new to Krishna consciousness, who take on the same vows of renunciation as a *sannyasi*. They usually go to the airport or work in the temple maintenance department. After an apprenticeship they are allowed to marry and live in household life until the appropriate time for renunciation. For the ordinary follower, entering family life could mean getting a job outside and moving away from the community. Full-time workers were important to the hierarchy, so in ISKCON there was much pressure for a *brahmachari* to go directly to the stage of *sannyas* without stopping to have a family. When a promising *brahmachari* succumbed to female companionship other renounced men considered it a sad occasion. When Subhananda eventually married, I heard whispers of "it's too bad. He would have made a great *sannyasi.*"

An even lower place in the institutional hierarchy was held by the female counterpart of the *brahmachari,* the *brahmachar-ini.* Women were expected to follow the same strict vows of renunciation during their apprenticeship, but the stereotype was that most *brahmachar-inis* couldn't wait to get married because of their attachment to material life. In this scenario, women were criticized for luring formerly renounced men into a life of toil to support a family.

The color of clothing went a long way to indicate a particular devotee's marital status. For men, saffron meant "not married" and "not interested." White meant "already married" or "courting." A change from saffron to white let everyone know there might be a relationship. For women, wearing white (or white saris with colored borders) meant renunciation. A colorful sari meant the woman was either married or open to marriage. As with men, a change from renounced clothing to nonrenounced meant the possibility of marriage. Although the customs seem confusing, within ISKCON they were as effective as wearing a sandwichboard.

Accepting initiation meant that I had fully entered the ISKCON society. It was the single most important thing I could do to fit in, almost like marrying into a family. I was so immersed in the situation that I couldn't see the hierarchy or its effects on those of us who found our identities within it.

5

Jonestown Fallout

Summer ended, and talk around the temple turned to the Christmas marathon. Rumors went around that the L.A. airport might be closed to ISKCON because of bad *sankirtan* practices. Mukunda and Ramesvara spent hours negotiating with LAX officials, finally reaching a compromise. LAX painted red safety lines around the escalators, and ISKCON promised that their solicitors would stay behind the lines and not buttonhole traffic coming off the escalator. It seemed like the compromise would guarantee a great Christmas marathon. Unfortunately, the reputation for aggressive fundraising, combined with a mass suicide in an obscure country on the northern rim of South America, meant a world of trouble from the media.

I didn't hear about Jonestown for a few days because I had been ill, and the ashram managers had a knack for suppressing unfavorable information. When I started coming into the office again there was plenty going on. The media rode the breaking wave of cult news from Guyana with intensity, carrying the public with them. ISKCON had no direct connection with Jim Jones and the People's Temple, but every newspaper article suddenly listed ISKCON in his category. To the world outside, Jonestown, Scientology, the Unification Church ("the Moonies"), the Children of God, and Hare Krishna were all alike. Packets from the news clipping service bulged with articles naming ISKCON as one of a dozen "dangerous cults."

To educate reporters and editors, Ramesvara and Mukunda planned to publish a booklet about ISKCON's authenticity. Subhananda, as BBT staff writer, came to L.A. to work on the project. He spent every day in meetings with Mukunda and Ramesvara. Meanwhile I answered telephone calls and read news clippings in the office. The situation was stressful, and we all needed a break. Mukunda encouraged me to accept my father's Thanksgiving dinner invitation. Devotees were allowed to visit relatives, but usually temple leaders, gurus, and those who trained new devotees conveyed the message that family ties were a distraction from spiritual life. My case was different because Mukunda and my father considered each other colleagues in the P.R. business.

On Thanksgiving afternoon I drove to a vegetarian restaurant on Sunset Strip. Dad was waiting on the covered patio, enjoying a frothy green drink. "Over here," he said, waving to catch my attention. He was wearing a suit because he was on his way home from work.

"Let's get a table inside," he said. "It's cold."

The din of afternoon traffic disappeared once we went in. As I adjusted to the relative darkness, I could hear Indian flute and sitar music. A tall man in pressed white clothes and a turban guided us to a table with a view of the parking lot next door. Followers of another guru operated the restaurant, but beyond the vegetarian connection the place was a Sunset Strip landmark.

"How's business?" I asked my dad once we were seated. His post-production studio was a leader in the emerging Hollywood video industry.

"Going great, really picking up," he said. "We're doing a show about Los Angeles."

A waitress, also a Sikh dressed in white clothes and a turban, brought water and menus. She was a Scandinavian blond with freckles and a pleasant smile. Dad and I opened our menus and studied them.

"You know, we have a new P.R. disaster," I said, tipping my menu back for a moment.

"No kidding?" he said without looking up.

"This crazy guy in South America and all his followers killed themselves with poisoned Kool-Aid. Did you hear about it?"

"All that crap at the airports makes your group look like a cult."

I tried to detect a note of sarcasm or a smile that would indicate that my dad was playing devil's advocate. Maybe he was having a bad day, how did I know? At first he stared gently at his menu without flinching, but when he looked up with his mischievous, fatherly grin, I knew he was inviting me to explore the issue.

"We're not a cult," I said. "We're part of an ancient religion."

Just then our waitress asked if we were ready to order.

"I'll have the lamb chops," Dad said, grinning. When the waitress hesitated, he laughed slightly. "Seriously, I'll have the Thanksgiving special. And refill my lime whatever-this-is." He held his glass up for her to identify.

"I'll have the fruit salad," I said, handing her my menu. As a good devotee I didn't want to eat grains cooked by anyone but a *brahamana,* and I wasn't sure if members of another guru group qualified. ISKCON had strong rules about these things. According to the Vedic medical system, the Ayurveda, we were also supposed to avoid mushrooms, garlic, and onions for various reasons. Devotees partake only of food offerings made to the deity of Krishna. In private kitchens, devotees offer their food by bowing down and reciting Sanskrit prayers. I planned to do the best I could in the restaurant.

When the waitress walked away, I continued, "We're not a cult. Our religion has roots that go back to the fifteenth century. Lord Chaitanya started the *sankirtan* movement, and his disciples' disciples' disciples still live in India. They have temples like ours where they chant Hare Krishna. We even dress like they do. There are 550 million Hindus in the world."

"Nobody in America knows from Hindu," Dad said. "Over here you just look like a bunch of kooks."

I blinked away his criticism. "That's why we have to educate the media. Our booklet will explain that we're a real religion."

"Whoa, wait a minute," he said. "What is a religion, anyway? And what is a cult? You were a sociology major. A cult is just a subculture, a subgroup that sets itself apart, right?"

I nodded.

"Anything could be a cult," he continued. "Stamp collecting is technically a cult. Face it, you guys dress differently, you chant mantras and subscribe to a different set of beliefs."

"Okay, you're right in that sense," I admitted.

I sat quietly for a moment, listening to the hum of conversations around me and the Indian music in the background. I watched the waiters and waitresses run from table to table, carrying plates of vegetarian food. They seemed so efficient, so self-assured, despite their obvious adherence to their Sikh faith. There was nothing wrong with what they were doing, just as there was nothing wrong with what I was doing, I told myself. I was unaware of any corruption in ISKCON and had complete faith in the leadership.

"But Dad, if we admit we're a cult, the media will accuse us of brainwashing people. We'll look like Jim Jones."

The waitress came back and set our plates in front of us. I looked at her religious clothing, then down at my own sari. She smiled at me.

"Everything okay?" she asked.

"Looks good," I said.

"Call me if I can get you anything else," she said, smiling at my father before turning to leave. He had a way with pretty waitresses.

I silently offered my food to Krishna, then started on a green melon slice while I tried to understand Dad's point. Surely we were a cult as he said, but what about the media's definition? Suddenly "cults" had come to mean heinous organizational monsters that stole American children and brainwashed, tortured, and even killed them. Mukunda and Ramesvara thought it would be best to distance ourselves from the concept. I could hardly disagree.

"It's not going to be easy," Dad said, as if reading my thoughts. "Why not just tell the media that although you're a cult of sorts, you're a benevolent cult. Tell them the good things your group does, like getting young people off drugs, giving them some goals in life."

"We want the media to know we're a sect of Hinduism," I said.

"A sect, a cult—they're just labels," he said. "Your leaders are too concerned with the labels. If the media calls you a cult, just show them how good your group is. That will set you apart from the rest."

I thought for a few minutes while I worked on a chunk of pineapple. "They're going to call us a cult, aren't they?"

"Over and over, no matter what you do."

"I wish you could explain this to Mukunda instead of me."

He only smiled. I began to realize that Dad's solution was a paradox that the Hare Krishnas could not yet understand.

That weekend I tried to tell Mukunda the things Dad and I talked about, but the more I pressed, the more he resisted. I realized that the two men had different ways of doing things. My dad had a telephone that he always answered himself at his office and at home. Mukunda never answered the telephone. My dad wanted ISKCON to face the Jonestown cult issue head-on. Mukunda issued a statement accusing the media of "dog-pack journalism," implying that dragging ISKCON into the cult debate was like a random attack of feral dogs. He also tried to add a positive spin to the disaster in his *Public Affairs Newsletter,* a publication offering instructions to temple presidents on how to deal with the media. Mukunda wrote "Keeping Up with the Joneses," leading a call to spiritual arms: "The 'Jonestown Era' of Krishna consciousness preaching has begun! The bizarre and brutal deaths in Guyana have become the news story of the decade. This news is already providing the most spectacular preaching opportunities in the history of Vaishnavism! 1979 will undoubtedly be the biggest year ever for spreading Krishna consciousness in the media. This newsletter will deal primarily with suggestions on how to take advantage of the sudden surge of interest in the Hare Krishna movement arising out of the Jonestown tragedy."

During the Jonestown fallout, Mukunda asked if I knew any famous people who might like to come to the temple for dinner. He and Ramesvara had cooks and an elegant dining room in Ramesvara's quarters for "cultivating" VIPs. It was a new feature of the department, and I was flattered that they wanted to entertain one of my friends. I suggested Art Seidenbaum, an editor at the *Los Angeles Times*. He had been a neighbor in L.A., and I had grown up with his children. I hadn't seen Art in four years, but Mukunda convinced me to show up at his door, dressed in a sari and with my Ratha-yatra scrapbook, and tell him about ISKCON. I gathered my courage and did as Mukunda asked. Art not only agreed to come for lunch but also offered to get us an article in the *Times*.

A week after Art's visit, Ruth Ryon, then *Los Angeles Times* real estate editor, came over with a photographer to do some reporting. Ramesvara and Mukunda showed the journalists around the community and took them to the Pyramid Center for Krishna Consciousness in Topanga Canyon. The custom-built pyramid houses were set on a parcel of land at the end of a winding road in the canyon, with a postcard view of the Santa Monica Mountains. The pyramid residents practiced a regulated devotional life-style, including the morning program and Sunday love feast. Nrsimhananda, the owner and builder, headed ISKCON-TV, producing videos about Krishna consciousness. His wife Mohana, a disciple of Ramesvara, taught at the community grade school on Watseka Avenue.

Ryon's article appeared on the front page of the Sunday *Times* real estate section during the critical period of Jonestown reporting. After quoting the full *maha-mantra*, she explained that devotees, in addition to chanting, had "flourished in Los Angeles and elsewhere in the United States as well as overseas in terms of business ventures and real estate holdings." She described Ramesvara's "kingdom," which included the buildings on Watseka Avenue plus fifty thousand square feet of leased commercial property in Culver City (the BBT warehouse and FATE art studios) and the Pyramid House.

The article temporarily erased all pessimism. We celebrated the victory, and Mukunda enclosed copies with his *Public Affairs Newsletter*. Unfortunately, *Time* and *Newsweek*'s simultaneous front-cover headline "Cult of Death," and images of corpses piled in front of the jungle compound, came out in late November, at just about the same time.

In late December, Subhananda's sixteen-page booklet *A Request to the Media: Please Don't Lump Us In* came back from the printer. The professional-looking pamphlet offered six reasons why ISKCON was not a cult. For example, point one:

> *"The Cults":* Generally recent creations, without definite roots in traditional religious or cultural systems.
> *Hare Krishna:* An ancient and principal denomination of Hinduism (the world's oldest religion), with a long-standing spiritual, philosophical and cultural heritage.

To build a case for ISKCON's authenticity, the booklet quoted professors, psychologists, medical researchers, journalists, and devotees' parents. *Please Don't Lump Us In* concluded with six points for the media to consider, for example:

- When researching or writing, please try to be sensitive to the possibility of personal bias.
- Please get our side, too. It's only fair. We're always ready to speak frankly and openly with members of the news media.
- Please avoid "lumping." Although objective observers usually find many more differences than similarities between the Krishna consciousness movement and other groups, nonetheless we are often found guilty by arbitrary association.

When the booklets arrived, my job was to type cover letters and mail a copy to every reporter and editor who had published an article naming ISKCON as a cult. Mukunda took several cases and traveled to major ISKCON centers around the country. Subhananda returned to Denver.

I spent Christmas Eve with my father and his girlfriend Brit, exchanging gifts and talking into the night. When I showed Dad a copy of *Please Don't Lump Us In,* he said it was a good attempt but warned that the booklet alone would not erase the specter of Jonestown.

I believed public opinion was a pivotal issue for ISKCON. There was so much to do—and so much we couldn't do. ISKCON's ratings were low and out of our control. Hollywood was already joining the fray. Production was underway for *Airplane!* starring Leslie Nielsen, Robert Stack, Lloyd Bridges, and Peter Graves, a film that offered a collection of gags about Krishna airport solicitors. Paul Simon was already producing his movie *One Trick Pony,* with its opening scene of a devotee persistently asking Simon for a donation in the Cleveland Airport.

I felt sorry for the devotees who did *sankirtan* at the airport that winter. A man named Mitch Egan, a restaurant consultant from Burlingame, California, became fed up with airport solicitors and started the FROGS club. The acronym meant "For Repelling Obnoxious Grabby Solicitors." He traveled the nation's airports, distributing metal clickers to as many people as possible. Anyone who took one automatically became a FROGS member. An article on the *Chicago Sun-Times* wire explained, "A person with a toy clicker begins clicking when he or she becomes the target of a solicitor or sees a particularly brazen solicitor trying to rip off somebody else." Others with clickers gather round, distracting the solicitor and ending the transaction. FROGS members harassed *sankirtan* women across the country. I remember seeing one of my girlfriends at the end of a hard day of encounters, frustrated and exhausted. Still, she didn't give up.

Sankirtan revenues were down, and sending out more solicitors seemed to be necessary. Because I lived in the *sankirtan* ashram, some expected me to go to the airport.

"When was the last time you went out?" the temple president asked, stopping me in front of his office one day.

I always cringed at the thought. "Four weeks ago, why?" I said.

"It would be great if you could go out every weekend," he said, smiling. "If you stay away from *sankirtan*, cooped up in that office with all that negative propaganda, you'll forget the real nectar of Krishna consciousness— preaching."

"I'll ask Mukunda," I said—my standard answer to anyone who wanted me to work outside the department. Mukunda was my authority who helped me arrange my schedule and said whether I could work for a different department, including *sankirtan*. The L.A. temple was quite corporate. Every devotee answered to a manager, and all managers answered to Ramesvara. Officially, our department supported *sankirtan*, but I ignored the $100 a week quota they had given me. Some people gladly gave donations and wanted the books, but so many copies ended up in airport trash cans. Considering the bad publicity, it probably would have been wiser for ISKCON to lay low that Christmas.

6

A Spiritual Disneyland

In April 1979, Kirtanananda, the guru for the Krishna commune in West Virginia, announced ambitious plans to turn his rural community into a "spiritual theme park." He wanted to chart a ten-year publicity plan, and when he called the P.R. office Mukunda told him about my father. I'd been a devotee barely a year when Kirtanananda sent tickets for Mukunda, my dad, and me to fly to New Vrindaban for a P.R. consultation.

We landed in Pittsburgh at dawn, and the temple president met us at the gate. He and Mukunda talked all the way to the baggage claim, while Dad and I followed along half-asleep. We claimed our suitcases and got on the highway in a temple station wagon. I fell asleep in the back seat as the car wound its way seventy miles southwest to New Vrindaban, West Virginia. I awoke when the car turned onto a dirt road. We rounded one bend and then another, and there it was, atop a distant emerald green hill: a miniature gold Taj Mahal framed in the morning mist. The building was a monument to Prabhupada and had already garnered national publicity for ISKCON.

We drove into the compound, parked in the center of the community, and the driver got some men to carry our bags to our rooms. We had two hours to rest, then at ten o'clock the guru wanted us to tour the palace. I stopped in my room for a few minutes to wash, then went on to the temple to get some rounds done. In ancient India, greeting the deities was the first business a traveler took care of when they arrived in a new town. I liked to do the same.

The simple, barnlike temple structure had an area outside the door for leaving shoes, and I left mine there and went in. At the altar I paid obeisances to the Radha and Krishna deities dressed in embroidered gowns and garlanded with wildflowers from the surrounding hills. Prabhupada himself had sent these deities from India, and their images appeared in ISKCON's books, movies, and magazines. I had always wanted to see them. A priest worked quietly on the altar, gathering up flowers left during the morning program, while I chanted *japa*.

Just about everyone in ISKCON was aware that the history of New Vrindaban included a 1973 attack on the deities. According to an Associated Press report, six men from a Kentucky motorcycle club broke into the temple during the morning program and "ripped two star-shaped chandeliers from the ceiling, cracked the marble altar, smashed idols and fired pistols into the air." Four devotees were wounded, and two suspects were arrested but a grand jury would not indict them. One of the men was looking for his fifteen-year-old daughter.

The deities had beautiful, delicate features, but scars of the attack were still visible. New Vrindaban itself bore scars because media suspicions of weapons stockpiling hung over the commune from that time onward. I didn't know of any weapons anywhere in ISKCON, and I certainly didn't suspect that a community so obviously absorbed in glorifying Prabhupada would ever host a criminal enterprise.

At exactly ten o'clock I stepped out of the temple, into the morning light, and saw my father walking down the path from the residence hall. He was a hearty traveler who had visited many countries. He always wore a hat and carried his bulging camera bag with extra lenses, film, and filters.

"Did you get any rest?" he asked me, stopping at the temple door.

"No, did you?"

"Sure did," he said, setting his bag down.

We both spotted Mukunda walking toward us with another man who used a cane to maneuver his way down the path. It was the guru, Kirtanananda. He and Mukunda had known each other since 1966, when Prabhupada became a feature of Manhattan's Lower East Side. Both men had been eligible for initiation at the first ceremony. Mukunda went through with it, but Kirtanananda languished in Bellevue Hospital, undergoing psychiatric evaluation. It didn't seem fair; although he was thirty years old he had needed a legal guardian to get him out.

Kirtanananda was the first man in ISKCON to become a *sannyasi*, a position Mukunda was still trying to achieve. He did not have a spotless reputation, though. As soon as he accepted the renounced order from Prabhupada in 1967, he returned from India, grew a beard, and started wearing black vestments. He believed that the saffron robes of the Vaishnava religion didn't have a broad enough acceptance in the United States and told others that Prabhupada had sanctioned the change. Although only a few devotees traded their dhotis for black robes, Prabhupada denounced Kirtanananda, writing at least forty letters on the matter to his disciples in New York. In one he wrote, "It is clear that [Kirtanananda] has become crazy and he should once more be sent to Bellevue. . . . if he is not sent to Bellevue then at least he should be stopped from speaking such nonsense." Kirtanananda and his long-time male companion Hayagriva split from the New York temple and wound up starting New Vrindaban. Within months Prabhupada forgave his repentant disciple, and Kirtanananda began developing Prabhupada's vision for the property, along with more than a few of his own ideas.

"Jaya Srila Bhaktipada!" some nearby disciples shouted before offering their obeisances. (Everyone, especially disciples, addressed Kirtanananda by his terms of honor.)

"Welcome to New Vrindaban," Kirtanananda said with a wry grin. He shook my father's hand. "Want to go for a tour?" he asked, turning toward his Jeep. One of his male disciples dropped a polishing rag to open the doors, remembering to bow down as Kirtanananda hopped in and slammed the door.

As we drove along, devotees on the roadside bowed down at the sight of their guru. We parked in front of the palace, which was still under construction. Its golden dome glimmered in the warm sunlight, and the scent of pine trees filled the air. Bird calls mingled with the sounds of machinery and people working.

"We're almost ready for the grand opening," Kirtanananda explained, tapping the cement foundation with his cane. The workers acknowledged Kirtanananda's presence by bowing or at least bowing their heads to offer *pranams.* He escorted us around the outside of the building, describing the construction process in his exotic accent. "I think this place picked me," he said, drawing a deep sigh and looking out over the hilly vista. He led us through a portico, where some workers were pouring cement. "This started out as a house for Prabhupada," he said, "but now it's ISKCON's most glorious monument." He took us through several more doors and a hallway, leading us like a hobbit to his magical place, the inner sanctum he called "Prabhupada's room." In the center of the room, sitting on a raised platform, was a life-sized icon of Prabhupada. We paused for my father to take pictures, then made our way back to the Jeep. Kirtanananda drove us to the barn, the dairy, and over the ridge to the proposed construction site of yet another temple. At last we returned to the residence hall, where Kirtanananda escorted us to his private quarters. All of us, including my father, sat on mats and flat pillows, while Kirtanananda sat on a white cotton futon that took up most of the room.

"Now that you've seen the palace and know what we have to offer, we can get down to business," Kirtanananda said.

"Not much competition in this state," Dad said. "I believe you could become a major tourist attraction. You could set up bus tours, go to travel conventions, get a package deal with the local Holiday Inn."

"We're planning a theme park with a monorail connecting the sections, like a spiritual Disneyland," Kirtanananda said.

"You could use that phrase, 'Spiritual Disneyland,'" Dad said.

"We thought it was an East-Meets-West thing," Mukunda added. "What about 'Krishnaland'?"

I sat quietly and listened.

"You need to think of a name people can relate to," Dad said.

"We were kicking a few ideas around," Mukunda said.

"One of the things we're thinking about," Kirtanananda said, "is 'Prabhupada's Palace of Gold.' What do you think, Bill?"

"Prabhupada's Palace of Gold, Prabhupada's Palace of Gold," Dad repeated. "Say it a thousand times to the media and then another thousand. It has a good ring to it."

While the men talked, a schoolboy came in and bowed before Kirtanananda. His mother watched shyly at the door, tugging her sari over her face so she could remain unseen. The boy left a flower and a dollar bill on Kirtanananda's feet, but Kirtanananda barely noticed.

At the end of the weekend, my father and I flew home, while Mukunda stayed on the East Coast. During the flight, Dad turned down the steak, opting for chicken when the cabin attendant came around. I thought that was a positive step because we had argued about it on the way out. In a fatherly way, he had advised me to leave him alone to eat whatever he wanted.

"How were the rest of the meetings?" I asked, folding down my tray table.

"Productive," he said. "Your people have a potentially good thing going there."

"Have you ever heard of life membership?" I cautiously explained that some people supported ISKCON with donations, even though they didn't become devotees themselves. It was a subject Mukunda had wanted me to bring up at the right time, because my father donated a percentage of his income to charity every year. Most life members were Hindus, but anyone could join for $1,111. (Odd numbers are popular because they're believed to bring good luck.) Life membership was important to ISKCON, especially in large centers such as London and Bombay.

The metal service cart pulled up to our aisle, and a woman set our meals on the tray tables. My vegetarian plate had a plastic dish of buttery noodles and steamed vegetables, with a side of cantaloupe.

"Looks better than mine," Dad said, opening his plastic utensils. "How did you get that?"

We both ate in silence for a few minutes, then Dad said, "If I donated money, where would it go?"

"Mukunda has a deal with Ramesvara, so whenever he makes someone a life member he keeps the money for our department. It's like *sankirtan*. He's made a few life members already."

"Better than getting it a little at a time at the airport," Dad said. "Well, hell, I'll join."

I was thrilled that my dad was so agreeable. He wrote a check for $111 that night and mailed us $100 payments for the next ten months. His name was later added to a life membership plaque in the Los Angeles temple room. Although a small amount, it was dependable income and helped the P.R. office get started.

Over Labor Day weekend that year, New Vrindaban's grand opening of Prabhupada's Palace of Gold was the media's place to be. As if to prove that a major temple opening, some good P.R. planning, and a little luck work wonders, the palace received favorable reviews on the front pages of *The New York Times* and the *Washington Post* "Style" section. The *Post* article by Lynn Darling began, "Forget limestone, we're talking marble here, two hundred tons of it. White Italian marble and blue Canadian marble, marble walls and marble floors, inlaid with Iranian onyx. Crystal chandeliers, teakwood doors. Stained-glass peacocks. Four pounds of twenty-four-karat gold leaf—a mere $60,000 worth. $60,000?" The article noted that the commune was perhaps two thousand acres and called "Krishnaland." The *L.A. Times* reprinted the *Post* article. *Saturday Review* published an article with an illustration of "Krishnaland" that showed tourists lined up to go in, then coming out the other side as devotees. Mukunda liked that one.

The good news echoed overseas, and Prabhupada's Palace of Gold received positive coverage in India, where the *Times of India, Illustrated Weekly of India,* the *Organiser,* and many other news organizations did stories praising the West Virginia monument. Kirtanananda put many of my father's ideas to work. He eventually printed a color souvenir book, and even the *Delta Queen* offered passengers a bus tour to the palace from a stop along the Ohio River. By the mid-1980s the Palace of Gold was West Virginia's third-largest tourist attraction.

I believed that New Vrindaban was great, but devotees who came from there had strange tales to tell. One former resident said that lax attendance at the morning program meant no food in the communal dining room. Rumors of child abuse dated back to 1974, when a nineteen-month-old boy died from abdominal injuries. The place of women at New Vrindaban was low, possibly the lowest in all of ISKCON. Women who left the *sankirtan* teams told stories of physical and sexual abuse, and despite 1977 and 1978 Governing Body Commission resolutions on the subject they still slept with their male *sankirtan* leaders. Women were considered property, and Kirtanananda believed it justified for men to slap their wives, if need be, as part of the women's training, an idea he later explained on national television. Strange ideas were commonplace in the isolated commune, where every devotee was fixed on the single goal of making the Palace of Gold successful.

My enthusiasm for the palace blinded me to the possibility that Kirtanananda ran the most corrupt zone in ISKCON. Years later my dad told me that he knew something was amiss. He reminded me of the boy who had bowed at Kirtanananda's feet while the mother looked on. Dad called it a "fearsome abuse of power" that a man could accept adoration from women and children without having to acknowledge it.

The L.A. temple was completely different and integrated with the real world, I thought. I easily dismissed rumors about New Vrindaban because Kirtanananda appeared to be a scapegoat for early problems in ISKCON. Besides, New Vrindaban was in the "back hills," and the isolation could account for many things. Living in West L.A., near Beverly Hills and UCLA, gave me a feeling of civilized security. My aunt worked nearby at MGM studios, and I ran into her occasionally when I did errands in Culver City. I grew up in L.A. and believed I had complete freedom to be myself at the temple.

When someone suggested that I flush my radiator to make it stop overheating, I didn't think I would become a spectacle on Watseka Avenue. I was wrong. Every man who passed had something to say. Finally, the temple president sent a woman over to tell me that leaning under my hood was unladylike and would "agitate" the men. In other words, the sight of me holding a hose to my radiator was inconsistent with the dogma that women had best depend upon men for everything throughout their lives.

I had taken a year of auto mechanics in college and did my own car maintenance up until then. I lost my timing light, sparkplug socket wrench, screwdrivers, and set of metric wrenches when we moved the office to a different apartment. I had forgotten them in a kitchen closet. When I went back, the new devotee tenant said she had found the tools and thrown them away. I was disappointed, but it wasn't just the loss of the tools. The incident provided evidence that I didn't want to face: my college professor had been right about women's place in ISKCON.

Having our office in the new location was great though, and I put the problem out of my mind. The P.R. department was given a 1,500-square-foot apartment next door to Ramesvara's BBT headquarters in the green building. We shared a courtyard patio with him, and our back door faced the secretarial room where Koumadaki worked. She and I saw each other every day and did a lot of work together. We became roommates, and the BBT paid my portion of the rent. It was much better than living in the *sankirtan* ashram.

Koumadaki and I were the equivalent of executive secretaries, but we worked for spiritual ideals instead of salaries. She was my best friend, and we talked about everything. Her younger sister in the material world had died from a drug overdose the year before; perhaps I reminded her of her sister.

Koumadaki wasn't afraid to speak up to Governing Body commissioners to voice her opinion, and she did so whenever she felt the need. She knew the men as her equal godbrothers, and they all knew her as Ramesvara's trusted secretary. People said she had "the body of a woman but the intelligence of a man." Sometimes the statement seemed a warning rather than a compliment. If not for her gender she would have gotten much more credit for the publishing work she and Ramesvara did. Most women toiled contentedly, serving their husbands or male authority figures without offering a critique or asking hard questions. That was not her style, nor did I want it to be mine.

7

Drug Busts, Guns, and Gangsters

My first year of doing ISKCON's P.R. had been a challenge, especially because of Jonestown. Mukunda didn't let Jonestown get to him. It probably seemed like nothing, because his first year in ISKCON P.R., 1977, had been much worse, especially October and November of that year.

In October 1977, a former devotee named Robin George (initiated by Prabhupada as Rajanath-devi Dasi) and her mother, Marcia George, filed a multimillion-dollar civil lawsuit charging seven ISKCON branches and two individuals with kidnapping, brainwashing, and false imprisonment. One of the individuals named in the suit was Rishabdev, the longtime Laguna Beach temple president. Rishabdev admitted to helping the girl hide from her parents because she wanted to be a devotee and her parents didn't approve. Any temple president would have done the same in the early days, with little concern for legal implications. In 1977, however, Mukunda found that big lawsuits can draw big publicity. Newspaper, TV, and radio news covered the Georges' initial filing, along with ISKCON's response, but a court date was far away.

November 1977 was memorable for Rishabdev, Laguna Beach, and the P.R. office. In addition to the kidnapping indictment, Rishabdev was indicted for conspiring to murder Steven Bovan, a Newport Beach drug dealer. Rishabdev was not a murderer, but he went on the run to avoid the two indictments. His service in ISCON was to cultivate "congregational members" and get them to give large cash donations to the BBT. He had received encouragement from above, even though his flock happened to include international drug smugglers from the Brotherhood of Eternal Love. The Brotherhood had roots in Eastern spirituality and was associated with Timothy Leary when LSD first became popular during the early 1960s. The Brotherhood tried to instill Eastern philosophy along with the psychedelic drugs its members manufactured and marketed. One former Brotherhood follower joined ISKCON and eventually became one of the eleven gurus. Over the years the Brotherhood had drifted apart, but the few who remained in Laguna Beach made friends with Rishabdev because they appreciated Krishna consciousness. These congregational members gave generously to the ISKCON mission, and Rishabdev welcomed their donations with an open heart. He was the Brotherhood's Hare Krishna mentor and friend on the path. They had their connection with Krishna consciousness, and the BBT had the money it needed to realize its dreams. Devotees seeking private support for their projects flocked to Laguna Beach for the abundant cash that seemed to circulate there.

Rishabdev, the link between ISKCON and the Brotherhood, made the necessary introductions for those who wanted to become smugglers. Despite the moral questions involved in such practices, some devotees willingly risked their freedom for the promise of quick financial independence and the ability to support chosen projects. New couriers had their photos taken with Dridha-vrata, the ringleader, and the photos became their identification cards for the hash oil connection in Pakistan. Dridha-vrata lived and worked outside the temple; the other man involved, Alexander Kulik, was not initiated but had long revered Prabhupada. Their "service" was confidential, of course, because ISKCON prohibits intoxicants, but it would be foolish to say that the Governing Body Commission was completely innocent. "Money is money once it's in the coffer" was the rationalization of those who took the cash.

Hare Krishna men in business suits carried the hash oil through Pakistani customs in hollow plastic typewriter cases. Muslim officials who organized the drug trade didn't know they were helping an American Hindu group that worshiped Radha-Krishna. There was every chance that they could turn against the devotees because of their religion. After landing in Canada and mailing their luggage home, operants returned to Laguna Beach to package the hash oil in baby bottles. Each bottle sold for $11,000, a profit of $10,000 per liter. Those at the top of this pyramid bought expensive properties, customized cars, and made six-figure donations to the BBT.

The drug ring included a restaurant in downtown Laguna Beach, Govinda's, and a money-laundering facility called PDI, short for Prasadam Distribution, Inc., *prasadam* being the Sanskrit word for sacred vegetarian food. Officially, PDI sold "Bionic Bits" snack food and Hawaiian fruit juices, but another activity was pumping money through faltering companies they bought. PDI managers also let other criminal figures launder money in exchange for a cut of the profits.

In late 1977 the devotee-dealers became irritated that some associates were embezzling from PDI. They hired five Italian enforcers who were—unbeknownst to them—members of the federal witness protection program under orders to infiltrate PDI. In time, two of the Italian gangsters grew impatient with Stephen Bovan, a PDI "employee" who owed them money. They urgently wanted Bovan to pay so they could reimburse federal agents for fronted cocaine. To raise money, Bovan kidnapped Alexander Kulik and extorted $100,000 in ransom from PDI, but instead of paying his debt, he kept the money. The protected witnesses reacted by shooting him nine times in front of a Newport Beach restaurant. Local law enforcement officials solved the case in a matter of days when they found the getaway car, a customized green and white Cadillac convertible, for sale in a used car lot. High-powered attorneys helped clear the devotees of murder charges; the two notorious protected witnesses disappeared before the trial.

When the case broke, the media assumed that ISKCON was running a drug ring. One paper even carried an article that tried to link Kulik with the BBT. Ramesvara and Mukunda issued press releases and held what the Orange County *Daily Pilot* dubbed a "barefoot press conference" inside the Laguna Beach temple. Ramesvara had just appointed a new temple president to "purify" the atmosphere and drive drug dealers away. Agnidev, originally from Trinidad, had been serving in the New York temple as a cook and *kirtan* leader. Although Agnidev had never managed a temple before, Ramesvara believed that he was the right man for the job because of his integrity and honesty. The press conference was a panel discussion that included Mukunda, Ramesvara, Agnidev, two ISKCON lawyers, and a Hindu life member, who all attested to ISKCON's benevolence, its roots in India, and its innocence of any crime. As a result, the *Daily Pilot*'s headline read "Krishnas Disavow Link to Newport Beach Slaying," and the *Los Angeles Times* followed with "Hare Krishna Officials Deny Link to Four." Despite ISKCON's efforts to distance itself, however, *The New York Times*'s account was headed "California Slaying Case Involves Ex-Mafia Figures and Krishnas."

In the media flurry that followed, Ramesvara characterized the Laguna drug ring as a "splinter group" and filed federal trademark suits against PDI and Govinda's Restaurant. He accused PDI of violating ISKCON's "Hare Krishna Movement" trademark and "Govinda's" service mark. He told *Daily Pilot* reporters that Rishabdev was a "self-styled guru" who twisted the philosophy to justify his illegal activities. Reporter Michael Paskevich described Ramesvara's maneuver as "an attempt to erase alleged links between the Hare

Krishna movement and murder suspects." Weeks later, the *Los Angeles Times* published a four-page round-up, "Mystics and Mobsters: Focus on a Curious Alliance," by Evan Maxwell, who detailed the twists and turns of the case chronologically.

Agnidev succeeded in clearing drug smugglers out of the ashram, but Laguna Beach was more than just a temple. The former members came to the Sunday feast dressed in their devotional clothes to chant in the *kirtans*. They acted and talked like most other devotees and seemed respectable to anyone who didn't know what they did for a living. There was a gray area, and the media smelled blood. It was true that the Krishna consciousness movement had followers who were black-marketeers. Some were more devotee than crook. Others perhaps used ISKCON, just as criminals who are Roman Catholic might use their church. Such people might make large donations to enhance their respectability or assuage their guilt. Some may even visit the confessional and, wishing to reform, make themselves over with religion. Hare Krishnas believe that the power of the Holy Name is great enough to bring about such a salvation, and Prabhupada wrote to ask the PDI devotees to earn a living by honest means.

It's doubtful that anyone told Prabhupada what was happening in Laguna Beach that winter. He was terminally ill in India, preparing to leave his body. Other problems were developing, too. Certain *sannyasi* leaders were grabbing power and enforcing their own rule as the guru's health dwindled. When Prabhupada died in November, ISKCON was slipping into disarray. It was a devastating year for ISKCON's public image, and yet few within the organization knew of the troubles. There was only one story on everyone's mind by the end of 1977: Mukunda and Ramesvara wrote Prabhupada's obituary and distributed it to the media. *Yoga Journal* and *Rolling Stone* published heartfelt condolences; major news media noted his passing.

I looked over the old clippings and filed them, so I was aware that the drug murder had taken place just when I met the devotees in Santa Barbara. It never occurred to me that dealing was still going on, but yet another drug bust happened five months after Dad and I returned from New Vrindaban. For the second time in two years, authorities arrested Rishabdev, Dridhavrata, and others in Laguna Beach. This latest bust, an undercover operation of the Drug Enforcement Agency (DEA), happened in November 1979, just in time for the first anniversary of Jonestown. The *Orange County Register*

announced the news on its front page with the headline "Krishna Hash Bust: Eleven Indicted in Orange County Crackdown." Similar headlines appeared in the *Los Angeles Times* and other papers, but "Krishna Hash Bust" was unique for its size and its tabloidlike impact.

The *Register* later called the drug-smuggling ring one of the largest in Southern California history. They were right about the Hare Krishna connection, too, even though the P.R. office denied it. At the time I didn't know that in the 1970s ISKCON accepted money from a number of different drug-dealing operations. I was unaware of these facts and defended ISKCON because I believed the overall organization was benign. Thousands of devotees in a hundred temples innocently worshipped Krishna and led a Vedic religious life-style. I was naive. Like many devotees, I believed that book distribution provided all the money that built ISKCON.

The Hare Krishna hash bust happened when the P.R. office was moving from one side of Watseka Avenue to the other. Despite the chaos of unpacked boxes, we plugged in a typewriter and pounded out a six-page statement. Our new office was a mess, but Mukunda held a press conference in Ramesvara's quarters. Reporters with cameras and tape recorders spilled onto the courtyard, where we had set out a table with press materials. CBS, ABC, and NBC vans pulled up outside, ready to transmit reports in time for the evening news.

Mukunda read his statement accusing the media of "persecution so severe as to immediately bring to mind the mood of the witch hunts of Salem and the McCarthy era." He said, "The Southern California and other media have been having a field day victimizing the Hare Krishna movement, seizing every opportunity to discredit this religion and avoiding obvious opportunities to report on its true activities. This post-Jonestown dog-pack journalism and broadcasting is an example of persecution so intense and so unconscionable in this country of religious freedom that we have at last had to call a news conference just to expose the media itself."

The camera people took their best shots as Mukunda held up the "Krishna Hash Bust" headline, covering the word *Krishna* with printed index cards to make the headline read "Jewish Hash Bust" and "Catholic Hash Bust." He said, "We don't read of a 'Jewish' hash bust or a 'Catholic' hash bust because it's unfair to implicate an entire religion for the alleged aberrant behavior of a tiny handful of its members, almost all of whom are excommunicated or not in good standing." Just as the media shouldn't blame all of Islam for radical terrorist acts, so Mukunda tried to convince the Southern California reporters to back off of ISKCON. Unfortunately, crying foul was all we could do. It seemed an encouraging victory when *Esquire* magazine published Mukunda's catchphrase "post-Jonestown dog-pack journalism."

I believed Mukunda when he said that the drug ring was an aberration that the Governing Body Commission would soon eradicate. I saw the crisis as a chance to prove my loyalty. Little did I know that the situation was not at all what it appeared. Rishabdev went back to fundraising for ISKCON yet another time and was arrested again in 1982. The judge gave him a year in jail, which he spent meditating on how gurus could accept his donations yet publicly deny him to preserve their reputations.

When the bad press finally died down after Christmas, Mukunda convinced Ramesvara to fund the P.R. department. Our office would be tied in as a branch of the BBT, although independent. Ramesvara consulted fellow Governing Body commissioners and BBT trustees, then ordered Mahendra, his accountant, to begin giving our department $1,000 a month.

Ramesvara used the Bhagavatam class to explain how the newly funded department would resolve ISKCON's media situation. Temple devotees generally didn't read newspapers or watch TV, but they heard questions from relatives and people at airports. Bhagavatam class was the best place to prepare them for the *maya* they might face. Ramesvara didn't talk about the drug bust. Instead, he criticized the media's overreaction to simple airport handshakes and the pinning of flowers:

> In the Middle East there is constant agitation by Arab groups against Israel. Their methods are reprehensible. The whole world has been focused on their methods and therefore everybody hated them. . . . Even though they're using abominable methods of murder and sabotage and torture and all other kinds of abominable activities, because they've been so persistent in trying to get the world to look at their cause, they've actually achieved that goal. . . . So we can learn from this. Our methods, by comparison, are so gentle, and yet they have attracted the attention of the media. They have attracted, practically, the attention of the world. So that is very good. We have a good opportunity, a good position. Without having to resort to terrorism, we have the media focusing on the Hare Krishna movement.

ISKCON's notoriety could be transformed into acceptance once people understood Prabhupada's books, he said. Distributing books made it all seem so simple. Everyone could forget about the two thousand news clippings in the P.R. files, including about fourteen hundred on *sankirtan* conflicts, drug busts, lawsuits, and cults. Mukunda felt the same optimism when he asked me to transcribe Ramesvara's lecture for the *Public Affairs Newsletter*.

Whether it was a coincidence or something Mukunda and Ramesvara saw coming, our biggest P.R. challenge started just as the official support began. On March 4, 1980, law enforcement officials raided Mount Kailash, guru Hamsadutta's 480-acre ranch in Northern California named after the home of Lord Shiva, the god of destruction. Police seized ammunition and clips, rifles, shotguns, and a grenade launcher. The weapons proved legal, but only Hamsadutta's inner circle knew that the cache the police had sought—nine rifles and handguns purchased with stolen checks and credit cards—had been spirited away the night before. Local papers and TV stations carried the story.

A few weeks later, reports of gunshots brought police to a Bay Area garage full of ammunition and bullet-making equipment, including nine pounds of gunpowder. The business was legal, but they charged the German devotee-owner with passport fraud. When *The New York Times* reported the raid, Mukunda and one of the gurus flew to the Bay Area to stage ISKCON's official response. Mukunda read a statement about the organization's roots and warned the media against "post-Jonestown dog-pack journalism" again. Hindu businessmen filled out a panel of members who answered reporters' questions.

Mukunda kept criticizing the media's handling of the situation as envelopes of clippings piled up at the office. The *Oakland Tribune* ran "Hare Krishna Sect Faces Growing Police Scrutiny," and more inflammatory articles followed, including *Hustler* magazine's "The Hare Krishnas: Drugs, Weapons and Wealth." The four-part, front-page *Sacramento Bee* series "The Krishna File," detailing all the scandals, was the result of a three-month investigation by three reporters. *High Times* magazine's "Hare Krishna, Hare Krishna, Guns 'n' Ammo, Guns 'n' Ammo" began with the statement that although an ISKCON devotee may claim to be on the "path of peace . . . if you peek under his robe, you just might find a .45. And if you look into his *japa*-bead bag, there could be a pound of cocaine." There were a few good photos, like Eddie Adams's "Changing Bodies" from Topanga Canyon. Unfortunately, the biggest photo was of a devotee look-alike dressed in dhoti and holding an M-16 automatic rifle, a bandolier of shotgun shells over his shoulder and his left hand in a bead bag. We knew the photo was a fake, because even a drug-dealing devotee with a big gun would never put his *muchi* left hand on his *japa* beads. To an outsider it looked menacing enough, however.

The drug and gun bust exposure harmed ISKCON's public image and damaged membership allegiance. I wasn't allowed to talk about the Bay Area situation with anyone outside the department, but major media covered Mount Kailash as if they were presenting the sequel to Jonestown. Jim Jones had started out in the same county, they liked to point out. It was a small consolation when Mukunda assured me that the articles were exaggerated. Based on an erroneous initial report from the Bay Area Associated Press bureau, *The New York Times* had cited nine tons of gunpowder in the raid but then printed a correction that it had really only been nine pounds. Mukunda confided that the Governing Body Commission would probably suspend Hamsadutta.

Apparently some devotees actually were packing drugs and guns in their bead bags. Drug dealing and fascination with guns were rampant in certain ISKCON circles, as in the rest of society, surprising only because devotees portray themselves as nonviolent people. I had visited the Berkeley temple but only vaguely sensed the darkness that investigative reporters later confirmed. Hamsadutta and his band of German gangsters ran their temple like Rome in its later days. A covey of airport women slept with their male leaders, including the guru, and took speed to work long hours. Importing illegal German cars, using drugs, collecting weapons, and playing rock and roll were the mainstays of temple life, along with worshiping Krishna.

From the earliest days, Hamsadutta was famous as one of ISKCON's best *kirtan* leaders. He hoped for a career as a rock star and began to record with some of his associates. His first album, *Nice but Dead*, featured the song "Guru, Guru, on the Wall," which begins with the sound of machine gun fire and then the lyrics:

> Did you ever see a guru behind a gun?
> Did you ever see a guru flying a plane?
> Thin as a cane? Looking insane?
> Did you ever see a guru driving a car,
> Porsche or Mercedes? Singing in a bar?

To promote the album Hamsadutta and a few associates traveled the zone, from San Francisco to Seattle to Singapore, but apart from an audience of disciples the only place it seemed to catch on was in the Philippines. In the United States his obliging followers sold thousands of copies in parking lots all over the country, violating zonal gurus' boundaries. Ramesvara was especially piqued to learn that Hamsadutta's disciples were selling the records near his Denver temple. Ramesvara and Hamsadutta, rivals since the early days, were an odd couple to share California.

The Governing Body Commission didn't discipline Hamsadutta during the Mayapur meeting, which fell right in the midst of events, but weeks later twenty GBC members gathered for an emergency meeting in Los Angeles. In light of continued bad publicity, they requested that Hamsadutta give up his responsibilities in the United States. Still, he remained.

In mid-May, after another month of media focus, Berkeley police arrested Hamsadutta for having an illegal submachine gun in the trunk of an unregistered, illegally imported Mercedes-Benz. The Governing Body Commission called a press conference to announce that Hamsadutta had stepped down from his local duties, although he remained on the GBC. They put Ramesvara in charge of all of California and thought they had Hamsadutta under control. In a prepared statement, Bhagavan, chair of the GBC, told reporters, "The collective spiritual power of the GBC is greater than that of any individual leader, irrespective of whether or not that member can initiate students." Unfortunately, fist fights broke out when Ramesvara sent his men to occupy the Berkeley temple.

During the crisis, newspaper reporters bared ISKCON's soul on their pages, exposing things that insiders could not talk about. UPI reporter Todd Eastham wrote, "Since Prabhupada's death in 1977, the society, which numbers at least five thousand sworn devotees in the United States alone, has come under the control of eleven disciples, hand-picked by the master, who have taken their respective followers along paths which seem to diverge ever more from the principles of its founder."

The Governing Body Commission discussed the media coverage at their Mayapur meeting and raised Mukunda's operation to the level of an official ministry. The 1980 GBC resolution ordered that "an all-ISKCON office of Public Affairs be established with Mukunda das Gouravanacari as Minister of Public Affairs. He and his office will assist local GBCs [Governing Body commissioners] in developing their public affairs programmes, and oversee the collection and distribution of international public affairs materials."

Few things become a crisis overnight, even in ISKCON. When Prabhupada died, his final instructions had been to "cooperate together" to preserve ISKCON. The eleven gurus took that to mean "cooperate to keep ourselves in power" and preserve the zonal guru system. Had the Governing Body Commission been more proficient, it could have confronted Hamsadutta at any number of critical junctures. His preoccupation with guns and gangsters was known to date back at least six years, to the time he managed a small empire of Hare Krishna properties in Germany. His *sankirtan* team of a hundred devotees was based at Schloss Rettershof in Frankfurt, a mansion built of stone, and traveled throughout Germany in a fleet of sixteen Volkswagen buses. In 1974 police raided the Frankfurt temple, and fourteen devotees, including Hamsadutta, stood trial for fraud, larceny, and postal and weapons violations. They were convicted on the weapons charges. *Back to Godhead* printed an article after the 1978 trial but presented the situation as a case of religious persecution. Hamsadutta's integrity, inside the movement at least, was unharmed.

Dealing with ISKCON's dark side was stressful, but, like Mukunda, I believed Prabhupada's goodness would shine through. At the end of that year I traveled to Bombay for a worldwide public relations seminar that Mukunda and one of the gurus hosted. Men and women from France, Italy, England, India, and Berkeley exchanged anecdotes from their fledgling P.R. departments. The man from France had persuaded the *International Herald-Tribune* to give ISKCON equal time in three foreign-language editions after it printed an unfavorable *New York Times* article about the Berkeley gun busts. Small victories like that assured us that we could do something about ISKCON's problems. We convinced each other that ISKCON's media situation was no worse than that of any other organization held under the spotlight of public scrutiny.

After the conference, the P.R. delegates traveled to Vrindavana to observe Prabhupada's disappearance day. In the evening we gathered around Prabhupada's deathbed, now covered with flowers, for a slow, solemn *kirtan*. One of the gurus read aloud from his manuscript of Prabhupada's official biography. The ceremony was emotional; everyone cried. Prabhupada was gone, but ISKCON needed him more than ever.

My first experience in India, seeing ancient Vedic temples and pilgrimage shrines, made me feel more dedicated to healing the American organization. The devotees I knew were honest spiritual aspirants. Some had been searching, like me, and had found their answers to the mysteries of life in approximately the same way I had. Some newer devotees in the temple were people I had encouraged to join. ISKCON was my family, and the temple had become my home. This was not the second or even the third family in which I had been; it was neither the best nor the worst. I just needed a place where I felt accepted and understood. Hamsadutta's problems paled next to my own need to prove that there was nothing wrong with my Hare Krishna family.

Around this time my dad showed me a video he had made for an ordnance manufacturer. His work made the company's new product, a cluster bomb, look like the most ingenious thing the U.S. military-industrial complex had ever invented. Dad said he didn't like bombs, but he liked the pay. The only difference between Dad's P.R. business and mine was that I had to live in ISKCON.

8

❖

Who's Watching the Children?

My father once commented, "You can win more people to your side with pictures of kids and animals than with any other gimmick." This rule applied to the April 1980 *Life* magazine cover of two beautiful Hare Krishna girls wearing colorful saris and big smiles. Fortunately for ISKCON, the magazine was on the stands in every market in the United States throughout most of Hamsadutta's upheaval.

Life photographer Ethan Hoffman had originally contacted our office shortly after Jonestown. He told me that he wanted to shoot pictures of the Los Angeles *gurukula*, the private school for Hare Krishna children. I suspected that *Life* planned to capitalize on the cult issue, because the *gurukula* and the question of how ISKCON raised its children were controversial subjects. Troublesome media reports had plagued the schools from the beginning; all media hype, I believed. I told Hoffman that he would have to get permission to take pictures at the *gurukula* and that the minister of public affairs was out of town.

While I tried contacting Mukunda in Europe, Hoffman received permission to shoot the New Vrindaban *gurukula*. Kirtanananda, anxious for publicity, put up no resistance. When Mukunda found out, he flew to New York and deputized a devotee to act as New Vrindaban's P.R. man. (Most P.R. devotees got their training in hands-on, real-life situations.) Mukunda hired Paul Kurland, a New York attorney who had defended Daniel Ellsberg during the Pentagon Papers trial. In their negotiations, *Life* signed an agreement to print a prominent photo of Prabhupada's Palace and leave out any references to Jonestown, cults, brainwashing, physical or psychological coercion, deceptive recruitment techniques, or airport solicitation. Although agreeing to skirt the problem areas, the editors knew that Hoffman shot searing black-and-white photos and that reporter Hillary Johnson wrote compelling copy. *Life* didn't lose an ounce of impact by signing off to the demands. It was more like cutting a key to a lock.

"Children of a Harsh Bliss" began with a fifteen-inch-wide, black-and-white photo of three bald *gurukula* boys, holding their hands out to Kirtanananda as if begging. Kirtanananda, sniffing a flower, looks them over. Gurus sometimes passed out flowers during worship time; the children wanted the flower that Kirtanananda held to his nose. The lead paragraph said, "The children with the outstretched hands have already begun their training as lifelong members of the sect of Hare Krishna." ("Sect" not "cult" was a small concession to Mukunda's legal front.)

Life printed a good picture of the palace, but the rest of Hoffman's black-and-white photo essay was moody and bleak. In one picture, a group of men bow to someone on a bare, rutted road. In another, a sari-clad woman shaves her son's head. Bold type beneath a photo of children in a classroom reads, "The study of Sanskrit in a climate of few comforts." On the seventh page of the eight-page article is the heading "Strict rules to separate the sexes" and a photo of a *gurukula* girl receiving a sewing lesson. Finally, a full-page photo shows a teenage girl with almond eyes, her face partially illuminated by rays of sunlight. "The fourteen-year-old at right, caught in a reflective moment, was married recently. 'She was developing a lot of crushes,' a devotee explained. Her sister, sixteen, is married and pregnant."

The day *Life* magazine hit the stands, we went to my father's office for a meeting. Mukunda admitted that the article was bad, but he hoped the cover could be counted as a victory because many more people would see the magazine than buy it or read it. Dad confirmed Mukunda's hunch and said to purchase as many copies as we could find. He also suggested making a media kit with one-page fact sheets on each facet of ISKCON: festivals, philosophy, dress, spiritual vegetarianism, Srila Prabhupada, restaurants, humanitarian programs, art, and architecture. Dad also advised us to put together a video of footage for TV news segments about ISKCON. He said if we provided good footage of things like festivals and temple worship, news programmers might use that.

Back at the temple, ISKCON-TV started on the videotape, while everyone in our office put in ten-hour days to get the press kit ready. Mukunda termed the final product a "preaching weapon" and titled it "Universal Media Kit, Number One," with the shortened code name "UMK-1." Maybe the nickname stuck because of all the worry over guns. The next *Public Affairs*

Newsletter announced the UMK-1 and encouraged temple leaders to order at least one copy. Mukunda envisioned a P.R. branch office in every center, with the UMK-1 a big step toward that goal. Many temples bought the materials, which we sold for $5; extra photos were $3. The P.R. office ran on a shoestring.

In his newsletter Mukunda described the *Life* cover as a victory and printed comments by the guru Hridayananda:

> Concerning the part on women, it says that we segregate the sexes and stress chastity for women, which are values that most Americans respect. Don't forget that the Equal Rights Amendment failed in America. America, as a nation, does not believe in the equality of women. It's a proven fact, because ERA failed. . . .
>
> The mention of a sixteen-year-old pregnant wife and a fourteen-year-old who will get married came off very well. The article mentioned that one is married and the other is getting crushes. These days, there's a big movement in America against illicit sex, and these early marriages show our concern for not letting women become polluted.

In controversies like this I wanted to take ISKCON's side, but such inane arguments by the leaders gave me new doubts. I trusted my father above anyone else because he knew P.R., and I was glad Mukunda respected his opinion. As far as *Life* magazine, Dad and Mukunda were right. The cover was remembered. *Life* readers voted it one of the best of the year, and the magazine published several letters about it. The Hare Krishna girls even appeared on a Bombay billboard advertising *Life*. Ethan Hoffman won praise for the photo, and it remains one of the most memorable and well-known of all his prize-winning shots.

The article was not as bad as some that had been published in 1974. That year the media focused on the Dallas boarding school where parents could visit their children only twice a year. The arrangement was supposed to increase students' attachment to Krishna and ISKCON. Instead, overcrowding and mismanagement led to neglect and countless abuses. That year the *Los Angeles Times* published an article quoting Dr. Emileo Alonzo, a Dallas physician who treated the devotees, who said, "These people are regressing into the thirteenth and fourteenth century." Around that time, *Personality*, a foreign tabloid-style weekly, printed "A Crackpot School That Teaches Kids to Die," quoting Dr. Jack Leedy, a New York psychiatrist: "Children have been known to die from lack of love, and these children are being deprived of love by being taken away from their parents." An anticult group reprinted the "Crackpot School" article as a pamphlet.

The *Houston Chronicle* Sunday magazine also carried a cover story about the Dallas *gurukula* that year. In the lead paragraph, writer Connie Lunnen called the schoolhouse a "gray tombstone in a low-rent district in east Dallas." The headmaster, a Marine Corps veteran, told the reporter, "When a child gets to be six years old, austerity is fun. It's a way of life." He demonstrated his love of austerity for the reporter by throwing away a stuffed animal, a present that his wife's parents had mailed to his own daughters.

The article included quotes from some of the eighty students, whose innocent words told more than pictures. One five-year-old girl said, "Fun is nonsense activity." An eleven-year-old said, "Footballs, dolls, kites. That's sense gratification. We don't do those things here." After the age of ten, boys and girls were segregated "to keep them from thinking about sex," according to the report. One preadolescent girl, already concerned with female shame, said, "I don't wear my hair loose because it will attract men's minds. And I wear saris so the men won't get attracted to my body." In short, the article was a disaster, but if its premise was true, so was the school itself. The reporters' hyped presentation just drew attention to a situation that was already bad.

The same year, *Harper's* magazine published a more favorable article, "Raise Your Hand if You're a Spirit Soul," by Judith Wax. The writer, the mother of a devotee, presented the same issues of austerity and discipline but handled them sensitively. For example, she compared *gurukula* to the boarding schools of Oxford and Cambridge, where students are groomed for elevated social positions.

Another report came out in 1974 in a book titled *The Children of the Counterculture* by John Rothchild and Susan Berns Wolf. The authors described the students in Dallas as "chubby little boys with shaven heads and pink pajamas, adorable replicas of the people who chant on the streets." However favorable some of their comments, Rothchild and Wolf accurately portrayed the despair of *gurukula* in this observation: "One of the smallest boys, who was wearing a cardigan sweater over his Krishna outfit, kept coming over to the teacher and trying to sit on his lap. The teacher, with dispassionate authority, patted the boy on the head and sent him back to his place. . . . Finally, with all his excuses taken away, the boy broke down and started to cry. He said he wanted his mommy, and with the mention of that word 'mommy' he was immediately led out of the room by the teacher."

By the time the Dallas *gurukula* closed, many temples had their own schools. Parents could enroll their children in local ashrams and see them more often. The smaller, decentralized schools were an improvement but still repressive. Children often followed the same rigorous morning schedule as adults, and it took severe discipline to get classrooms of eight-year-olds to sit still for chanting *japa*. Some schools were free from abuse, but ironically the *gurukula* in Vrindavana, India, the land of Krishna's youthful pastimes, was the setting of the worst child abuse. The most dedicated ISKCON parents sent their teenage boys there because it was the only *gurukula* that offered a high school curriculum. The prevailing wisdom was that public schools were bad and a strict religious education in a *gurukula* high school would set boys on the righteous path. Tragically, there were men on the staff who never should have been around children. Students were slapped, kicked, beaten, and slugged when blindfolded, held under water faucets, locked in bathrooms for days without food or blankets, sodomized, and threatened with death. The most abusive aspect of *gurukula* life was that the teachers employed the older, more experienced boys as "monitors" to enforce discipline and corporal punishments. Teachers looked the other way when monitors abused and sodomized younger children.

ISKCON defiled the holy land, and an offense there is said to be more serious than the same act committed anywhere else. Unfortunately, the problems were systemwide in the organization. Family incest is usually accompanied by demand for blind obedience to authority, poor communication, lack of loving and playful touch, duplicity, deceit, and family secrets. ISKCON's offenses in Vrindavana could be characterized as organizational incest.

Communication was seriously breaking down. Rumors of abuse spread as perpetrators moved from one *gurukula* to another, with authority figures' blessings. The Governing Body Commission probably wanted the problem to go away on its own, and ignoring it was just easier than facing it. Or perhaps they believed the violent pedophiles might reform themselves. The Catholic church has had the same problem, to its great liability. After dealing with a 1984 abuse case at the L.A. community nursery school, Mukunda tried to convince other Governing Body commissioners to face the issue. Incest doesn't go away on its own, it gets passed along to the next generation. The only way to stop it is to bring it out in the open.

Institutional attitudes about women added to the problems. Gurus and temple leaders who may have known of the abuse asked mothers to "surrender" their children to the *gurukula* system because "Prabhupada said" that was the right thing to do. Women foolishly thought that surrendering to God meant overcoming their natural motherly instincts. Prabhupada never would have approved of the abuse; he once reprimanded the teachers in Dallas merely for using a paddle. Nevertheless, many women naively enrolled their teenage boys in Vrindavana and collected money to support the school. These are the darkest secrets of the organization, which the women and children have had to bear alone.

The *Life* cover was a metaphor for the children of ISKCON. On its face, the picture seemed like good publicity, with innocent, smiling faces, but it hid a growing desperation. All the children in ISKCON during those years felt it, even if they were not assaulted. Some adults sensed the tension, but most trusted the GBC leadership and left childcare to the *gurukulas*. Perpetrators told the children it was their karma that they were abused, but that's not true. It was neglect on the part of idealistic and irresponsible adults.

I knew of the negative articles from Dallas but didn't know they were true. I believed that no matter how good the schools were the media would still write something negative. In my mind, ISKCON was innocent but misunderstood. Ramesvara himself lectured in Bhagavatam class that the media always tends to focus on negative details to play up the cult stereotype. He compared their behavior to flies looking for a sore. In the *Public Affairs Newsletter* Mukunda published a cartoon of cameramen and reporters flocking to examine a small black spot of dirt on a devotee's saffron robes. Insiders wanted to believe that everything was okay; their denial even let them overlook the welfare of their own children.

9

The Gurus Start World War III

Externally, ISKCON was exposed and suffering from the backlash of negative press. Within the organization there was an abundance of gossip, distrust, and backbiting but little real communication. Some devotees said it was better to continue in one's service, ignoring the confusing political situation, while others wanted accountability from the leaders. It takes two to tango and there are two sides to every story, my mother taught me. If a war were to start in the Hare Krishna organization it would be between two distinct parties: those who supported the Governing Body Commission and those who felt the GBC betrayed Prabhupada by instituting the eleven-guru system.

In 1980 a few brave disciples of Prabhupada openly stated that the GBC had made a terrible mistake. The young Western gurus didn't have Prabhupada's charisma, and soon many devotees were openly discussing the subject. As a second-generation disciple, I was tossed on the waves. I heard the grumbling but didn't want to accept any of it because my faith rested on the assumption that Ramesvara connected me to Prabhupada. I didn't want to lose that link. I still believed that ISKCON was functioning according to Prabhupada's will. In L.A., as in many temples, insiders supported the GBC, whereas Prabhupada's disciples on the outside—"fringies"—were skeptics if not outright opponents of the GBC.

I was surprised to learn of all the splinter groups that had sprung up around Watseka Avenue. A rash of BBT workers had quit their jobs, moved away, and opened an alternative preaching center nearby. When a much-loved *kirtan* leader criticized the zonal guru system, temple authorities banned his recordings, warning the rest of us that hearing his voice could make us lose faith. Some ISKCON dissidents sought refuge with Sridhar Swami, an elderly godbrother of Prabhupada's from the Gaudiya-math. A former L.A. temple president took initiation from Sridhar Swami and opened a center near Watseka Avenue.

Siddha-svarupa, one of Prabhupada's disciples, had gone back to being a guru of his own followers in Hawaii. Another man in Mississippi started his own organization and rural community, attracting disenchanted ISKCON members who still wanted to follow the life-style and morning meditations. Most splinter groups circulated their own publications, however modest, criticizing ISKCON. The Governing Body Commission still controlled all ISKCON properties, while dissenters had to get a footing in the outside world. With strict boundaries of "inside" and "outside," the atmosphere was tense. The GBC refused to negotiate with these factions, hoping that they would just go away. Outsiders were considered deviant, philosophically or morally, and Governing Body commissioners refused to look to their own behavior to explain why so many people left. As Ramesvara once put it, "Good fences make good neighbors."

As the ISKCON world divided into factions, most of the eleven gurus embraced the revelation of an apocalyptic world war. According to the widely accepted scenario, only core ISKCON members and a few thousand chosen souls would survive, with the insiders leading the others into an age of spiritual enlightenment. In ISKCON's disarray, it seemed that a devastating nuclear war between the United States and the Soviet Union might be God's plan to usher in Lord Chaitanya's golden age of Krishna consciousness. Fear bolstered the GBC's position because commissioners had the vision to prepare everyone else for the Apocalypse. The fear also distracted people from the real issues.

The Bhagavatam class became a forum for discussing "the war," which some said was imminent now that Prabhupada had "left the planet." The way they talked, it seemed the war could start in a matter of months. Leaders implored devotees to stand by their posts on the front lines of preaching, collecting money, and selling books until, upon the Governing Body Commission's command, it would be time to retreat to rural strongholds. They said guns would be necessary to fight off looters and refugees. Upon civilization's collapse, nuclear warheads would fall on cities like L.A. and New York. I had nightmares about hiding in the temple's walk-in refrigerator, not knowing whether I would survive.

To establish outposts of shelter and defense, gurus raced to acquire retreat properties. ISKCON already had property in India, Hamsadutta had Mount Kailash in Northern California, Tamal Krishna had a farm in Oklahoma,

Harikesh had his headquarters in Zurich and estates in Scandinavia, Bhav-ananda bought property on Australia's Gold Coast and a fifteen-thousand-acre sheep ranch, and Kirtanananda had his palace in West Virginia. When Ramesvara sought land, his assistants relied on a U.S. Department of Defense map showing nuclear fallout zones for expected California targets. His pur-chase of a former dude ranch in central California was based on its location in a mountainous, untargeted area. He relocated the *gurukula* to the ranch because children would be the most vulnerable in a war. Many families moved there for the sake of their children.

Some of ISKCON's rural properties were the self-sufficient Vedic farm-ing communities that Prabhupada had wanted, but others were extravagant purchases whose practicality in the event of social collapse was debatable. In December 1980, the guru for England, Jayatirtha, bought an estate in Worces-tershire, twenty-five miles south of Birmingham, known to local residents as Croome Court. He renamed it Chaitanya College, looking forward to the day when ISKCON would offer its children and others a college degree in the Vaishnava tradition. The two-hundred-room mansion, a chapel, and vari-ous outbuildings had been built in 1750 for the Earl of Coventry by Lancelot "Capability" Brown and the designer of interiors Robert Adam. The prop-erty included forty acres of fields, landscaped park land, and a way station where feudal tenants used to bring their grain in payment to the earl. The Queen of Holland had stayed there during World War II. When the Coven-try family sold the property in 1950, the tapestry room, including its doors and famous Gobelin tapestries, went to the New York Metropolitan Muse-um; books and shelving from the library went to the Victoria and Albert Museum in London. A photograph taken in 1894 of the Duke of York (later George V) at a Croome Court party remained in the house, and oil portraits of other royalty hung prominently in the grand ballroom. Jayatirtha spent hundreds of thousands of pounds restoring the estate and turning the chapel into a Hare Krishna temple.

Bhagavan bought similarly historic properties, including a sixteenth-cen-tury villa outside Florence, Italy, where in his last years Machiavelli wrote *The Prince*. I visited the radio station there, Radio Krishna Centrale, which broad-cast from one wing of the mansion.

For all the time and money spent worrying about it, the World War III panic was based on sparse evidence. Most came from the "World War III tape," a conversation recorded in 1975 during a morning walk with Prabhu-pada in Mayapur. He and a few disciples had discussed the tension between Pakistan and India and how the superpowers seemed to be lining up behind the opposing countries. They also discussed twentieth-century warfare, with its nuclear weapons and other technological wonders. Prabhupada, unimpressed with the superpower arsenals, dismissed it all as the glitter of *maya*, illusion. He said the Vedas speak of nuclear energy, so it is nothing very remarkable. He said such technology only serves to distract humanity from spiritual life. Prabhupada added, "Next war will come very soon. Your country, America, is very much eager to kill these Communists, and the Communists are also very eager. So, very soon there will be war. And perhaps India will be the greatest sufferer." The mysterious statement seized everyone's attention, as if Prabhupada had revealed a cosmic prophecy.

"Will that help our preaching Prabhupada?" one disciple asked.

The rest laughed.

"Preaching will be very nice after the war, when both of them [the United States and Russia], especially Russia, will be finished," Prabhupada said.

"What will the devotees do while the war is going on?" the disciple asked.

"Chant Hare Krishna," Prabhupada answered.

"Is there something we should do to prepare ourselves for this coming disaster?" another devotee asked.

"You are simply to prepare for chanting Hare Krishna," Prabhupada said. Everyone laughed in relief.

"That's all?" the devotee asked.

"Yes."

The conversation went on, with little more in the way of predictions or specific warnings. A year before, *Back to Godhead* had quoted Prabhupada as saying, "In fact, because of our Krishna consciousness movement, there will be no nuclear war." After war fears became established, the magazine quoted Prabhupada as saying that the superpowers would be compelled to use the nuclear arms they had amassed. They also printed editorials suggesting that war was inevitable and that it was best to be prepared. Regardless of Prabhupada's intentions or wishes in the matter, fear won out, and gurus everywhere were preparing for war. Hamsadutta's activities were extreme, but only because he seemed so outwardly militant in his plans take advantage of the chaos that might ensue. It was rumored that he bought a decommissioned battleship in the Philippines to fix up and sail into San Francisco Bay during the height of the war.

There was no central arsenal and no official policy requiring gurus to buy guns. That would have been a real challenge for the P.R. department. Our press releases said that ISKCON was a peace-loving organization and that Hamsadutta's problem was an aberration the GBC was working to correct. It was not a complete aberration, considering that other temples had guns—and some even stockpiled them—but usually the arms were perfectly legal.

Gun laws in the United States made it easy for any group to own military-style weapons. Devotees in New Vrindaban and Berkeley even became federally licensed firearms dealers. Gurus claimed that they would welcome a war because Prabhupada had said, "Preaching will be very nice after the war."

The public affairs department was part of the establishment, an extension of the BBT and GBC, and our purpose was to uphold the institution. Despite its current state, Prabhupada had designated the Governing Body Commission to manage ISKCON in his absence. Mukunda supported Prabhupada's heirs right or wrong, hopeful that they would soon become mature enough to handle their responsibilities. He believed that overthrowing the GBC would be a disaster even worse than what was already happening.

As a member of the public affairs department I was expected to repress my fears and continue working. When my doubts arose, Mukunda advised me to read and chant extra rounds to fortify my faith. I overlooked a lot and rationalized even more in order to feel at peace in the organization. Ramesvara, visiting Governing Body commissioners, and Bhagavatam speakers encouraged naive devotees to overlook everything. They twisted scripture to suit institutional needs. "Blasphemy of the great saintly persons who are engaged in the preaching of the Hare Krishna mantra, is the worst offense at the lotus feet of the holy name," a commonly memorized verse, became a credo to forbid discussion of GBC problems. According to them, listening to gossip about an authority figure could result in turning a "mad elephant" loose on one's fragile, vinelike creeper of devotional service. The mad elephant would surely crush the creeper and make a person "bloop," or jump ship and sink like a stone into the ocean of material life. The leaders quoted from scripture, but the mad elephant offense probably didn't apply to situations as dysfunctional as the one in which I found myself by 1980. Had people talked more, then they might have done something.

Instead of direct and honest disclosure, the GBC seemed to withhold information. Commissioners discussed the secrets in their meetings, but in the name of "cooperation" they suppressed anything distasteful. GBC meetings were exclusive. Observers were rarely allowed, and minutes were circulated only to a mailing list of temple presidents, Governing Body commissioners, and a handful of other VIPs in the organization. Some resolutions simply appeared with the word "unpublished." Thus, no one could learn the intimate secrets of the GBC. The commissioners didn't even know all of each others' secrets.

Devotees did not talk about the guru controversies openly. Even critical senior devotees hesitated to disrupt a younger devotee's faith in the gurus because of their own belief in the concept of the guru-disciple relationship. For its part, the GBC didn't want to risk disrupting anyone's faith in ISKCON, because a higher awareness of the troubles could cause many members to leave. It would have been much more convenient for them had Hamsadutta been the only guru with an integrity problem, but there were others.

Jayatirtha had been holding twelve-hour-long *kirtan* sessions, during which he would laugh, roll on the ground, and cry out incoherently. He lectured about the divine love of Radha and Krishna in the spiritual world and told his disciples that he was experiencing devotional ecstasy. Only the GBC knew that his ecstasies were symptoms of a drug-induced psychosis. In Vrindavana and Mayapur during the 1980 GBC meetings he went out of control on heavy doses of LSD. Later he revealed that he had never fully stopped taking the drug, despite having been a devotee for ten years. When the GBC met in L.A. to deal with Hamsadutta's problems, they also suspended Jayatirtha for one year and required him to renounce his wife and take *sannyas*. Kirtanananda performed the ceremony in the L.A. temple room.

The GBC hoped that his new status as a *sannyasi* would help Jayatirtha, but he was unhappy in ISKCON after that. During the 1982 GBC meeting he walked off the Mayapur property and defected to Sridhar Swami's Gaudiya-math temple. As an elder who was concerned about the growing tension in ISKCON, Sridhar Swami tried to mediate problems but usually only drew fire on himself. Several dozen of Prabhupada's disciples, disillusioned with the zonal guru system, had turned to the Gaudiya-math for spiritual renewal. The GBC saw Sridhar Swami as a threat, especially when long-standing members such as Jayatirtha took his side as a statement against ISKCON.

The GBC resolved to expel Jayatirtha for not acting as a "bona fide spiritual master" and for failing to "work cooperatively within the ISKCON movement." They turned Jayatirtha's zone over to the guru Bhagavan, who "reinitiated" all the Jayatirtha disciples who were willing. Devotees in the United Kingdom went on a year-long marathon to save the British properties, but Bhagavan eventually sold Croome Court because of high mortgage payments. Jayatirtha went away mad, and many of his disciples followed him to India to form a splinter group. Jayatirtha issued a statement addressed "To All Devotees of Srila Prabhupada's Lotus Feet." In it, he lamented his position: "I, who am an outcaste from the many beautiful temples which my Guru Maharaja [Prabhupada] founded, am not able to take *darshan* of the same Deities which I in many cases installed and looked after for years." Jayatirtha's new group was based in London, and he renamed his former ISKCON disciples with biblical names.

Yet another guru crisis of 1980 involved Tamal Krishna, who, after leading the Radha-Damodar bus party that had originated many deceptive *sankirtan* techniques, realized that doing so created bad publicity. The guru stopped all public solicitation in his zone and encouraged his devotees to open restaurants or start their own businesses. Book distribution came to a standstill in the U.S. portion of Tamal Krishna's zone, Texas, an affront because the zone also quit giving money to Ramesvara's BBT. The zone even snubbed Mukunda's P.R. efforts and objected to his plans to send mailings to media representatives in Texas. Tamal Krishna's worst problem was that he advised his godbrothers and godsisters to worship and obey him as their living intermediary to Prabhupada. Insulted, many took their complaints to the Governing Body Commission, which suspended him for a year. He found himself in the same boat as Hamsadutta and Jayatirtha, and ISKCON found itself with three "pure devotees" accused and suspended for their impure activities.

When the GBC came to Los Angeles in April, I felt sure that the Governing Body Commission was strong enough to overcome its illusions. When the gurus came to the temple for the morning program, I had my camera handy, and I attended all their *kirtans* and Bhagavatam classes. It was the guru groupie in me that made it seem like fun rather than the tragicomedy it really was. Logistics were complicated. Each GBC man needed comfortable accommodations, along with meals and housekeeping. In addition, the eleven gurus had to be worshiped simultaneously on eleven *vyasasanas*. Carpenters and seamstresses worked all week before the meeting to fashion wooden pedestals and red velvet cushions. The miniature thrones lined the walls of the temple, leaving little room for the rest of us.

On the last morning of the visit, I left the crowded temple to sit outside with Jadurani, one of the women at the ashram who could collect $1,000 a day. She was an accomplished BBT artist whose oil paintings are reproduced in BBT books and was one of the first women to join ISKCON.

"It must be purifying to have these senior devotees visiting," I suggested as I sat down.

"We can't imagine the layers of impurities being washed away by their presence," Jadurani said. She continued chanting on her beads.

I chanted with her, wondering if she felt any connection with her former husband, the guru Satsvarupa, who was being worshipped in the temple. If she did, I had never heard her mention it. Some of the other widows had spoken to me of their loneliness, pride, jealousy, or anger. I knew some who felt bitter because their former husbands enjoyed comfort and fame as *sannyasis,* while they raised their children alone, dependent on the temple.

A few days after the GBC meetings ended, community routines returned to normal. Upstairs in the temple balcony one morning, while meditating on all that had happened, I heard a woman screaming outside. I ran to the window and saw two men chasing Jadurani down Watseka Avenue, toward the traffic on Venice Boulevard. The first grabbed her white sari, which was falling from her shoulder. The other tackled her and held her down on the sidewalk while another man opened the door of a waiting car. They forced her in, and the car sped away.

I ran outside as devotees gathered on the street and learned that Jadurani had been ejected for blaspheming Satsvarupa, saying that he wasn't a "real" guru like Prabhupada.

Jadurani sought refuge in New Vrindaban, but during her brief stay there some women violently attacked her for her continued outspoken blasphemy. Jadurani moved on to Florida, where the political climate was different. The guru there gave her a sympathetic welcome, so she settled down to continue her art career at the Miami Beach temple.

After the emergency GBC meetings and the incident with Jadurani, things were never the same in L.A. Ramesvara's band of *kshatriyas,* Sanskrit for "warriors," took to guarding the temple twenty-four hours a day. I thought the guards were for the stated purpose of protecting the deities. I didn't realize they were armed, but they were. A gun closet was in one of the buildings. To those of us who lived there and trusted the temple, the men were nothing more than private security guards who cooperated with police if there was a problem in the neighborhood. Anticult deprogrammers or other critics could have pointed to the gun-toting devotees as evidence that ISKCON was a violent cult, but truth be told, the organization was in deeper trouble than anyone outside could know. Without Prabhupada, there was no accountability, no place for the buck to stop. An organization with no ultimate accountability is a dangerous thing; women such as Jadurani were its victims.

10

The Storm Within: The Guru Issue

Just as all inside devotees were practically next of kin, we also shared a host of common symbolism. When a man shaved his head, it was an act full of meaning for himself and everyone he met. Most people would interpret it to symbolize the renunciation and spiritual transformation of someone entering into ascetic life.

When someone said the gurus were not "real" gurus like Prabhupada, that was also symbolic and charged with meaning. Prabhupada was the *acharya,* the spiritual leader, and he was the *sik-sha* guru (instructing guru) for all his followers. He was also the *dik-sha* guru (initiating guru) for thousands of men and women. Hundreds more received initiation from him through *ritvik* priests, ritual gurus who chanted on disciples' beads and performed the fire ceremony on Prabhupada's behalf when he was too weak to travel. The Sanskrit words to describe gurus had strong symbolic significance.

The problem within ISKCON was that subtle esoteric concepts that most people wouldn't spend five minutes thinking about were crucial to the violence spreading within the society. A chasm of controversy formed over what kind of guruhood Prabhupada had intended for the eleven: *acharya, sik-sha, dik-sha,* or of much lower status, *ritvik.* Tamal Krishna said of the *ritvik* guru, "It's not a question that you repose your faith in that person—nothing."

In late 1980 several devotees who were part of a fledgling opposition movement combed the Bhaktivedanta Archives on Watseka, looking for evidence of Prabhupada's wishes in the guru issue. They found passages in letters Prabhupada had written to disciples, such as the following: "Anyone following the order of Lord Chaitanya under the guidance of His bona fide representative, can become a spiritual master and I wish that in my absence all my disciples become bona fide spiritual masters to spread Krishna consciousness throughout the whole world." That was a much broader interpretation than the one the GBC had endorsed.

They also found Prabhupada's comments criticizing the GBC itself: "What will happen when I am not here, shall everything be spoiled by the GBC?" and "I do not think the leaders are themselves following, nor they are seeing that others are following strictly. That must be rectified at once." Photocopies of such letters circulated through underground channels, and grapevines buzzed daily as new puzzle pieces appeared.

One odd puzzle piece was an American from Calcutta, Amogha-lila, who claimed to receive messages from Prabhupada through dreams, trances, and visions. ISKCON doctrine rejects the possibility, but a *sannyasi* named Trivikram became interested in Amogha-lila's writings and circulated them on the insiders' grapevine. Amogha-lila (channeling Prabhupada) added fuel to the anti-guru fervor with statements like, "I never wanted this big fanfare for these eleven disciples. Now you stop treating them as special. That is their own concoction. You are all gurus, as much as you repeat my instructions and follow them."

Ironically, the most controversial materials in the debate were the appointment tapes and subsequent July 9, 1977, letter that introduced the eleven gurus. The GBC's official position was (and still is) that Prabhupada appointed eleven men *ritvik* gurus to deliver initiation on Prabhupada's behalf while he was living, and that after his passing they were allowed to initiate disciples of their own. Some of the men understood it that way at the time, whereas others of the eleven found out about the sacred command after Prabhupada's passing. The GBC cited the transcript of the appointment tapes, especially the statement where Prabhupada specifically used the term "grand-disciple," then added, "When I order you become guru, he becomes regular guru. That's all. He becomes disciple of my disciple. Just see."

Opponents read the transcripts differently. They cited the phrase "when I order" and said Prabhupada never gave the order. They pointed to the word *ritvik,* which appeared in the letter and tapes, to argue that Prabhupada intended that the eleven gurus remain *ritviks* to deliver the initiation on his behalf. The *ritvik* proponents believed that Prabhupada should remain the eternal spiritual master, with his disciples offering initiation on his behalf. This is similar to the understanding that priests and ministers witness on behalf of Jesus, the supreme spiritual teacher of Christianity. The GBC rejected the evidence that they were only *ritvik* gurus because Prabhupada had never spoken of a guru giving initiation posthumously. The GBC said there must be a "living guru" to connect the aspiring disciple with God through *dik-sha* initiation.

When this controversy broke out, Bhagavatam speakers were carefully screened to keep out troublemakers. A few people were asked to move away from Watseka Avenue and stay away. Those who believed the *ritvik* theory migrated away from ISKCON to form splinter groups of radical guru reform. Although similar episodes took place in other temples, Los Angeles was one of the main stages for the drama to play out.

The GBC and its critics pointed to the exact same materials but came up with opposite viewpoints. When controversy arose over the subtleties of the different ranks of gurus, rumblings of dissatisfaction were heard everywhere. People said, "Prabhupada is the only real guru, these others have no right." No one could honestly communicate or figure out what to tell the second-generation disciples. Trivikram wrote a letter to the editor of *Back to God-head* magazine calling for an end to zonal guru worship. Although the magazine never published it, each guru received a copy.

Meanwhile, in a spate of sincere humility, my guru had come to a similar conclusion. Ramesvara took his *vyasasanas* out of the temple and from his salon in the green building, then wrote back to Trivikram, confessing that guru worship was wrong. He commissioned Subhananda to compile quotes from Prabhupada's books, and together they wrote Ramesvara's statement, "On the Position of the Initiating Guru in the Western USA Zone." After twenty-nine pages of supportive Prabhupada references, Ramesvara wrote: "In carefully analyzing Srila Prabhupada's books and letters regarding the position of the guru, I have come to the understanding that I have created a great offense against Srila Prabhupada by allowing myself to be regarded and worshiped on his level, along side His Divine Grace. I can honestly say that it was never my conscious intention to be thought of in this way. . . . Now I am seeking to rectify this situation."

In July 1980 Ramesvara presented his paper to the GBC and to temple presidents in his zone. He knew it would be dangerous, and he expected to be reprimanded, but "On the Position of the Initiating Guru in the Western USA Zone" went over like an ice-carving in hell. The GBC wrote a lengthy, harsh reply overruling Ramesvara's conclusions. Fellow gurus traveled to Los Angeles to make sure Ramesvara put his *vyasasanas* back and felt good about accepting adoration.

When we disciples heard "rumors" that Ramesvara was in trouble with the GBC, we didn't listen. Everyone knew that several gurus had experienced spiritual problems, but our guru was different. The feeling among Ramesvara's disciples in L.A. was that his essay had been an act of inspired humility, which made him even more worthy of our worship. It was exactly what the visiting Governing Body commissioners told us in their lectures at the temple.

Ramesvara was in much deeper than any of us suspected, with other problems besides his guruhood. One dilemma concerned the BBT's financial situation. At one time, the BBT office in L.A. had been the main BBT branch for all of ISKCON. Since 1977, however, separate branches had sprung up everywhere. BBT branches in Europe and Asia published in different languages; everyone needed to save shipping costs, including other English-language branches in Australia and England. Ramesvara tried to maintain international control as the Los Angeles office diminished in prominence. Originally, the North American BBT held the copyrights to all of Prabhupada's writings, but Ramesvara had little power to collect royalties when another guru reprinted the books. Hamsadutta, for example, considered the books his property as much as Ramesvara's. Prabhupada had named him a BBT trustee in 1974, and despite his suspension Hamsadutta saw nothing wrong with offering his own editions of all the books. Ramesvara fretted that unauthorized reprints were not up to the BBT standard and should be condemned, but his real problems were political and financial.

The only North American temples regularly contributing money to Ramesvara's BBT were his own (in L.A., Laguna Beach, San Diego, Honolulu, and Denver), several that had outstanding loans, and a dwindling few others that still gave priority to book distribution. In late 1980 Ramesvara launched a campaign to "Save the BBT" from bankruptcy, urging temples to have a good Christmas marathon and make a pledge to the BBT.

Ramesvara looked for new fundraising ideas and became convinced that the food business could be his big opportunity. Devotees offer their food to Krishna, so in that sense his business plans were based on a spiritual premise. Ramesvara's followers in Colorado manufactured "Bliss Bars," natural, honey-based candy. Restaurants were another venue for blessed food. Ramesvara's temples in L.A., Laguna Beach, and San Diego each opened a restaurant as the idea caught on in other countries around the same time.

Ramesvara's breakthrough in food-based fundraising came at the end of 1980, when he set up a bakery at Govinda's Restaurant on Venice Boulevard. It made three varieties of cookies: oatmeal, peanut butter, and carob chip. During the 1980–81 Christmas marathon, every available disciple spent ten hours a day in front of department stores selling cookies. I went out for two weeks with another P.R. secretary. After realizing how lucrative cookies could be, Ramesvara purchased an oven that turned out six thousand an hour. In

Bhagavatam class he ordered every devotee in the temple to sell cookies every weekend, pressuring us with guilt and reminding us that we took our budgets from the BBT without giving anything back. After the lecture, he privately warned Mukunda that he would cut off the P.R. budget unless everyone cooperated.

I pitched in. Cookies gave disciples a way to appease Ramesvara by doing *sankirtan* without having to go to the airport. My dad thought the cookies were delicious and encouraged me to fulfill my duty to sell them. Dad, who was an army photographer in World War II, always valued his military training. Perhaps he thought selling cookies would be good for me. Partly out of dedication to my guru, and partly because of pressure from my guru, I spent hundreds of hours selling cookies in front of department stores. In the 1983 marathon my partner and I sold $8,000 worth and came in fourth place among the other teams. That year sixty devotees sold a million and a half pieces—bringing in more than $200,000. All cookie sales were done undercover, in plain clothes. Marathon organizers at the temple misled the department stores to believe the cookie tables represented non-Krishna charities. Ramesvara sometimes drilled us, "What are you going to say if they ask if you're a Hare Krishna?" We were supposed to say, "Not me, no way!"

The cookie business brought in lots of cash, but flour, carob chips, and butter made for a high overhead. Another method of *sankirtan* was practically pure profit: "the pick." The techniques were the same as book distribution, but without the books. A devotee would "pin up" a potential donor by sticking a smiley-face pin to his or her lapel and then ask for a donation. A quarter, a dollar—it added up to big money. *Sankirtan* teams "blitzed" malls, stadiums, and concert halls until the places got hot with security guards. The pick was a covert operation. Part of the solicitor's pitch might be to flash a document praising ISKCON for humanitarian work without revealing his or her identity as a Hare Krishna.

"Pick it to the bone or don't come home" was nonvegetarian but common parlance among *sankirtan* devotees, and there were a host of other slogans. The public media had something else to say about the practice. San Francisco District Attorney Arlo Smith told the *Sacramento Bee* that he considered the pick "misdemeanor organized crime." From our viewpoint in the P.R. office, it seemed that whole law firms were kept busy defending ISKCON's First Amendment rights.

Ramesvara opened his "Pin Up the World" factory in Culver City to mass-produce buttons and stickers for temples across America. New Vrindaban later became the leading sticker manufacturer, turning out a variety of easy-to-sell items. Among the favorites for rock concerts were stickers and hats that said "Party Animal" or the name of the band. Managers at New Vrind-aban came up with the ingenious but illegal idea of printing their own National Football League team logos and Charles Schulz's Peanuts characters. The pirated Peanuts characters were the most offensive. As Schulz later said, Snoopy would never appear with a beer in his hand. Still, some enterprising cartoonist depicted him that way with the caption, "Are We Having Fun Yet?"

Book *sankirtan* generally meant revealing one's identity as a Hare Krishna, even if only at the last instant of an exchange. As San Diego Temple President Badri-narayan told the *San Diego Union* in 1978, "We aren't trying to hide or we wouldn't be handing out books telling who we are." This was not true of the pick, and selling stickers supplanted book *sankirtan* in many temples. Other things devotees have sold to raise money for *sankirtan* include incense, candles, knife sets, cut-out records, and water purifiers.

"Painting *sankirtan*," selling cheap oil paintings of the kind normally featured at "starving artist" galleries in malls and hotels, were popular and profitable for years. Mass-produced in Hong Kong and Korea, the paintings were signed with made-up Western names and exported. A twenty-four-by-thirty-six-inch canvas cost $15 wholesale but could bring up to $500 retail. The usual markup was more reasonable, but as in the pick and the change-up routine paintings had the potential for high profits. It was not generally known that Hare Krishnas had taken up art sales, but at least one report was published in 1981. Police in Bangor, Maine, told the *Boston Herald* that six ISKCON fundraisers from Philadelphia had been arrested for going door to door without a permit, telling customers that the paintings were original oils by Maine artists. The article quoted a Bangor art dealer, "It's not what they sold, it's the way in which they sold the paintings" that was deceptive.

Selling books was acceptable because Prabhupada's guru had encouraged it, but ISKCON had stretched the meaning of *sankirtan* to the limit. The literal meaning of *sankirtan* was "congregational *kirtan*," or group chanting. Lord Chaitanya's *sankirtan* in the sixteenth century certainly did not refer to aggressive fundraising activities. Corrupt *sankirtan* was a big factor in the growing sentiment against gurus because people accused them of being materialistic. The BBT became big business, and many felt its initial purity had been compromised. Non-guru godbrothers watched helplessly as ISKCON deviated further from its traditions.

Another revealing symbol was ISKCON's pyramid, which was located in the Western U.S. zone. It's more than a coincidence that some of the society's most volatile issues were hashed out at the Topanga Canyon Pyramid House. Pyramids symbolize order in the cosmos, with higher and lower planes of consciousness; the apex symbolizes attainment within the cosmic hierarchy. Pyramid residents submissively turned over their living room and facilities whenever a contingent of leaders descended for a meeting. At the meeting in December 1980, talks revolved around the appointment of gurus and the way power was handled at the top of the organization. The men at the meeting hoped the GBC would circulate guruship more widely because there was abundant evidence that Prabhupada would have wanted it that way.

As fate had it, the leading participants at the Pyramid House talks were Hamsadutta and Tamal Krishna, two of the suspended gurus. According to the transcript of those meetings, Tamal Krishna espoused the *ritvik* theory when he said, "Actually, Prabhupada never appointed any gurus. He didn't appoint eleven gurus. He appointed eleven *ritviks*. He never appointed them gurus. Myself and the other GBCs have done the greatest disservice to this movement the last three years because we interpreted the appointment of *ritviks* as the appointment of gurus." Tamal Krishna stated that most of ISKCON's problems (including Hamsadutta's, Jayatirtha's, and his own) could be attributed to this original mistake. He further said, "I think that if there had been a whole different mentality, there would be seventy-nine gurus or 122, instead of eleven." It was a breakthrough for the resistance. They hoped Tamal Krishna's revelations would change everything for the better. Unfortunately, the buried treasure—the answer to the mystery surrounding guruship—still eluded ISKCON.

The Governing Body Commission held its annual meeting in Mayapur two months later. They rejected the conclusions of the Pyramid House talks based on Prabhupada's statements on the appointment tapes and the precedent of the living guru. Hamsadutta and Tamal Krishna sided with the GBC on the matter and were reinstated with blessings from elder authorities. The GBC endorsed a paper called "The Descending Process of Selecting a Spiritual Master." Their edict on the guru question said:

> By Prabhupada's grace we are successfully discharging the duties of spiritual masters [of the *dik-sha* and *acharya* distinction] in Krishna consciousness, but we are becoming increasingly aware that it is a difficult and demanding burden. We, as the initiating gurus who have to nominate a new candidate, as well as the GBC, who has to consider whether to confirm our nomination—do not feel our own qualification is as yet such that we can bestow guruship upon others as an act of our mercy. We have to be aware that such "mercy" on our parts could

possibly be an act of violence on those [to] whom we prematurely bestow it, as well as to their disciples. If a guru were selected under less than ideal circumstances, and later had major difficulty, the bad karmic effect of such a mistake would also come back heavily to us.

There were no new gurus that year or the next. The GBC supported the theory of divinely empowered *dik-sha* gurus. They claimed that the system could still work and asked the rest of us to overlook the deviations that had already taken place.

The media didn't hesitate to report ISKCON's internal politics. Just after the Pyramid House talks, two reporters from the *Los Angeles Times* called to verify tips about conflict within the organization. Mukunda negotiated for fair play and invited the reporters over for lunch. This was to be his and Ramesvara's best shot for damage control. I remember the day that Evan Maxwell, an investigative reporter, and Russell Chandler, a *Times* columnist, came over. They ate with Mukunda and Ramesvara in the conference room while another secretary and I served lunch. We were glad that our guru had this opportunity to explain the spiritual rationale behind *sankirtan*. Mukunda gave the journalists an array of press materials.

"Lost Innocence: Krishnas—a Kingdom in Disarray" came out on the front page of the *L.A. Times* Sunday edition, with a circulation of well over a million. Newspapers across the country picked up the Times Wire Service version. "Kingdom in Disarray" stretched over six pages, including eight photos and three sidebars. It began with a comprehensive discussion of *sankirtan* practices and lawsuits, then launched into a description of the Laguna Beach drug busts and Hamsadutta's gun problems. The article hadn't turned out the way Mukunda and Ramesvara hoped.

Maxwell and Chandler exposed the scuffles between the gurus, singling out Hamsadutta, Kirtanananda, and Ramesvara as the "leading figures in the power struggle." They wrote, "Some observers feel the ill will could break into open fratricide." Ramesvara denied the situation, but Kirtanananda and Hamsadutta said it was possible that one of the three of them could emerge as the single, "all-powerful successor" to Prabhupada. The article said of Ramesvara, "More than any other Krishna guru, he operates through a well-organized and efficient staff at his temple in Culver City. He shares *prasadam* meals with visitors in a conference room that appears to function as an executive dining room. His publications and multi-media presentations are smooth, slick and effective." It was fine that the P.R. department had been mentioned, but the end of the article didn't strike me as being so great: "When Prabhupada steamed into New York in 1965, he had little reason to worry about the material world. He owned no earthly kingdom. Prabhupada was innocent of the world, in much the same way the young people who flocked to him were innocent. The loss of that innocence has been painful. It is a process that continues. Where it will lead only Krishna, or God, knows."

11

❀

P.R. Publications Promote ISKCON

In addition to playing the piano, Mukunda's other passion was writing. He no longer played, but he wrote for publication all the time. In 1980, he, Ramesvara, and another guru dreamed up a plan that made our operation the ISKCON propaganda headquarters for the world. The *L.A. Times* had already dubbed Mukunda's press kits "smooth, slick and effective," and Ramesvara took that as a good sign. He raised the P.R. budget to $2,000 a month so Mukunda could work on a series of best-selling paperback books under a new BBT imprint, the Vedic Contemporary Library Series.

Ramesvara knew that ISKCON would have a broader acceptance if the BBT produced philosophical books tied to the concerns and interests of the outside world. My father agreed that the concept was simple enough. The paperbacks were designed to fly out of the hands of devotee book distributors, bringing *sankirtan* back to its original intent.

Mukunda recruited three writers to work on the books he envisioned. Drutakarma, the first man, worked for *Back to Godhead* magazine as a staff editorial writer. The second, Maharudra, had been an editor at a Cape Cod newspaper but had given up his job and family to join New Vrindaban in 1971. The third man, Bhutatma, had been a Berkeley devotee in the 1970s. When Hamsadutta came there after his crisis in Germany and took up being a guru, Bhutatma retreated to Thailand, the most distant part of the zone. He wore his hair long by devotee standards and resisted wearing devotional robes. When he did appear in a dhoti, he wore saffron. Bhutatma was a writer and also acted as Mukunda's general manager and treasurer. He and Mukunda kept things going, always joking and entertaining friends, gurus, reporters, or celebrities such as Steve Allen or Annie Lennox. They spent their mornings at the temple and their days in editorial meetings with Ramesvara. As senior management they encouraged everyone in the department to attend the morning program, give Bhagavatam classes, chant *japa* in the temple, and go on marathons. When they had to concentrate on writing, they got away to Laguna Beach to stay with friends.

In my role as a secretary, I typed and photocopied their manuscripts. Luckily, I was a fast typist, so between edits I had time to read. Subhananda had told me to read the Srimad-Bhagavatam from the beginning, and I did so three times. I'd studied Lord Chaitanya's biography, the *Caitanya-caritamrita,* even more thoroughly. Unfortunately, as a woman, I was the only one in the department who couldn't give Bhagavatam class or lead a temple *kirtan.* I always wished for the chance to try.

The P.R. department's first book, *Lennon '69: Search for Liberation,* featured a conversation between Prabhupada, John Lennon, Yoko Ono, George Harrison, Mukunda, and other devotees. The transcript came from the Bhaktivedanta Archives' collection. The writers added frontmatter and appendixes, and the first printing, off the presses shortly after Lennon's murder, sold in airports and parking lots faster than the temples could reorder from the BBT, and for a while faster than the printer could ship.

With that success behind them, the writers wanted a book about chanting. Ramesvara decided that the best angle would be to interview a celebrity who chanted Hare Krishna, namely George Harrison. Mukunda flew to England twice one summer and ended up with six hours of recorded talks from the second trip. The material was condensed and edited, and Harrison approved the final manuscript by telephone from England. After the first printing of seven hundred thousand, the writers mixed in material from the John Lennon book, bringing *Chant and Be Happy: The Power of Mantra Meditation* to a highly readable 118 pages. BBT branches in South America, Europe, and Asia translated and reprinted it; literally millions of copies were circulated in a dozen countries. Next came a book about reincarnation, *Coming Back,* and a cookbook that had similar international appeal, *The Higher Taste.*

Besides best-selling *sankirtan* books we published *As It Is,* a newspaper for college students. We also published *Who Are They?* a one-time promotional magazine-style brochure with articles about the ISKCON life-style and testimonials from famous people. The guru Bhagavan was the first to think of such a publication. He published the French and Italian editions—*Qui sont-ils?* and *Que son ells?*—for distribution in his zone. On the front cover of the French and Italian versions was a close-up of two beautiful people, a man and a woman, dressed in Hare Krishna clothes and adorned with *tilak.* The woman in the photo, Satarupa, was a Danish devotee who had just moved to L.A. to continue her modeling career and work with our office doing P.R. At age eighteen she had been Miss Denmark and then cover girl for *Officiel, Vogue, Mademoiselle, Paris Match,* and *Elle.* When she joined ISKCON in 1973, magazines printed stories of her conversion, featuring "before" and "after" photos. As a devotee, Satarupa would not accept modeling jobs to promote cigarettes, meat, or alcohol, but she always worked.

A photographer friend of Mukunda's shot a new cover photo for the American version of *Who Are They?* This time Satarupa posed with a handsome fringe devotee from Santa Cruz. Devotees throughout Ramesvara's zone hung the magazine on doorknobs and gave away hundreds of thousands of copies in shopping centers, airports, and on street corners.

Some devotees didn't like *Who Are They?* because it seemed to compete with *Back to Godhead* at a time when the magazine was already losing money and morale. Others said the P.R. books should wait in line behind all of Prabhupada's lectures that had gone out of print. Still others complained that the man on the cover should have shaved his head for the picture and that he was standing entirely too close to Satarupa, considering that they weren't married.

Ignoring all criticism, our office advertised the books through newsletters and telephone calls to temple leaders. On balance, the publishing venture was judged a success. *Sankirtan* devotees genuinely liked the books and felt good about handing them out. They were inexpensive enough to give away free, as long as the temple had credit on account with the BBT. Cartons of books moved out of the warehouse almost as well as in ISKCON's good old days. When the Vedic Library series became successful, Ramesvara raised the P.R. budget to $3,500 a month but never offered a royalty as Mukunda and Bhutatma had hoped.

Besides books, Mukunda wanted a newsletter to send to the public media. He recruited Maharudra, the former New England journalist, to design *ISKCON Report,* which would offer a monthly barrage of news we wanted reporters to cover. The bulletin published photos with short, promotional items praising ISKCON. British Prime Minister Margaret Thatcher, Queen Elizabeth, Pope John Paul II, and Indian Prime Minister Indira Gandhi all had their pictures in *ISKCON Report* in relation to ISKCON. The newsletter apparently did its job because we found a quote about Prabhupada's Palace of Gold in *Time* magazine that came directly from the *ISKCON Report.*

Maharudra was the editor as long as he was in our department; after that a woman editor took it over.

Mukunda's final goal was to start an internal newsletter. He found a capable person for the project: Uddhava, a former student from Syracuse University's graduate school of journalism. Uddhava joined ISKCON in Denver and met Subhananda, who was working for his ticket to India. Subhananda introduced Uddhava to Mukunda. In those days it was difficult to "hire" a devotee if they already owed allegiance somewhere else, and Uddhava was tied down in Denver as the temple treasurer. After trying to work through channels for Uddhava's transfer, Mukunda simply sent him an airplane ticket with orders to "sneak away." Once Uddhava was in L.A., Ramesvara reluctantly approved the change.

I gave Uddhava my office, and the department rented another apartment for me. Having my own place in the green building was like getting a promotion. Mukunda and Bhutatma had their apartment; Ramesvara had his apartments; and Mahendra, the BBT accountant, had his office upstairs. Uddhava later received one and so did another long-time secretary, Yasodamayi. We had a pool of secretaries and helpers who came to work each morning. Our department, Ramesvara's BBT operation, and a few other offices occupied most of the green building, with everyone living and working around the central garden patio.

Uddhava assumed responsibility for the *Public Affairs Newsletter* with instructions from Mukunda to make something of it. Printed as it was on bond paper, the newsletter cost 50 cents a copy. That seemed expensive to Uddhava, so, on a lark he called several web press printers for quotes. A tabloid-sized publication on newsprint would cost only 10 cents a copy, with a minimum print run of five thousand. Uddhava proposed selling advertising and subscriptions to make the venture self-sustaining, and Mukunda told him to go ahead.

Because the BBT Press couldn't handle extra work, Uddhava needed phototypesetting equipment. Bhutatma stepped in with money from his personal savings, and Uddhava located a used machine that fit the budget. It was primitive, but it was a typesetter, and it belonged to the P.R. department. When it arrived, we put a garland on it and worshipped it to bring good luck.

With the enthusiasm of cub reporters, we considered names for the new publication: *ISKCON Plain Dealer, Hare Krishna Inquirer, ISKCON Citizen,* or perhaps the *Screamer, Enterprise, Guardian, Blade, Tattler,* or *Gazette.* Mukunda settled on calling it the *ISKCON World Review: Newspaper of the Hare Krishna Movement.*

The office worked at full capacity for two months to produce the first issue. When Uddhava brought it back from the printer everyone stopped to read it, and we studied and admired it for days. The front-page picture was of a forty-foot sailboat, a donation from a wealthy philanthropist. The Honolulu temple president had refurbished the boat and outfitted it with sails lettered "Hare Krishna." The first issue also included an article I had written, along with a photo I shot. I rushed to Dad's office with a dozen copies. He congratulated me and said that although he liked all our publications, he liked this one the best. He knew how exciting newspaper publishing could be because he had been on his college newspaper. He told me he preferred it to broadcast media.

An editorial in the first *ISKCON World Review* explained that the paper was meant to replace the *Public Affairs Newsletter*. Another article called for stories, and people started sending them in. Although it was meant to be an internal publication, the *ISKCON World Review* instantly became more. Our domestic circulation doubled, then tripled, and we easily sold advertising for festival gatherings, products, and devotional services. Temples ordering a thousand copies a month got free advertisements and discount rates, so Chicago, New York, Texas, and all the temples in Ramesvara's zone sent thousands of addresses for our bulk mailings. We had twenty thousand names within the first few years. Layout flats and film negatives went to our representatives in Bombay, Calcutta, South Africa, and England, where devotees raised money from local advertising and printed the paper for their congregations. At the end of the third year our circulation reached fifty-five thousand worldwide. When temples in faraway countries bootlegged our articles, we took it as a compliment.

After the third year, the BBT Press manager invited Uddhava to go in on a lease for state-of-the-art typesetting equipment. Our $15,000 terminal worked in conjunction with the processing equipment at the BBT Press, which was all the more expensive. We joined the big league of ISKCON publishing when we were finally able to typeset transliterations of Sanskrit words, using custom-made diacritical fonts. Uddhava and I were the only ones in the office trained on the Varityper, so whenever a typesetting job came up it was ours. We sometimes worked on five deadlines at once.

I loved the publishing business and jumped at every opportunity to write. When Uddhava asked me to become an assistant writer, Mukunda freed me from my secretarial duties to work full time on the newspaper. As soon as Uddhava and I finished shipping out an issue, we started working on the next. Our deadline was the first of each month, which meant a frantic week of last-minute stories, headlines, and filling empty spaces. Deadlines could be miserable if we felt overworked, or they could be ecstatic, like the night George Harrison came to my door looking for Mukunda.

After a few years, Uddhava and I got married in a happy, two-day celebration that started with a ceremony at the L.A. temple. My mother and stepfather traveled from Phoenix, and my dad was also there with his cameras. While Dad fussed with his light meter, loaded film, and tried different lenses, the priest started the ceremony. Hare Krishna weddings ordinarily include a fire ceremony that goes on for an hour or more, but because Uddhava had already been married once in the traditional ceremony, Ramesvara recommended that ours be a simple exchange of flower garlands. We said our vows and that was about it. Dad looked up from his camera bag and said, "I want to get a picture. Can you do that again?" The next day we held a party at his house for family and friends.

Not much changed for me after filing the marriage license. Neither of us wanted to give up our apartments. We continued living as before, working together to serve the P.R. effort. It was ideal for me because I had always assumed that marriage would interfere with my devotional service. It turned out quite the opposite. It was a valuable alliance; Uddhava and I made a great team. He taught me graphics skills, and we split up the task of designing pages for the *ISKCON World Review*. We also got my father involved. Every month we asked him for advice on our headlines, layouts, and lead paragraphs. There were months when Dad insisted on complete rewrites. His input was welcomed, and Mukunda asked me to list him on the masthead as our media consultant. Working for the paper was my real career, my calling. I had the editorial freedom to propose stories, do the research, and work independently. Publishing my own writing gave me the feeling of satisfaction that I imagined I would get from giving Bhagavatam class. In fact, it was better.

By design, the *ISKCON World Review* was limited to pro-ISKCON good news from GBC zones around the world. We also printed profiles and covered the activities of preachers in the movement. One of our favorites was Bhakti-tirtha, a Princeton graduate who once called himself Toshombe Abdul, president of his university's Association of Black Collegians. Bhakti-tirtha had a way of striking up spontaneous friendships with celebrities such as Muhammad Ali. In one issue we reported Bhakti-tirtha's visit to the Zambian statehouse, where he had dinner with the country's president, Dr. Kenneth Kaunda. He met the president through a judge, Aiyadurai Sivanandan, who had become a devotee. We also printed a photo of Justice Sivanandan dressed in his black judge's robes and powdered wig, with *tilak* on his forehead.

The judge resigned his post in Zambia to serve an ISKCON temple in India. One of ISKCON's predecessors had predicted that in the dawning of Lord Chaitanya's golden age judges would wear *tilak* and become devotees. I spelled this out in a sidebar story. The prediction also stated that entire nations would become Krishna conscious. Naturally, we wanted to promote this notion, and at the time the Hindu kingdom of Nepal seemed the most likely to convert. Nepali officials visited the Kathmandu center for festivals, and the ruling monarch, King Birendra, was already a life member. An ISKCON *sannyasi* in Nepal paid the subscription, and our paper went directly to the royal palace every month. The queen of Nepal and her son, Crown Prince Dipendra, once dropped in on the Soho Street temple for lunch. Our London correspondent sent us a photo to publish, of course.

Mauritius, another predominantly Hindu country, welcomed the Hare Krishna movement. We ran the headline "Mauritius: The First Vedic Country? Prime minister wants Krishna Consciousness spread throughout island." South Africa was another contender because of its Hindu population. The government gave ISKCON land in Natal to build a temple, a project that rivaled Prabhupada's Palace of Gold for its opulence.

Fiji was another country with a large Hindu population. Tamal Krishna had supporters in the Hindu government, which later fell in a coup. He also preached in the Philippines and sent us photos of himself meeting Ferdinand and Imelda Marcos, just a year before they fled the country. Having a picture printed in our newspaper was highly desirable for a guru, regardless of the circumstances. Tamal Krishna wasn't joking when he included pictures of himself embracing the Archbishop of Manila, Cardinal Jaime Sin. *Back to Godhead* also printed the photo.

The land of Bangladesh, the former East Pakistan, was the origin of much tradition for ISKCON. Lord Chaitanya's family roots were in the region and, despite Partition and the creation of a Muslim state, Vaishnavas stayed in Bangladesh to worship and protect the holy sites. ISKCON also had a presence, and correspondents sent us news and photos constantly.

Although there were no Hindus there, the Soviet Union was another place where Krishna consciousness took root. People behind the Iron Curtain read and distributed smuggled BBT books, learned to sing *kirtan,* and had their own Sunday love feasts. The guru Harikesh had been facilitating Soviet preaching from his headquarters in Zurich but kept operations secret because of danger from the KGB. The first Russian devotee, Prabhupada's disciple Ananta-shanti, had been confined to a Soviet psychiatric hospital, and many more devotees had been arrested and detained in labor camps, hospitals, and jails.

At first the only concrete news the *ISKCON World Review* could print came from a pair of *New York Times* articles, "Hare Krishna Chant Unsettles Kremlin" and "Soviet Says Hare Krishna Cloaks CIA." Then, at the beginning of Mikhail Gorbachev's glasnost reforms, Harikesh gave Mukunda the goods: a folder of information and photos that we could publish. Gurus usually communicated with Mukunda, so I didn't know Harikesh personally, but he became one of my favorite gurus when he gave us that scoop. A two-part series in 1984 introduced the Soviet Hare Krishnas. From then on, the *ISKCON World Review* followed the campaign to free two-dozen imprisoned devotees. One memorable front-page story concerned a woman who fasted, dressed in a wedding gown, in front of the Soviet embassy in Sweden for twenty-one days to demand the release of her fiance, an imprisoned Soviet devotee. We ran a photo of the woman in her gown, surrounded by protest signs. The Soviets gave the groom freedom and passage to Sweden.

Hare Krishna leaders conceded that distributing books in communist countries could prevent the impending world war. Prabhupada had predicted a war between the superpowers, but clearly said that chanting (not to mention book distribution) could help. His exact words had been, "Prepare to chant Hare Krishna." Some devotees still believe that the end is near, but my own fear of the war dissipated as the campaign to free the Soviet devotees soared in popularity and provided a positive, common cause to unite all ISKCON zones. Perhaps institutional angst diminished as well.

With the Soviet dispensation in place, we editors started to promote the idea that Chaitanya's golden era would start not by war but by electing ISKCON devotees to political office. In the past, several of Prabhupada's disciples had run for political office. Folklore among Ramesvara's disciples held that he would someday make his decisions from the White House. We had already declared him the king of book distribution. Breaking down the barriers between church and state in 1984 was a Guatemalan devotee named Rupa-manjari, a descendent of a British counsel general. His first political act after being elected to the Guatemalan congress at the age of twenty-two cleared the way for ISKCON's tax-exempt status after four years of strife. Hardly anyone in ISKCON would have known of this political victory unless they read it in our newspaper.

Our publication tried to imply that ISKCON's mission to save the world would succeed any day. Nations such as Nepal and Mauritius would soon be Krishna conscious, and the rest would follow. It was the Hare Krishna domino theory. The early *ISKCON World Reviews* ran outrageously hyped headlines, for example, "Ecstatic Ratha-yatra Liberates New York City." Not all New Yorkers were liberated by the modest procession, of course, but we liked to project an optimistic image. Mukunda, as executive editor, wanted the paper to report ISKCON's strides, and so did Uddhava and I.

All the good news in *ISKCON World Review* made it seem that ISKCON was getting better after four years of internal and external turmoil. Alienated disciples of Prabhupada didn't join in the optimism, but enthusiastic, second-generation disciples had faith that good news was all they needed to know about ISKCON. They loved their gurus, and enthusiasm for preaching reached a new crest. In 1982, nearly a thousand devotees gathered for the Mayapur festival, more than in any previous year. Mukunda and Bhutatma held P.R. workshops for temple presidents while I staffed a P.R. booth that displayed all our publications. Mukunda took *sannyas* initiation that year in a ceremony on Lord Chaitanya's appearance day. It was a great honor for him and a proud moment for P.R. devotees all over the world. Due to Mukunda's efforts, most temples were starting their own P.R. branch offices.

At the next Mayapur festival Mukunda acquired even more responsibility when he became the Governing Body Commission's minister of public affairs. We had a party in the office to celebrate his new status and his forty-first birthday. I had a store print the words "Cult Leader" on an orange T-shirt. When he opened the present, he laughed and wore the shirt the rest of the day.

Our department had grown quickly, along with our productivity. A GBC *sannyasi* led us, our headquarters occupied the same prestigious building as the local guru, and millions of our books, newspapers, and magazines circulated worldwide.

The P.R. department projected an image that ISKCON was doing well. In a sense it was, because we always had plenty of good news for the *ISKCON World Review*. Temples opened in places no one ever heard of, books were coming out in dozens of languages, and VIPs were reaching out to ISKCON. New members were joining and turning their lives over to their gurus. They took initiation in the ancient faith but found themselves on local *sankirtan* teams, doing the pick to finance their gurus' newsworthy projects. Contrary to media reports, gurus like Ramesvara and Bhagavan didn't have stockpiles of cash. They spent it all as soon as it came in because they believed their empires would keep "expanding." This was yet another deviation from the philosophy. There is an esoteric teaching that Krishna's pastimes are expanding, but this isn't the spiritual world. Under material laws, even the stock market doesn't go straight up.

Some gurus were sensible, but others went into debt with leases, mortgages, and loans. It was an excess that ISKCON's top men led lives of luxury, surrounded by adoring and aspiring disciples. They were chauffeured in fancy cars and had their feet bathed in ritual ceremonies. Whenever gurus met with celebrities or government dignitaries they sent us photos of the event. To some readers, the gurus seemed to have it all. Remarkably enough, many were successful even without following the austerities required of ordinary devotees. In the interest of organizational unity, the *ISKCON World Review* gave good coverage equally to all gurus, even if it meant overlooking their tragic flaws and the trouble in their zones. This policy amounted to an intentional internal cover-up.

Mukunda Goswami, ISKCON's public affairs executive, during the publicity campaign for the Venice Beach Ratha-yatra festival in 1978. (Margo M. Shapiro/Mohana d.d.)

Hamsadutta Swami at the 1979 Venice Beach Ratha-yatra festival. (Bill Muster)

Bill Muster and Nori Muster at the 1978 "elephant press conference" on Watseka Avenue. (California Communications, Inc.)

Nori Muster at the elephant press conference. (Bill Muster)

The author's father, Bill Muster, at his studio on Santa Monica Boulevard in Hollywood. (California Communications, Inc.)

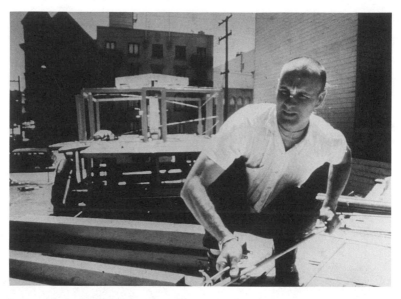

Jayananda, building Ratha-yatra carts. (The Bhaktivedanta Book Trust Int'l © 1983)

The Ratha-yatra parade on the boardwalk at Venice Beach. (The Bhaktivedanta Book Trust Int'l © 1992)

The lead cart of the Venice Beach Ratha-yatra parade. (Bill Muster)

The crowd at the Venice Beach Ratha-yatra festival, as seen from the main stage. (Bill Muster)

Srila Prabhupada (right) after taking *sannyas* initiation in India in 1959.
(The Bhaktivedanta Book Trust Int'l © 1980)

Srila Prabhupada in the United States, flanked by Tamal Krishna (left) and Ramesvara (right). (The Bhaktivedanta Book Trust Int'l © 1977)

Ramesvara garlanding Srila Prabhupada. (The Bhaktivedanta Book Trust Int'l © 1977)

The Los Angeles Hare Krishna temple on Watseka Avenue.

The deities of Radha and Krishna. (The Bhaktivedanta Book Trust Int'l © 1988)

Nori Muster and her mother, Paula Hassler, at the University of California, Santa Barbara, in 1978. (Bill Muster)

Wedding photos in the L.A. temple room. (Bill Muster)

The author's family, left to right, Bill Muster, Nori Muster, the priest Ramadas, Dave Schiller, and Paula Hassler. (Don Hassler)

Nori Muster in 1984. (Bill Muster)

Uddhava (Dave Schiller), working on the *ISKCON World Review*.

Dave Schiller now lives in
Toronto, Canada.

Kirtanananda Swami at Prabhupada's Palace of Gold in New Vrindaban in 1979. (Bill Muster)

A "Krishnaland" illustration appeared in the *Saturday Review* following the grand opening of the Palace of Gold in West Virginia. (Reprinted by permission of The Saturday Review 1979, S.R. Publications, Ltd.)

Bharata, the P.R. department's graphic artist in 1986. (Photo by Bill Alkofer; reprinted with permission of the *Orange County Register,* copyright 1986)

The *ISKCON World Review* and *Back to Godhead* magazine published this publicity photo of Tamal Krishna in the Philippines embracing Cardinal Jaimie Sin. (The Bhaktivedanta Book Trust Int'l © 1983)

Annie Lennox with the British punk stars Poly Styrene (left) and Laura Logic. (The Bhaktivedanta Book Trust Int'l © 1983)

Indira Gandhi honors a portrait of
Lord Chaitanya on national Indian
television. (The Bhaktivedanta
Book Trust Int'l © 1983)

George Harrison at ISKCON's temple complex in Mayapur,
India. (The Bhaktivedanta Book Trust Int'l © 1996)

Ramesvara Crashes

While the P.R. office chugged along at a steady pace, I didn't notice that my guru's world was deteriorating. Ramesvara's woes were typical of the gurus. In L.A. he had trouble keeping the good Prabhupada disciples and went through several temple presidents in a few years. At one point he felt obliged to take on the role himself, which only added to his stress. Senior devotees formed a temple board to make decisions, including what to do about Ramesvara himself.

Revenues to the BBT were down, too. Ramesvara's *sankirtan* teams couldn't deliver like they had in the 1970s, and other zones resisted making donations. Ramesvara sold the lease on the Culver City warehouse and moved the mail order department to Watseka Avenue. Many of the creative programs had to spin off and support themselves, like Golden Avatar Recording Studio. International projects suffered too. The BBT had been sending funds to Mayapur and Vrindavana to build Prabhupada memorials, called *samadhis,* but these were still not completed years after the fact. Instead of building monuments to the founder, bricks were disappearing as critical observers made accusations of mismanagement and embezzlement.

Ramesvara let Koumadaki go because fellow *sannyasis* criticized his keeping a female secretary. He couldn't find a qualified man to replace her; perhaps that was when his world actually started to crumble. Things to which we paid no mind seemed to really bother Ramesvara. He despised the media, especially the religion editor at the *Los Angeles Times,* John Dart. When Dart refused to cover the Venice Beach Ratha-yatra festival one summer,

Ramesvara took it personally. He seethed with anger every time someone mentioned Dart's name.

In the P.R. office we had a more casual attitude about the press. Maybe we were in denial, but it helped to keep a sense of humor. When an imprisoned Prabhupada disciple named Ujjvala set mass murderer Charles Manson on fire, we knew we had a potential disaster. Ujjvala had been convicted of killing his father, a physician who performed abortions. According to Ujjvala, Manson taunted him for chanting *japa* and offering his food to Krishna. After taking Manson's abuse for too long, Ujjvala (Sanskrit for "illumination") stole gasoline from a prison workshop and set Manson ablaze. Although he wasn't seriously hurt, the story became front-page news in *The New York Times* and other papers.

As if setting fire to a notorious cult leader was not enough, Ujjvala told reporters that Krishna had inspired him to "kill the demon." Mukunda's press release, issued from the Washington, D.C., office, claimed that Ujjvala was no longer a devotee, that ISKCON had no link with him. It worked well enough. "Hare Krishna Lights Manson on Fire" made a fine headline, but most editors heeded Mukunda's press release and chose something less sensational. ISKCON suffered only slight damage, and after the media's interest passed, we joked about running the story on the front page of the *ISKCON World Review.* When Ramesvara heard that we were taking the matter lightly, he yelled at Mukunda and Bhutatma, blaming and condemning them as if they were the ones who had struck the match.

Ramesvara was most on edge during his Christmas marathons. He set up a *sankirtan* office in an apartment in the courtyard of the green building, where everyone checked in for their daily assignments. The nightly parties went on past midnight because Ramesvara liked to wait up for the devotees to come home with their collections. Whenever I saw Ramesvara during marathons he was either counting money, talking to widows in white saris, or yelling at someone. During the 1985 marathon, tension built between Ramesvara and everyone in the P.R. office. He already yelled constantly at the men, but beginning with that marathon he started screaming at me, too. He treated us like we were morons who couldn't do anything right. He said things like, "This department doesn't know what it's doing," and "the paper is terrible." When he was in town, I could expect daily incidents of anger and chastisement, which he called his "special mercy." I feared Ramesvara, while Uddhava nurtured a growing resentment.

Gossip circulated that Ramesvara didn't chant all his *japa*. To encourage him to do so, the temple board asked Mukunda to sit with him each morning. It was a losing battle, Mukunda later told me, because Ramesvara either called the East Coast at 5 A.M. or someone called him. Once he got on the telephone it was impossible to wrench the receiver from his hands, and his *japa* suffered.

To his dismay, Ramesvara had become ensnared in his commitment to chant the holy name. Sixteen rounds was required of all devotees, not just beginners. Gurus, especially, were expected to chant all their rounds—they were the ones asking others to take the vow. It was a disgrace for an ordinary devotee to admit to unfinished *japa*, but that could be forgiven in someone still striving for perfection. Part of the zonal gurus' charade was that they were blessed with purity beyond all the other men. Their own definition of a guru's character didn't cut any slack.

Ramesvara had climbed to the top of the wrong ladder. He should have been a business executive, a teacher, a lawyer, or a real estate broker, but instead he was a Hare Krishna guru. His lot had been unfortunate and painful at times. Besides fudging his *japa*, he often wore a suit instead of devotional clothing; he shaved his hair to conform to the guru image only for a time before letting it grow out again, and he didn't like waking up early. As a young man in his twenties he had taken on the vows of a celibate *sannyasi*, only to realize later that he was a full-grown, virile man. Trying to handle the power of a Governing Body commissioner, guru, *sannyasi*, and BBT trustee while leading a life full of duality and doubt took its toll.

The worst stress for Ramesvara was dealing with the *George v. ISKCON* case. Robin George and her mother Marcia had been suing ISKCON since 1977, seeking millions in compensation and punitive damages for alleged kidnapping, false imprisonment, intentional infliction of emotional distress, libel, and the wrongful death of Robin George's father, who had succumbed to heart disease after his daughter's ordeal. Although the plaintiffs had filed suit against each temple where Robin George set foot during her year-long odyssey through ISKCON, Ramesvara's BBT absorbed most of the legal bills. It was an important battle. If the Georges won, more disgruntled former members might file multimillion-dollar lawsuits, which could force some centers to go bankrupt. With the impending trial, Ramesvara demanded that our department perform some P.R. magic to turn public opinion in ISKCON's favor—and quickly. The legal affairs office, another branch of the BBT, had already issued news releases, but to no avail. Mukunda preferred to wait for the verdict, when getting coverage would be easier.

Had it not been for ISKCON's legal and financial troubles, people would have liked Krishna consciousness my father told me. He saw value in what I was

doing for Mukunda because he knew some of ISKCON's projects were benevolent and newsworthy. The grand opening of the Bhaktivedanta Cultural Center was one such event. The building itself was famous, having been
built in 1925 by Lawrence P. Fisher, president of Cadillac Motors. The fifty-
five-room mansion was an ornate Moorish-style estate on the Detroit River
that had ceramic tiled ceilings and floors, intricate wrought-iron work, gold
leaf, and hand-carved wooden details. The patrons of the center were also
newsworthy: Ambarish, Alfred Brush Ford, the son of Henry Ford's grand-
daughter, and Lekhasravanti (Elisabeth Reuther), the daughter of Walter Reuther, the long-time president of the United Auto Workers, had purchased
the Fisher mansion in 1972 as an offering to Prabhupada, and over the years
Ambarish had invested another $2 million in restoration. FATE artists from
Los Angeles had produced a diorama museum, as well as a collection of sculptures that decorated the estate's ten acres of formal grounds.

The grand opening would feature a ribbon-cutting ceremony with Ford,
Reuther, and the guru Bhavananda, who was co-Governing Body commissioner for the project. Mukunda had high hopes because Reuther's 1977 marriage
to Bushaya, another disciple of Prabhupada, received national publicity. Ford
had been the best man, and news reports celebrated the wedding as well as the
comradery between the assembly-line heir and the union boss's daughter.

Weeks before the grand opening, Ambarish flew to L.A. to consult my
father and Mukunda. We drove to Hollywood in Ambarish's rented car, and
during the meeting Dad gave his mini-lecture about museums. He told
Ambarish, "No matter what your museum houses, people will come see it.
People will visit the most eccentric, ridiculous collection, just because it's
there. They'll even have a good time."

On the way home, driving down La Brea Boulevard, we got a flat tire.
Ambarish jerked the car off the street, jumped out, changed the tire, and
within five minutes we were back on the road. He said, "It's a Ford. Every time
I drive a Ford something happens."

The May 25, 1983, grand opening of the Bhaktivedanta Cultural Center
received favorable coverage in *Newsweek, People, USA Today, The New York
Times, New York Daily News, Detroit Free Press, Dallas Morning News, Chicago Tribune*, and *India Tribune*, as well as numerous printings of the Associated Press and United Press International wire stories and coverage on radio and TV news shows. The *Washington Post* ran a photo of the two Detroit
heirs on the front page of the "Style" section, with the headline, "Temple of
Tomorrowland," referring to the Disney-like diorama museum featured at
the opening.

We celebrated at my father's house with a feast cooked by Magic Lotus, the P.R. office's celebrity catering service. Magic Lotus, which specialized in serving vegetarian meals to traveling rock bands, had started in Europe, and there was some Magic Lotus catering in the United States. For the event at my father's we brought the Magic Lotus chefs and their husbands; Satarupa, the model from *Who Are They?* magazine; Arnie Weiss, a man who was basing his doctorate on ISKCON; and Gaura Krishna, a Ph.D. from Italy. When Gaura Krishna had joined ISKCON and taken initiation from Bhagavan, several Italian musicians, artists, and philosophers followed his lead. My father met many ISKCON VIPs, and he enjoyed their company. He also loved *prasadam* (blessed food) and sometimes complained that it was my fault when he gained weight.

In 1983 Mukunda and my father stumbled upon a new venue for *prasadam,* which was based on the style of free food distribution that had been one of Prabhupada's preaching platforms. There was a famous story that when Prabhupada saw the hungry children of Mayapur, he declared that no one within ten miles of an ISKCON temple should go hungry. That started ISKCON Food Relief, financed with grants from the BBT, which provided millions of vegetarian meals in India and Africa. Sadly, the program had diminished without Prabhupada.

In P.R. consultations on the subject, Mukunda convinced my father that individual temples could afford to distribute free food, without relying on the BBT. They saw it as a way the temples could give back to society and propagate spiritual vegetarian food at the same time. Dad and Mukunda thought of the name "Hare Krishna Food for Life" and talked about dozens of ideas to promote the project. Mukunda revived his *Public Affairs Newsletter* to introduce Food for Life to the temple presidents and offered to fly to any center that wanted to start their own program.

Food for Life quickly caught on. Mukunda hired a graphic artist to design a logo for letterheads, vans, and storefronts. Temples in Cleveland, Dallas, and Philadelphia applied for, and received, government grants for thousands of dollars; the Food for Life center in Philadelphia included a shelter for women and children. These programs attracted much support from members of city councils, mayors, and the media. Within the first year, temples in England, France, Bolivia, Germany, Spain, and Australia were distributing Hare Krishna Food for Life.

Mukunda knew that these proactive steps were the right way to change public opinion. My father agreed and sometimes complained to me about the attitudes and issues holding the organization back.

The Robin George trial was five months long and troublesome, and Mukunda had to sit through many days of it, waiting to testify about a libelous press release that he and Ramesvara had issued. Mukunda heard hours of testimony from former *Back to Godhead* editor-in-chief Ed Senesi (Jagannath-suta), who had once worked in the P.R. department, replying to the charges of deprogrammers and the anticult movement. As an innocent and devoted follower, he had been shocked to find articles in the P.R. files linking Prabhupada's organization to *sankirtan* scams and drug smuggling. His disillusionment, coupled with his observation of the mounting turmoil in the Governing Body Commission, made Senesi tell a reporter, "Wow! This organization is really sick. But it's the devotees who are making it go wrong." In court he derided ashram life and recited a laundry list of organizational problems. Listening to Senesi testify, Mukunda said, was "like listening to a toilet flush all day." It was unfortunate that any devotee had to look through our files, but I believed that getting ISKCON into deeper trouble in court was no way to fix things.

Senesi's testimony had nothing to do with Robin George, but it seemed the judge would admit anything meant to prove ISKCON a cult. He let the jury consider verses from Srimad-Bhagavatam as proof that ISKCON had a negative attitude toward parents. There was the evidence of Lord Nrsimhadev, the Lion Avatar who killed a devotee's father. Taken out of context, this popular Hindu deity became a horrifying, cultish monster bent on destroying family values. Scriptures are protected under the First Amendment and cannot be used to convict a religion. ISKCON's attorneys took note of this infringement of constitutional rights.

Robin George admitted that she liked devotional life, including chanting. In fact, when she came home for a few days in the middle of her odyssey her parents had to chain her to a toilet to keep her from running away again, and they shoved a hose in her mouth to make her quit chanting. George stated under oath that the only thing she regretted about her experience was having to return home. Nevertheless, prosecuting attorney Milton Silverman argued that ISKCON, a "dangerous cult," had "psychologically kidnapped" Robin George and had used "mind control" to make her think she was happy. He urged the jury to punish ISKCON with "millions and millions and millions" of dollars in punitive damages to stop them from "stealing children and hiding them from their parents." We in public affairs thought the Georges could never win; people in the legal office were sure they would. Robin George had been a minor when she first ran away.

The jury deliberated two-and-a-half days and then on June 17 awarded Robin George and her mother $32.5 million. Multimillion-dollar judgments were rare in 1983, and $32.5 million was one of the largest in California history.

The day of the George verdict was a pleasant summer day in Los Angeles, and I had my sliding patio door open. Outside, a commotion suddenly took over. Mukunda, Ramesvara, and Narayan, a paralegal heading ISKCON's office of legal affairs, had just learned of the jury's punishment. Ramesvara screamed at everyone he saw on the way from the street to his office, while Narayan ran around ordering community residents to lock their doors and stay inside because county marshals might seize the buildings that day. Mukunda wandered back and forth on the patio of the green building, urging everyone into Ramesvara's quarters to write a press statement.

In the confusion, Narayan came to my door, pounding wildly until I opened it. He had once lent us an elephant; now he was dressed in a dark blue suit and dark sun glasses, and his hair was greased back, making him look a great deal like John Belushi in his role as Joliet Jake Blues in the *Blues Brothers*. Little did I know that I would see him like that on the evening news, talking to reporters in front of the green building. "I thought I told you not to answer your door," he shouted. I didn't know what was going on, then Ramesvara yelled to Narayan to leave me alone and come inside.

When he turned, Narayan noticed that the front door of the building was hanging open to the street. He ran over and slammed it shut, shouting, "Doesn't this building have a lock?" He kept his hand pressed against the door, as if holding the drawbridge of a castle during a siege. Finally, at Ramesvara's next urging, Narayan hesitantly stepped back from the door and walked across the patio. Perhaps it was that day the green building got its nickname, the "Royal Court."

Mukunda emerged from the meeting long enough to give me a three-page press release to type. It said, in part,

> Every true religion has endured the tests of time as well as attacks by opposing elements. Today's verdict in a Santa Ana court is an attempt to destroy one of the world's major religious traditions being practiced in this country. The decision is as outrageous as it is absurd. The figure the court recommended is so high that it is beyond the imagination that the Hare Krishna movement could meet it. Especially when the Hare Krishna religion is no more guilty of falsely imprisoning Robin George than the U.S. Army is of its enlistees or the Catholic church is of brainwashing its clergy. . . . Even the fascist regimes of the 1930s seem tame compared to today's decision. The verdict in effect said that a former member of our religion was brainwashed. This is as ludicrous as saying

for example that the Catholic church has brainwashed a former monk or nun who had renounced his or her vows and taken up another faith.

At the end of a frantic day I called Dad. "You won't believe what happened," I said. "You know that Robin George case?" I was sorry to have to break the bad news because his birthday was the next day. He would be fifty-seven.

"Let me read you our press statement," I said. There were few fax machines in 1983, so I had been reading the three-page document to reporters all day while they taped it or took notes. I started reading it yet again, to my father.

"What are you trying to say there?" Dad asked, stopping me after the first few paragraphs.

"Say? What do you mean? I'm reading this to you."

"You can't have a statement like that," he said. "It's too long. The media will never get it. Your statement should be no more than a short paragraph. Then they'll quote the whole thing."

I pictured him running his hands through his hair. Mukunda had really done it this time, I could almost hear him thinking. We said goodbye cordially, and I hung up, feeling lost. Unfortunately, it was too late to change anything; besides, no one would have listened to me in the uproar of the day.

The George verdict was devastating, and the final outcome would be important to ISKCON, so Dad encouraged us to deal forthrightly with the situation in the *World Review*. Mukunda wrote an editorial that month, and we followed the case from then on. I weighed the significance of *George v. ISKCON* against dozens of stories we were covering all over the world. Weapons and drug dealing had been subdued since 1982. I was grateful that only one part of the sky was falling at a time.

Unhappily, it seemed to be the part right above Ramesvara. He failed to take an optimistic view of the fateful legal situation he shouldered, and the week ahead brought him only more misery. Three days after the verdict, one of his temple presidents happened to be speaking to a reporter on the front steps of the San Diego temple when two vans from the Berkeley temple pulled up. Twenty of Hamsadutta's renegade *sannyasi* disciples jumped out with picket signs saying, "This Temple Belongs to Everyone" and "We're Hare Krishnas Too."

The GBC was mad at Hamsadutta for initiating the *sannyasis* without their approval. Hamsdutta was angry with the Governing Body Commission for their dictatorial management style. He and Ramesvara resented each other more as BBT disputes about copyright infringement and unpaid accounts wore their relationship thin. Mount Kailash and the illegal machine gun just made things worse. After the fist fights in Berkeley, Ramesvara banned Hamsadutta's followers from visiting his zone, but the *George v. ISKCON* verdict somehow triggered the protest.

The resulting *San Diego Union* article, "Harried Krishnas Picket Pacific Beach Temple," stated that the incident "marked the first time that one Hare Krishna group had ever picketed another." According to reporter Arthur Golden, the temple president confronted the picketers with "arms folded across his white robes like an Old Testament prophet" and told them to "get lost." Instead of leaving, the picketers marched back and forth in front of the temple for four hours. Golden described the incident as a "public schism" and observed that "the bizarre scene offered an unusual insight into friction within the mysterious cult."

Mukunda said it must have been destined arrangement that the reporter was there when the picketers arrived. Ramesvara, however, was incensed. When the picketers showed up in Los Angeles, Bhutatma spoke to the ones he knew from his Berkeley days. The group went away peacefully, perhaps to reconcile themselves to their fate as followers of a black sheep, a strange aftermath to their seemingly aimless invasion.

Tensions broke for all of us a few weeks later when Judge James Jackman of the Santa Ana Superior Court reduced the *George v. ISKCON* award to $9.7 million and appointed a receiver to oversee ISKCON's assets. The L.A. temple would not have to give up buildings or turn over money while the Robin George case made its way to appeals court. Ramesvara and the legal department vowed to take the case to the Supreme Court if necessary. One *sankirtan* case had already been there, and another was on the way.

After that matter was settled, Mukunda decided the time was right to deal with Hamsadutta. He flew into action when he heard rumors that the guru had shot a cow that wandered onto his target range at Mount Kailash. Cows are sacred to Krishna followers, and killing one is considered as bad as killing a human. In an emergency operation, Mukunda notified each Governing Body commissioner that something had to be done. Within three weeks of the picketing incident, the full Governing Body Commission assembled in Miami Beach to expel Hamsadutta. Mukunda told reporters that the expulsion was the outcome of Hamsadutta's "attempt to initiate new principles which are unacceptable to ISKCON" and his allegiance to a spiritual master outside ISKCON (Sridhar Swami). He said nothing specific about the picketing incident or the dead cow, or of a GBC investigation that found

Hamsadutta using barbiturates, opiates, and alcohol and breaking his vows of celibacy with female disciples.

The GBC confirmed the expulsion at the 1984 Mayapur meeting. Sunk in depression after that, Hamsadutta got drunk and shot at the windows of a Cadillac dealership and a liquor store near the University of California, Berkeley. He was convicted on gunfire and felony vandalism charges two years later. The biggest negative for ISKCON was that Hamsadutta teamed up with Kirtananda at the Palace, and they fought for the Berkeley property in court. Several Governing Body commissioners were appointed to oversee the turf battle, but Hamsadutta's followers occupied the Berkeley property for several more years.

When there are family feuds, the tension inevitably spreads. The situation was worse within ISKCON because devotees weren't supposed to "speculate," listen to blasphemy, or talk *prajalpa* (idle talk). Outsiders who read newspapers knew more than the actual members. Yet my job was to publish good news that would encourage optimism. Inside, I knew what I was doing was wrong. The dualities wore on me, and I sometimes felt depressed. To pull myself out of it, on Lord Chaitanya's appearance day in 1983 I went to Hollywood Boulevard to chant with about forty other devotees.

It was a dreary, foggy March afternoon and slightly cold. When the chanting party stopped in front of the Chinese Theater, tourists gathered around us to watch. Alongside our party, some young breakdancers performed to the beat of the devotees' drums. I sang with eyes half-closed, remembering myself placing my hand in movie stars' cement palm prints. It may as well have been a different life. The traffic was noisy, and someone shouted "Hare Krishna" from a car. I struggled to feel peaceful within the meditation of chanting.

We walked deeper into the boulevard's madness, toward the Garden Court Apartment Hotel. I would be glad to see the historic old building yet again. I thought of my life before ISKCON but felt cut off from it. Ramesvara had told me that before meeting devotees I was wasting my life like an animal in deplorable material activities. Humility is required to surrender to a guru, but that day on the boulevard I was struggling to find some scrap of pre-ISKCON life, something of my old identity. I couldn't feel anything. Lately, Ramesvara's lectures had been peppered with even more violent warnings against lust. He didn't just suggest that we had sexual desire, he railed against it. It was difficult to explain his anger to aspiring disciples. I longed for the days when Ramesvara didn't yell all the time. Lately, I had been losing faith.

The chanting party stopped in front of a construction barrier surrounded with a chain-link fence. Perhaps my family had messed me up, I thought. For whatever reason, I was irritable. Not acknowledging that ISKCON was convulsing with guru wars, I blamed myself for the inner turmoil that kept me awake at night. When I leaned against the fence, I was startled to see someone about my age and height standing on the other side, looking at me.

"I'm a Christian," the woman said.

"That's great," I said, noting about twenty of her friends standing in the parking lot near a blue and silver bus. Some Christians I liked; I had even let a mysterious Christian woman anoint me once when I was chanting in Westwood. On this day, however, I wasn't in a mood to meet anyone who might try to influence my faith.

"I don't talk to Christians," I said, struggling to avoid the confrontation that was sure to follow. Jackhammers sounded from the construction site. I looked around for the Garden Court Hotel and suddenly realized that it was being demolished. It's a landmark! Don't tear it down, I thought. The sight nearly made me burst with urgency, as if the workers were tearing down part of my psyche. When the hammering stopped the woman asked, "Did you know Jesus said, 'You can only come to the Father through Me'?"

"Excuse me?" I said. I'd been a Hare Krishna for five years, but I had twenty-one years of history that came before. Now, a symbol of my past was being dismantled and a Christian wanted to chip away at what made me a Hare Krishna. A tear rolled down my cheek as I strained to see what was left of the hotel.

"Why do you worship Krishna, don't you know he's the devil?"

"If you're so holy, why do you eat meat?" I blurted out.

Several more Christians came over from the bus, and on my side of the fence some of the women had turned from the chanting to watch.

"Animals are living beings with souls just like you and me," I said by rote. "You Christians are hypocritical because you say you follow God's word, but you kill innocent animals. What about the commandment, 'Thou shalt not kill'? Doesn't that mean anything to you? I wish you would just leave us alone and let us worship God the way we want. We're not hurting anyone, especially anyone who's a real Christian." I could practically hear Ramesvara's voice dubbing over my own.

"I'm fasting today," the Christian woman said. Her last words were barely audible over her sobs, "I'm a vegetarian too. I didn't want to fight."

She turned away, and I followed the chanting party when it moved on. I didn't speak of the incident because it was too hard to reconcile what I had become. Officially, Ramesvara was my guru, a direct descendent of Prabhupada. I wanted to serve Krishna, but yelling at Christians hardly seemed the way to do it. I had joined ISKCON to learn love and compassion. None of that had sunken in, apparently, despite my years of study. I felt ashamed and isolated, anything but spiritual. I was sorry I was mean to the Christian, I was sorry ISKCON was cracking apart beneath my feet, and I was sorry someone tore down the Garden Court Apartment Hotel.

13

The Revolution of Guru Reform

There is an old story about eleven blindfolded men trying to describe an elephant. One man touches the tusk and says the elephant feels smooth and hard. Another inspects the ears and says the elephant is thin and flexible, another man touches the trunk, another the tail, and so on. The guru issue was like an elephant, with each zone representing a different part. Possibly the only person who ever fully understood it was Prabhupada himself, and he did not name a successor. He could neither predict how the family tree would evolve nor order it by decree. Only time and the perspective of passing generations would determine that.

Five years had passed since the Pyramid House talks were rejected, and not much had changed. The GBC had empowered additional men to initiate in under-represented zones like Canada, Africa, and South America, but once all the zones were covered, no more men were empowered in 1985. About half of the gurus stayed out of the fray to concentrate on fulfilling their sacred order. Prabhupada had said any of his disciples could become gurus; some would eventually prove themselves. Still, guruship hadn't opened up like reformers had hoped. A grass-roots movement, a revolution, was underway.

The guru reform movement had grown to about three hundred proponents, including about half of the leadership. Centrists, like Mukunda and others in the GBC, wanted to work within the system for change. Intellectuals on the left, like Subhananda, were naive about some undesirable elements but wanted the GBC to redefine the role of guru, especially abandoning the elaborate worship. Those on the far right blamed the guru system for all the criminal activity and everything else that had gone wrong in ISKCON. When they demanded that all the gurus step down and relinquish their disciples to Prabhupada, it seemed to some that anarchists from the United States were trying to destroy everything.

When a former zonal minister traveled to the United States with a portfolio of "evidence" against the guru for northern Europe, there were many who wanted to see the guru torn down. Angry reformers condemned Harikesh over rumors that he used a pendulum to make decisions in his zone, that he planted banana trees on his Swiss properties to take advantage of a coming weather change, and that he believed psychics in the Soviet Union were waging mental warfare against him and the whole Hare Krishna movement.

The Governing Body privilege committee discussed the matter but found Harikesh innocent and didn't want to start a witch-hunt. The GBC had nothing public to say about banana trees or pendulums, and nothing changed in Harikesh's zone. The rumors were exaggerated, but the GBC's secretiveness made it seem like there was something to hide. In the *ISKCON World Review* we continued to report news from Harikesh's zone, the Soviet Union, without any mention of the controversy. Distributing Prabhupada's books had become a priority because doing so was defeating communism. The way our newspaper presented it, Soviet domination would soon end, and ISKCON would become an accepted state religion. Then Lord Chaitanya's golden age would begin. We were such optimists.

The politics were bad, but *ISKCON World Review* was meant to offer an escape. In our meetings, Mukunda, Uddhava, Bhutatma, and I haggled over the details of each news story, seeking consensus on what would go on the cover, what would go on page one, what stories to pass on to *Back to Godhead,* and so on. Meetings were the time to discuss ISKCON's latest good news: Gurus were buying castles and throwing parties for royalty and rock stars.

We ran a story about Bhagavan's French Chateau d'Ermenonville, where, it was said, Jean Jacques Rousseau retreated in 1767 after having quarreled with David Hume. A front-page photo of the chateau, surrounded by a moat, made an inspiring image for those who wanted to believe all was well in ISKCON. The isolated castle was a metaphor for how the GBC operated, and our coverage didn't mention the unhappy details. Against better advice from some of his godbrothers, Bhagavan had sold the original Paris temple in rue Leseur in 1979 and bought the more prestigious Hotel d'Argenson. The purchase turned into a debacle when local opposition, bad press, a city-imposed ban on visitors, and a $25,000 fine for creating a nuisance forced devotees to flee to the chateau.

I tried to absorb myself in ISKCON's positive aspects. Lord Chaitanya's five hundredth anniversary would take place in 1986; perhaps the golden age would dawn in time for the anniversary. ISKCON badly needed a miracle, so the timing was right. Among Hindus in Bengal and elsewhere, Chaitanya is revered as the patron saint of Radha-Krishna worship. The Indian government had already issued a commemorative postage stamp of Chaitanya, which we enlarged and used for the cover of the *ISKCON World Review*. Prime Minister Indira Gandhi offered *arotik* worship to Chaitanya's portrait in a nationally televised ceremony in 1984, and her son, Prime Minister Rajiv Gandhi, later honored Chaitanya at a commemorative event in New Delhi. Our correspondents helped plan such events and supplied photos for our paper.

ISKCON's celebration included a *pada-yatra* (foot-pilgrimage) to Chaitanya's birthplace, Mayapur. Participants would not only walk but also chant *kirtan* along the route. In India, organizing a pilgrimage is one of the best ways to gain attention for a cause. Throughout 1985, ISKCON followers of every race and nationality walked for days, weeks, or months in the year-long procession. After meandering through scores of rural villages, the *pada-yatra* was scheduled to reach Mayapur just in time for the five-hundredth anniversary celebration. Our office helped publicize the event and, among other things, procured a portable public address system and shipped it to India. The *Public Affairs Newsletter* announced the itinerary and urged devotees to take part. The *World Review* regularly printed advertisements, schedules, and news from *pada-yatra* correspondents.

Mukunda was generally quiet about ISKCON's problems, but in one editorial meeting he told us the latest bad news from France. Bhagavan's real estate buying power had alerted French officials to look into the source of his money. As a result, authorities seized financial records and shut down all *sankirtan*. I found out later that several concerned devotees wrote to the GBC to warn them about Bhagavan's mistakes, including a former P.R. devotee from France who complained that Bhagavan's opulent properties amounted to symbols of bourgeois abuses that the French Revolution had sought to overthrow. The Governing Body commissioners brushed off the letters and took no action against Bhagavan.

For the unreformed, success was measured in materialistic terms. Ramesvara and Bhagavan had regularly compared print runs and *sankirtan* scores, and they competed to have the most prestigious followers. It was a friendly "transcendental" competition in which Bhagavan had clearly been ahead until this happened. Now his detractors told jokes about him. An astrologer once said that Bhagavan had the horoscope of a monarch, which led to the irreverent nickname "the Sun King."

In the editorial meeting we realized that we couldn't print a headline like "Sun King's Zone in Shambles"; our job was to make problems go away. At

Mukunda's enthusiastic urging, we ran a center-spread story about a festival in Bhagavan's zone. Instead of mentioning the devastating legal problem in France, we printed a good-news photo of a devotee dancing arm in arm with a robed Italian monk. A sidebar about the world-famous Ratha-yatra festival at Venice Beach explained that Hare Krishna festivals were happening all around the world in fulfillment of Lord Chaitanya's prediction. In our paper, Ramesvara and Bhagavan were still the kings of ISKCON.

It was our policy not to report problems because we saw ourselves as gatekeepers who had to maintain the pride and enthusiasm of other ISKCON members. In effect, our department perpetrated institutional denial and disinformation. We knew the dark side, but our motto at the paper might have been "Good news and good circulation go hand-in-hand." We believed that members wanted and needed good news.

As our editorial advisor, my father thought our attempts to disguise ISKCON's problems were ridiculous. He lectured Uddhava and me about our responsibility to present the whole truth. He had already earned our respect as an editor, but it was too hard to face the complex issues that Mukunda and practically every other ISKCON leader wanted to keep quiet. How could we tell fifty-five thousand readers about ISKCON's internal dissension when Prabhupada had warned from his deathbed that only internal strife could ruin ISKCON? Nine of the eleven gurus were having problems. In addition to Harikesh's pendulums and Bhagavan's troubles in France, Hamsadutta had been suspended and finally expelled, and Jayatirtha had abandoned ISKCON to start his own following in England. Tamal Krishna and Ramesvara were still licking their wounds from encounters with the Governing Body Commission in 1980, and their disagreements over the BBT continued. Bhavananda, a former Andy Warhol follower, was accused of being homosexual in an anonymous letter the GBC received. Satsvarupa, although still in good standing, suffered debilitating headaches that kept him from participating in management. Kirtanananda was in trouble for crossing GBC zonal boundaries to collect money and open temples. He'd had problems with the GBC ever since he declared that they should act as advisors only and that he, as guru, could do whatever he pleased.

The Governing Body Commission's internal squabbling added fuel to the mounting antiestablishment movement. In June, the North American Temple Presidents met at the ISKCON center in Towaco, New Jersey, for heavy discussions on the subject. Many brought along essays expressing their opinions, but the one that summed up everyone's feelings was "Under My Order: Reflections on the Guru in ISKCON" by Philadelphia temple president

Ravindra Svarupa, who held a Ph.D. from Temple University. The essay began with a quotation from Prabhupada describing the fate of the Gaudiya-math fifty years before in India:

> Bhaktisiddhanta Sarasvati Thakura, at the time of his departure [death], requested all his disciples to form a governing body and conduct missionary activities cooperatively. He did not instruct a particular man to become the next *acharya* [spiritual leader]. But just after his passing away, his leading secretaries made plans, without authority, to occupy the post of *acharya,* and they split in two factions over who the next *acharya* would be. Consequently, both factions were *asara,* or useless, because they had no authority, having disobeyed the order of the spiritual master.

The connection between ISKCON and the demise of the Gaudiya-math suddenly became crystal clear. Ravindra Svarupa's essay exposed the Appointment Tape controversy and concluded with a call to action: "To rectify the mistake, we must first dismantle the illicit institution of zonal *acharyas,* and reestablish the true position of guru under Srila Prabhupada's order."

"Under My Order" lit a fire that spread across the United States. Mukunda helped organize a late-summer gathering in New Vrindaban that would provide a forum for concerned disciples of Prabhupada to speak their minds to the Governing Body Commission. There were three meetings, in August, September, and November, when anti-guru sentiment was at its height. The participants voted overwhelmingly to accept the basic principles of Ravindra Svarupa's manifesto, namely that the zonal guru system was a mistake, the level of worship too high, and the gurus too powerful within the GBC. The cry for guru reform reached a crescendo. Women also attended the meetings, but their meek requests to have women gurus were ignored. Ultimately, the women were content to share in the men's victory, thankful that the zonal guru system might soon be overthrown.

As a result of the reform meetings, the North American Governing Body commissioners made up a list of resolutions to bring to Mayapur, including a call to end guru worship in all zones. Reformers also wanted to make it easier for men to become gurus. In the eight years since Prabhupada had died, two gurus had been expelled, three were added in 1982, and four more in 1984, bringing the total to sixteen. None were named in 1985. The American GBC proposed twenty men for guruship, hoping to flood the system and make being a guru a less elite position. Mukunda was on the list even though he had no prospective disciples.

The reform movement found support among fringe devotees in Europe. Fifty-six people in France signed a letter to the GBC to decry Bhagavan's administration. Thanks to Bhagavan's leadership, they pointed out, the temples owed $6.5 million in tax penalties to the French government.

Some of the targets of guru reform didn't like what was happening. Kirtanananda in particular boycotted the New Vrindaban meetings. Instead of attending, he loudly instructed his followers to continue their adoration of him. Retaliating to Ravindra Svarupa's "Under My Order," Kirtanananda wrote "On His Order," a defense of his position as an absolute guru and proof of his being the only qualified guru of the eleven. The GBC resented Kirtanananda's attitude and made several futile attempts to reason with him.

European zonal secretaries, regional ministers, and temple presidents opposed the reforms. In Europe, temples were filled with young disciples who knew little of the guru controversies; politics from the United States were seen as a disturbance that would only upset the status quo. The European Continental Assembly, composed of Bhagavan's *sannyasis* and administrators, met in France in November 1985 and January 1986. The chair sent out minutes and resolutions, informing the U.S. GBC of the assembly's intent to stop the guru reform movement.

Reaction in Australia and New Zealand was similar to Europe. Disciples of Prabhupada who had left ISKCON supported guru reform, while their godbrothers in positions of power fought against it. South Seas leaders resented the proposed resolution to suspend their guru on account of his being gay. Bhavananda publicly admitted his weaknesses, and the disciples didn't reject him.

Despite the institutional disarray, Mukunda hoped guru reform would be successful. In a series of departmental meetings, he explained the arguments for reducing guru worship. I realized, as Ramesvara had in 1980, that the worship was a folly that had been allowed to go on for eight years. The fight wasn't just about rituals; reformers disagreed about the absolute power of gurus who had divided ISKCON into fiefdoms. Mukunda didn't go into detail about the merits or arguments of each party, but he indicated that our department could do much to help. The *ISKCON World Review* was part of the solution, he said, but more important was strengthening "internal communications" in the GBC. For Mukunda, internal communications meant trying to work the bugs out of guru reform. He said he was obliged to Prabhupada to do what he could to keep ISKCON in one piece because there were others who wanted to tear it all down.

❖

I sat on the steps in front of the green building one quiet morning chanting *japa*. A series of small earthquakes had recently hit L.A. The biggest came one morning at 4:15 A.M., turning out devotees who hadn't been to the morning program in months. Fog hung over the coastal areas for days without lifting. On Watseka Avenue, devotees either paced the sidewalks or nestled in doorways, chanting *japa* in the darkness.

At about 6:45, a modified Econoline van with a homemade sheetmetal top cruised down Watseka Avenue and turned into the parking lot. The man in the driver's seat was Sulochan, a devotee who traveled around selling goods he imported from India. His family, a wife and two sons, lived in New Vrindaban. I'd known Sulochan for years as a friend of Mukunda's. Lately, one of Mukunda's responsibilities in internal communications was to take care of Sulochan. He didn't tell me the details, but only said to put Sulochan through whenever he called or stopped by. Few people had that access to Mukunda, so I knew Sulochan was an important man.

After the morning program I stopped by Sulochan's van to say hello and tell him Mukunda was looking for him. I was surprised at the van's spacious interior, which was like a small motorhome with bookshelves, a couch, chairs, and a kitchenette.

"Have a seat," Sulochan said. He had sandy blond hair and wore jeans and a T-shirt. "There's more room in here since I sold my books."

"Here's my pendant," I said, unhooking my neck beads and handing them over. Every devotee wore a choker of sacred wooden beads from the *tulasi* plant. I liked to hang a silver pendant on mine, but the picture in mine was faded and needed to be replaced. Sulochan sold pendants and had offered to fix mine. He carefully bent back the silver bevel and tried to pry out the faded glass picture of Krishna. It wouldn't budge, so he smashed it with a hammer. Pounding on the workbench seemed to rock the van, but Sulochan just smiled as he picked the broken glass from the setting. He offered me an assortment of pendants, and I picked one of Prabhupada. He dropped it into the setting and smoothed the bevel with a blunt tool.

"Here you go," he said, handing back my beads. "Are you a Prabhupada disciple?"

"No, Ramesvara," I said. "I like Prabhupada, that's all." I took the necklace and dropped it in my bead bag. "What do I owe you?"

Sulochan chuckled. "Not a thing. I'm just repaying the favor."

Mukunda encouraged me to respect all the disciples of Prabhupada, even the "fringies" whom Ramesvara referred to as "snakes." Their disagreements with the GBC were none of my business Mukunda told me. Later the *L.A. Times* would report that Sulochan carried a gun and made death threats to gurus. The *Times* characterized him as a vocal leader of a "growing internal reform movement."

Sulochan had threatened to publish a book he was writing, *The Guru Business,* which would expose the gurus' secrets. I knew nothing of Sulochan's writings, but he had called the GBC the Gang of Blasphemous Conspirators and mailed out sample chapters, which had titles like "How the Personal Ambition of the 'Top Men' Has Ruined Everything," "Cheap Gurus, Cheap Disciples: The Truth about the Spiritual Master," and "Just to Chastise the Evil Doers: But if There Is No Solution, We Must Act."

The Guru Business ranged from goofy to manic, from paranoid to deadly accurate. In it, Sulochan called upon temple presidents across North America to declare allegiance to Prabhupada above the GBC and suggested that it would be good P.R. to remove and destroy the gurus' *vyasasanas.* "The best way to do this is in a public ceremony, with media invited. This will reveal to the city that, 'The local Krishna Temple is taking part in a worldwide campaign to remove the corruption that has plagued them for the past decade.' Something like that makes a good caption and will bring the temple into good graces with the local populace, especially the Indians. The media also will appreciate the effort and will give you favorable coverage."

Sulochan had petitioned the GBC Privilege Committee to return his children, who had remained in New Vrindaban ever since Kirtanananda initiated his wife, and to investigate Kirtanananda's operation. Sulochan even threatened to take the story to CBS News's *60 Minutes.* Sulochan guaranteed, "This book contains enough filth on the new 'Gurus' to burn their little kingdoms to ashes—the fire starting at New Vrindaban." The privilege committee ruled in Sulochan's favor on the matter of his children but had special words of criticism for his anti-Kirtanananda campaign:

> The allegations made . . . in letters and papers distributed widely in ISKCON, have merely served to demean, slander and blaspheme the character of Srila Bhaktipada [Kirtanananda] in a manner unprecedented in ISKCON. Such unsubstantiated allegations, especially when accompanied with blasphemy, are clearly Vaishnava *aparada* [offense to a Vaishnava] to the highest degree. . . . Thus any complaint, legitimate or not, becomes distasteful and disgusting to one's brahminical sense when overshadowed by blasphemy and invective. Sulochan dasa should, therefore, seek forgiveness from Srila Bhaktipada for his offenses.

During the September guru reform meeting Sulochan placed himself in protective custody with the Marshall County, West Virginia, sheriff and spent the time relating stories of New Vrindaban drug dealing, prostitution, and child abuse. Sulochan spoke of a GBC "hit list" and said that he was the number-one most-wanted man on that list. From the safety of his jail cell, he called GBC leaders to demand that Kirtanananda be expelled. He also called reporters. For these activities, the GBC excommunicated Sulochan. When he emerged from protective custody, Sulochan drove to Los Angeles to try to work something out with Mukunda. He stayed on, debating the issues and sharing his views with anyone who would listen. He had friends living on the outside who believed as he did and supported his struggle for justice with the gurus.

ISKCON had become a house of mirrors in which motivations easily became twisted. Life inside felt increasingly untamed, as if violence could break out at any moment. Given the explosive situation in New Vrindaban, violence did break out. A devotee named Triyogi (Michael C. Shockman), angry after being rejected for *sannyas* initiation, had attacked Kirtanananda with a twenty-pound iron pike. Triyogi's repeated beatings to Kirtanananda's head and neck sent the guru into a deep coma. Witnesses caught the assailant and turned him over to police, while a helicopter flew Kirtanananda to a hospital in Pittsburgh for emergency surgery.

Kirtanananda was unconscious for twenty-six days and suffered a partial loss of hearing, but he returned to New Vrindaban and was eventually able to walk with a cane in each hand. After having polio as a child, this was yet another physical disability that would stay with him the rest of his life. He bought a German shepherd guard dog that became his constant companion. Triyogi wrote an apology to the residents of New Vrindaban from his jail cell, hoping to be forgiven in "some future lifetime." They did not forgive him; there was only anger and a need for revenge. Sulochan, however, wrote to Triyogi and congratulated him for his violent act.

A conflict arose over whether to report the incident in the *ISKCON World Review*. Mukunda and Bhutatma saw no harm in ignoring the attack because the paper was meant to be uplifting. They didn't want us to probe into issues surrounding Kirtanananda's volatile zone, which made up more than a third of the U.S. core membership. New Vrindaban's six hundred residents outweighed the L.A. and New York communities combined, and they had the most real estate of any U.S. ISKCON establishment—four thousand acres by 1986. Friction between Kirtanananda and the rest of ISKCON would be difficult to explain to the media as well since the Palace of Gold had practically become the logo for the U.S. Hare Krishna movement. Uddhava, Dad, and I wrote a concise, factual article that noted the beating; Mukunda allowed us to publish it on the front page.

The public media wasn't so sensitive. As usual they rushed to cover ISKCON's problems and point out things that most devotees found easier to deny. "Krishna Sect Splintering in Top Ranks," by Carl Remensky, appeared in the *Pittsburgh Post Gazette* and quoted Subhananda as ISKCON's director for interreligious affairs: "There is a feeling that each area is developing its own personality . . . rather than being a unified international movement, it is developing into a federation of individual ISKCONs." The reporter also interviewed Larry Shinn, an ISKCON observer from the academic world who warned that ISKCON was "in danger of being fragmented beyond recognition" because there was no longer a central authority. He said, "It's a spiritual versus temporal problem. How do you tell these gurus on the one hand that they are the supreme avenue to God, and then on the other hand tell them that they have to work cooperatively within an institutional framework?"

New Vrindaban had clearly rejected guru reform, but Mukunda hoped European leaders would see the light. The enlightenment came in December, when BBC Television broadcast *Persuaders,* a sixty-minute documentary that tells a story of manipulation and influence and how elite Hare Krishna leaders persuaded celebrities to join the fold. The subject of the documentary, British punk rocker Hazel O'Connor, became involved by meeting Ritasya (Anna Raphael), the filmmaker. Bhagavan wanted to produce the documentary and even paid for the production when it seemed as though the singer would become his disciple. Two other punk musicians, Laura Logic and Poly Styrene, had already taken initiation from Bhagavan, but no one had thought to film the story of their conversions.

Hazel O'Connor would have made a good movie for Bhagavan, except that she and Ritasya became angry and retreated with the footage. Ritasya finished the documentary at the National Film and Television School, weaving her longing for spirituality with the practice of guru foot-bathing and institutional chauvinism. In one remarkable scene Bhagavan's minister berates the women about their lack of submission to male guru superiority.

The London *Times* and *Daily Review* praised the documentary. Writing for *Film and TV Technician,* Bob Dunbar said, "The strained sincerity of the devotees and the complacent fascism of their leader were hilariously horrifying. The relentless insistence on the divine necessity of total humility, demanded by a hierarchy utterly devoid of that quality, resulted in unconscious self-satire almost beyond belief."

Mukunda showed *Persuaders* to the P.R. staff as a further briefing on guru reform. I was glad that I watched the show, and I was glad that Bhagavan had been exposed. It seemed like one more shoe dropping, however, because I knew of the trouble in Bhagavan's zone. I felt sorry for him, but my real concern was whether a similar blow could come to my guru. Ramesvara was a lot like Bhagavan, and I feared that he might be subject to the same weaknesses. I put the matter out of my mind, however, by telling myself that nothing could ever happen to Ramesvara. The movie was well done, and I was proud of Ritasya, whom I knew. She would no longer be welcome in Bhagavan's zone, but that was part of standing up to ISKCON. Anyone who tried it had to be ready to take a lot of flak, and I admired her ability to do so.

Dad watched *Persuaders* and commented, "There's trouble in paradise?" He urged us to review the show in the *ISKCON World Review* as a milestone of guru reform, but Mukunda declined. The movie fit that category of touchy issues that were okay to discuss around the office (or in a GBC meeting) but were not okay for the *ISKCON World Review*. He planned to bring the video to Mayapur to show to each Governing Body commissioner in the hope that it would bring about some guru reform. Meanwhile, reporters tried to reconcile ISKCON's good intentions with Kirtanananda's beating in New Vrindaban and Sulochan's warnings of death threats.

14

P.R. Bails Out of L.A.

The *ISKCON World Review* deadline loomed over the holiday season while Uddhava and I sold cookies in front of department stores. It was our duty to Ramesvara, but we were both getting sick of the routine. It was my sixth Christmas marathon; Uddhava had done as many and also worked parking lots and airports in Denver and Las Vegas. We were totally dedicated to the newspaper but only slightly patriotic about soliciting funds for the BBT. Nevertheless, completing the marathon and making the deadline would provide a sense of satisfaction. Our fiftieth issue, including the story of the assault on Kirtanananda, was about to go to press in January 1986.

Just before our deadline Ramesvara held an awards ceremony for devotees who had participated in the marathon. We put our work aside to join the rest of the community gathered in the temple room, including dozens of students from the *gurukula* school near Fresno. The children I had seen the first time I visited the temple were now teenagers and acting the part, expressing their individuality in terms of hair, clothing, TV, and dating.

I slipped in late and took my place in the balcony with the women. Ramesvara referred to a typewritten list to announce the awards for the various *sankirtan* categories (airports, mall blitzing, and cookies). Each time he called a name, others cheered and shouted "*jaya*," as the winners claimed their award certificates.

After that, Ramesvara gave out awards to students from the *gurukula*. Feeling a vague boredom, I listened as he announced the outstanding pupils, the most improved pupils, the best from each grade, and so on. The recognition was encouraging for the children, I decided. Next Ramesvara said he would name award-winners in the departments. I hadn't known he would do that, but he started with the BBT Press, giving his manager an award even though fifteen devotees, bitter from the experience, had left ISKCON from his department. Next he announced the awards for the legal office, for their hard (although unsuccessful) work in defending ISKCON against Marcia and Robin George. I started to fidget, realizing that only the P.R. department remained. Perhaps he would give Uddhava and me an award, or perhaps Mukunda.

"This goes to someone who has done a lot to help Srila Prabhupada in his mission, that is to say, Prabhupada's heart, the BBT. I don't know how to characterize it. Let's just say this person has been the workhorse of the public affairs department, the backbone."

My stomach filled with butterflies. I felt my heart beating in my throat. It wasn't possible he would call on me. I froze.

"Drutakarma, come on up."

Drutakarma, the staff writer, awkwardly rose and stepped forward to accept his certificate. My head swam with confusion. Drutakarma only worked part time in P.R. He kept his apartment in the BBT building and mainly wrote for the BBT and *Back to Godhead.* His receiving an award seemed unfair.

The ceremony ended with one of the male disciples starting a *kirtan.* The sea of people parted for Ramesvara to walk across the marble floor, followed by the *kirtan* chanters and more male disciples. As usual, the women stayed in front of the temple, while the men followed Ramesvara into the courtyard of the green building. I ran to the building before Ramesvara's entourage and locked myself in my apartment, feeling it would have been better if Ramesvara had not mentioned P.R. at all.

At times like that, I turned to chanting to calm my spirits. When the last of the disciples cleared away, I took my *japa* beads and went for a long walk. I had always denied any dissension among the gurus, but in the years that Mukunda had been a Governing Body commissioner the work had drawn me deeper into ISKCON's strife. I regularly came in contact with people and documents spelling out the specifics. Besides that, correspondents in each zone told me gossip and disaster stories along with the good news suitable for publication. I felt the pull of ISKCON politics whenever someone withdrew their support for the newspaper or when a story could only be presented a certain way. When Bhakti-tirtha, the black *sannyasi* from Princeton, appeared to take Kirtanananda's side in the guru issue, all news from his preaching in Africa was banned.

As I chanted, I chastised myself for losing faith. I wanted to surrender fully to prove my love for Krishna, but the discrepancies were hard to ignore. How many times had I heard the phrase "Krishna's in control" twisted to suit institutional goals? Ramesvara said that if we really believed in Krishna, we would do whatever ISKCON authorities asked. ISKCON was the "body" of Prabhupada now that he was departed. My job was to protect the body, but my life was breaking down despite the promise of guru reform. I was starting to see that the gurus themselves were destroying ISKCON, and my guru was one of them. The awards ceremony convinced me that Ramesvara didn't care about my work in the P.R. office. He never said anything nice about the paper, but only criticized it. It also seemed that he didn't care about P.R. anymore, except to keep up the public image for continued *sankirtan.*

When I talked to Uddhava later, he admitted disappointment over working for an organization that seemed to be sinking deeper into trouble each day. During the marathon I had spent my breaks huddled in a cold Toyota pickup truck loaded with boxes of cookies, wishing that I wasn't a Hare Krishna devotee on *sankirtan.* It seemed senseless to be out there seventy hours a week with all the P.R. disasters and internal communications breakdowns in progress. I didn't agree with Ramesvara's ambitions and quotas. I had no way of knowing that because his problems had consumed his entire being he could no longer do anything for anyone but himself.

I talked to my dad about my growing alienation. He asked me whether I was afraid, and I said no, just sad. He questioned further if I felt alone in the community, if I could turn to someone if I needed to do so. I told him that besides Uddhava I had many friends; there was security there. The women on Ramesvara's *sankirtan* team had always been friendly when I went to their classes or dropped in for a meal. Then there were my neighbors, the women who shared the hallway. We often met by our front doors to chat, and I knew their children as well. I told Dad there were also secretaries in the office who were my friends. He was satisfied with that.

When I told Mukunda about my stress, he advised me to get away for some much-needed rest after the marathon. He said things would look better when I got home, so I made plans to visit Texas, where there were thriving temples in Houston and Dallas.

One of the earliest centers, the Dallas temple filled a square block on the city's east side and included a half-dozen small houses, the former *gurukula* building (being remodeled), and an adjoining building with a restaurant and ornate temple room. The community was smaller than L.A.'s, but the friendliness and steadfast devotion of the Dallas devotees overwhelmed me with relief. I'd found an oasis in ISKCON's storm; one branch that wasn't caught up in the turmoil. With a popular restaurant and one of ISKCON's leading Food for Life programs, Dallas had been generating great publicity. *ISKCON World Review* printed a bit of good news from Dallas every month.

I spent the week recording interviews and shooting photos for future news stories. My trip to Texas was everything I wished ISKCON could be: carefree, devotional, and soothing—just dancing and making flower garlands for Krishna, as Subhananda had originally told me to expect. I dreaded going home to the paperwork and mail stacked on my desk and the telephone calls about problems and needs. I would walk in on a deadline already in progress. In addition to that, when I called home for the first time, Uddhava told me of Mukunda's plan to move the office to Laguna Beach. Mukunda had friends there and often stayed in Laguna Beach for several days at a time. It was his retreat, and he had always wanted to live there, but I had always resisted. My father and all my friends lived in L.A. Besides, there had been murders and drug busts in Laguna Beach, and it didn't seem like the best place to base the P.R. department. Uddhava said the move was happening for sure this time.

After finding out about my destiny, I hung up the pay telephone and noticed how alone I felt in the temple lobby. Friendly conversation and music came from the restaurant; across the hall, the jingling of bells meant that a priest was offering the last *arotik* of the day. The Krishna deity was a captivating black marble figure, a gift from the Queen of Jaipur to Prabhupada. I decided to take my grief to the deity. Inside the darkened temple room, I prayed as I often did, standing in front the altar. I didn't want to leave L.A., but all I could do was ask God to help me bear the transition. Then, as if hearing my prayer, the priest turned and dropped a yellow rose in my hand from the offering. I took it as a sign that Krishna would protect me.

My vacation soon ended. When I got home, Mukunda announced that we would move everything—eight apartments full of file cabinets, desks, and office equipment—on March 1. Despite the other challenges of moving, he wanted Uddhava and me to meet our scheduled *ISKCON World Review* deadlines at the end of January and February. Fillers such as children's coloring contests, photos of Prabhupada, philosophical essays, and reviews of our department's own publications helped spread out the news articles we had. Ramesvara disliked something about each issue, although practically none of our subscribers or advertisers complained or even noticed how sparse the paper became during those months.

Between the January and February deadlines I celebrated my birthday and reflected on how far I had come in thirty years. It had been sixteen years since my parents' divorce; sixteen years that I had been on my own. I was thankful to have made it to thirty. Mukunda offered his own input, convincing me that relocating the office to Laguna Beach would be a worthy achievement to mark this milestone. He recalled the excitement of his days in San Francisco and England, opening new outposts for Prabhupada. Temple life in L.A. had its comforts, he explained, but the best service was to break new ground. I appreciated his point. Perhaps things would work out for the best.

There were no residence buildings at the Laguna Beach temple as there were in L.A. When we went house-hunting, Mukunda asked Uddhava and me to wear Western clothes. I preferred to be up-front by wearing a sari, but he insisted that we conceal our identities. After a day of shopping with a real estate agent, we rented two expensive ocean-view properties: a two-bedroom house on a hillside and a tiny office space in a professional building near the million-dollar homes of Three Arch Bay.

Mukunda, Bhutatma, Uddhava, and I had been neighbors in the green building, but we would all live together in the house and work together at the office. Somehow we stayed optimistic even though the rent for the two places was more than we had paid for eight apartments in L.A. and four more people still needed housing: a graphic artist, a photographer, a writer, and Mukunda's secretary. Another inconvenience was the location. The rentals were in South Laguna, two miles south of the temple. That meant that Uddhava and I would be driving our car to the temple at 4 A.M. Worst of all, we would have to wear Western clothing to the office because the landlord didn't know we were devotees. My situation had a frightening resemblance to leaving ISKCON, but Mukunda assured me that I had not.

Moving posed other problems, such as where to print the paper and how to typeset it. Our typesetting terminal was useless without the equipment at the BBT Press. Fortunately, desktop publishing was evolving. My dad was about to invest in a Macintosh system, and he located a used Macintosh for us at the end of February so we could convert in time to make the next deadline.

I had no idea what motivated Mukunda to move south. There was a lot he wasn't telling us. Ramesvara seemed angry that we were leaving, but everyone, including Uddhava, told me that he was all for it. When doubts overcame me, I had nightmares. In one, Uddhava and Mukunda pushed us off from shore in a boat. I didn't want to go, so I jumped overboard and found myself thrashing in the water. Obviously, I feared I couldn't survive on my own.

The first day of March we rented a twenty-six-foot moving van and spent all day loading it. We left L.A. on March 2, in a caravan of cars and vans. We unloaded the vehicles in a hurry that night and left the six-hundred-square-foot office suite stacked with furniture. It was like a sadistic three-dimensional puzzle that took weeks to straighten out. Moving into the house was worse because I had forgotten to have the utilities turned on. The place was dark and cold until Monday morning. When we tried to return the van, it broke down on the way to the freeway. Uddhava waited for road service while I drove our car to the printer to pick up the March issue and start the mail-out.

After four days of anxiety over how we would publish the next issue, I went to L.A. to get the new computer. That night there was traffic on the freeway, and the hour's drive took longer than two hours. The delay put me in a bad mood, and as soon as I walked in the door Bhutatma and I started arguing. By the end of a frustrating evening the four of us had admitted that we would make terrible roommates, so we decided to break the lease and rent two separate apartments. Mukunda flew to India the next day for the Governing Body Commission meetings, where he would present the guru reform agenda and *Persuaders* video.

Uddhava and I had a deadline, and we had new software to learn. We found a computer store that would let us use their laser printer for a dollar a page, then at the Sunday feast we met a computer salesman from San Clemente who bought us a much-needed hard disk and helped us set it up. The desktop system cut our prepress work from ten days to ten hours, so despite the obstacle course we took the April issue to press only a few days late.

Our lead story was about Gopal's, a new vege-burger restaurant in Melbourne, Australia. I had always hoped a temple would open a vegetarian fast-food place, so I played it up on the front page. The article was optimistic, with no hint that everyone in ISKCON except the P.R. office was gossiping about the sexual misconduct of that zone's guru, Bhavananda. Even as the GBC deliberated his fate I wanted readers to believe that his zone was okay, just as Dallas had been for me.

Unfortunately, by the 1986 GBC meeting most North American temples were caught up in a deepening recession. Three of our biggest customers— New York, Chicago, and Houston—stopped their orders and pulled their advertising. When our circulation dropped to less than ten thousand, we needed Bhutatma to make a contribution from the BBT budget to print the next issue. He suggested making the paper a quarterly because it now cost money.

Just when I was feeling the most depressed, Mukunda called from Singapore with the good news that the Governing Body Commission had approved the entire list of twenty new gurus and that the American GBC had pushed through its guru reform agenda. Gurus in most zones agreed to think about removing the *vyasasanas* and dropping their terms of honor, especially the title "Srila," which they agreed to reserve for Prabhupada. There were still many areas of disagreement, but Mukunda said it was just a matter of getting all the zonal leaders to agree on the same standard. He wanted me to print the new gurus' names in the *ISKCON World Review*.

Bhutatma's pessimism paled alongside Mukunda's enthusiasm. Devotees from all over the world had given Mukunda material for future news stories, so he said not to worry about money or the state of the Governing Body Commission. He had received the internal communications responsibilities he asked for, and he planned to expand our department's role in reorganizing ISKCON.

Back in Los Angeles, Ramesvara, who had just returned from India, was under fire. I heard rumors that he was having a relationship with a fifteen-year-old *gurukula* girl and that some Governing Body commissioners were trying to drum him out of ISKCON. I knew the girl. Despite a regimented Hare Krishna upbringing, she was entering womanhood with beauty, sensuality, and mystery. Devotees acted as self-appointed spies, trailing Ramesvara whenever he went out alone in his car. Someone spotted him in Beverly Center with the girl, and a servant told of once finding her locked in the guru's bedroom. The temple board interviewed his housekeeper, who gave further evidence of his comings and goings.

Old rumblings about Ramesvara's *japa* also resumed. This time, critics said that Ramesvara had never been the type to chant all his rounds. That information didn't fit with my reality because he was supposed to be my guru. I felt cut off living so many miles away, but Ramesvara was scheduled to visit the Laguna Beach temple the last day of April. I was sure the bad dream would end if I could just see him again.

When the time came, I picked a blossom from a magnolia tree in our front yard. The temple was located in a split-level church building on a busy corner near downtown Laguna Beach, with a lunch and dinner buffet in the foyer. I had been at the grand opening of the building in 1980, and, for me, the temple held memories of wild *kirtans* from past years, where hundreds of devotees from Ramesvara's zone had danced together in celebration. When Uddhava and I entered, the temple room seemed empty except for Ramesvara, who was standing near the banister, and Mukunda, who was seated downstairs on a built-in wooden bench.

"Uddhava, Nandini," Ramesvara said, smiling as we offered our obeisances on the floor before him. He was dressed in *sannyasi* robes but had grown his hair out. He'd also been working out at a gym and had gained about fifteen pounds of muscle. He didn't look like a guru. I started to worry. After getting up, I noticed that others were present. Across the room from Mukunda were five teenage girls, including the one Ramesvara liked. There was an awkward silence, then I held up the magnolia flower.

"This is for you," I said. I took a step closer and held it out to him. Then I put the blossom on the banister.

"How are things?" he asked, finally taking my gift.

"All right," Uddhava said.

"Everything's fine," I said.

"Sure it is," Ramesvara said. "How can you say everything's fine when you live so far from the temple?"

"We tried to move closer," Uddhava said. "It's hard to rent anything around here."

"Don't give me excuses," Ramesvara said, throwing the flower to the floor. "I thought the temple president knew of an apartment."

"It fell through," Uddhava said.

"The timing was bad," I said, looking at the flower, which was already wilting.

Uddhava stood silently, hanging his head, then mumbled, "Is there anything special I could do to serve you?"

"Service?" Ramesvara said. "Just keep coming to the Sunday feast. Try to make some new devotees for the temple."

The teenage girls had moved into a huddle on the bench; Mukunda gazed at the floor. I was dressed for the office, not in my devotional clothes. I hardly felt like a devotee. Morning sunlight filtered through the windows, bathing everything in a haze of melancholy.

"Is that all Srila Ramesvara?" Uddhava asked.

"That's all. You can go now."

Just nine days later, two women from the Los Angeles community spotted Ramesvara at the Santa Monica Mall with the fifteen-year-old. They approached him to say hello and let him know that he'd been noticed. According to an account they later submitted to the Los Angeles temple board, Ramesvara said, "I'm dead. I'm finished. You guys have seen me here and I'm dead." He begged them not to tell anyone of the encounter and launched into a heart-felt confession. Among other things, he denied having sex with the girl but admitted that he was unable to give up her company. He mentioned keeping a gun in his office and said he had contemplated suicide. He said, "You don't know how [the Governing Body commissioners] work, how heavy

ISKCON can be. It's the heaviest movement on this planet. They won't accept it if I put on white [give up renunciation]."

Ramesvara's father had offered him a job in the family business, put a million dollars worth of assets in his name, and provided him with a credit card. Ramesvara revealed to the women that he had let his hair grow to please his father. He said that by taking a job from his family he would be able to donate millions of dollars to save the BBT. He didn't want to leave ISKCON or give up his renunciation, but he was sure that he didn't want to initiate more disciples. Of the 350 people he had initiated, more than eighty had already left ISKCON. The women recalled, "He said he was scared because no one knew what being a guru really meant in terms of what happens when a disciple falls down or bloops. He said he had asked all the gurus and no one knew, and that Krishna had not appeared to anyone to tell them what happens, and that he had some bad dreams about hell. He said he wasn't afraid of hell; he was in hell now."

In an emergency meeting the Governing Body Commission issued a letter recommending that Ramesvara travel in India for a year of atonement and purification. They approved his plan to work for his parents and gave him permission to get married to anyone but the girl. Finally, they ordered him not to make any moves until the next GBC meeting, eleven months away.

That year Ramesvara's disciples held a birthday festival for him in Laguna Beach as usual. We all hoped the situation would resolve itself and Ramesvara could continue as our guru. As in previous years, Uddhava produced a *vyasa-puja* book, a collection of disciples' letters of homage. Disciples read their letters aloud from the book, partook of a feast and birthday cake, and chanted at the beach. Although we tried hard to make the day fun, we were apprehensive. No one knew what would become of Ramesvara, and he wasn't saying.

15

1986: The Year of Crisis

Ramesvara's admission of weakness and his stern censure were blows to the movement, but the next week brought a harsher and more fateful event. Sulochan, the man who claimed to be on New Vrindaban's hit list, was shot to death in his van near the Los Angeles temple. When someone from L.A. called to tell us the news, Uddhava and I went out the door for a long, reflective walk on the beach. It was impossible to get back to work that day because neither of us could explain why being a Hare Krishna had suddenly become so dangerous. We were forced to realize the seriousness of Sulochan's attack on the gurus, as well as the fury with which it had been countered.

The next day I was back, writing a "good news" story about Lord Chaitanya's five-hundredth anniversary. Mukunda told me to publish a figure of five thousand devotees attending the Mayapur festival. The number seemed a bit exaggerated, but all I could think about was how sorry I felt that Sulochan was dead. As I struggled to grasp it all, sitting at my desk, staring at the computer screen, the telephone rang.

"My name is Terry Pristen. A mutual friend, Nancy Meyers, gave me your number."

"Oh yes, I know Nancy."

"She said you work for the public affairs department of the Hare Krishna movement, that you're in charge of the movement's newspaper."

"Yes, that's right," I said.

"I'm doing a news story for the *Los Angeles Times* about the recent murder. Can you answer a few questions?"

"Murder?" I said. Oh for God's sake, I thought, where's Mukunda? He didn't like me to handle these things myself and would be furious if I said too much.

"Actually, I'm just a secretary here," I said. "I can't give you an official comment."

"But you know about the murder, don't you?" the woman persisted. "I have a few simple questions."

"I can't make any comment. Let me take your name and number. I'll have the minister of public affairs call you back right away." If I can find him, I thought.

After hanging up I dialed Mukunda's private line to leave the reporter's name, number, and an urgent message to call her. Mukunda checked his messages but never got back to the *Times* reporter. In the days that followed, L.A. police detectives and certain investigative reporters kept Mukunda informed of the latest developments. Working on tips from Sulochan's friends and others, police in Ohio arrested Tirtha (Thomas Drescher) on a West Virginia warrant in the case of Charles St. Denis. Also known as Chakradhari, St. Denis had mysteriously disappeared from New Vrindaban three years earlier, and Tirtha was a suspect in his disappearance. The deaths, combined with the accusations Sulochan had made, precipitated a federal grand jury investigation.

The *ISKCON World Review* received a press release from New Vrindaban, but not about the murder. French photographer Pascal Matre had come to the palace to shoot pictures for National Geographic's upcoming book, *A Day in the Life of America.* I was relieved to have some good news to print because I thought doing so would lighten things up. I was wrong. After that issue, Bhutatma called a moratorium on New Vrindaban press releases or any news from New Vrindaban. Our newspaper was silent, but the *Los Angeles Times, New York Times,* UPI, AP, and most other news organizations reported the murder investigation. In its article "Troubled Karma for the Krishnas," *Time* magazine quoted Sulochan's allegation that New Vrindaban "was becoming like the Rev. Jim Jones' notorious People's Temple." The headline in *Hinduism Today,* widely circulated in the Asian community, summarized the unfortunate situation: "Murder Quickens Wider Crisis in Krishna Sect: In-Fighting, Succession Struggle and Demands for Reform Convulse ISKCON." We felt the convulsions in the form of telephone calls pouring into the office. What to do about the flood of negative publicity? we were asked.

Uddhava and I came to the office each morning, but the situation was discouraging. We were there with Mukunda one day, ruminating over the media coverage and trying to have an editorial meeting, when Ramesvara called. Uddhava answered.

"What the hell are you doing down there?" Ramesvara said. "There's a major media crisis going on! Where's Mukunda?"

Uddhava handed the telephone right over.

"What the hell are you going to do about this?" Ramesvara said. "What do you think I'm paying you for?"

"It isn't my job to make people stop killing each other," Mukunda said.

"Look, I can cut your budget off if you don't do something. Get out there and see what's going on!"

"Why didn't he double our budget?" Bhutatma joked later. "We could have stopped all the bad publicity for sure."

In the wake of his censure, Ramesvara was struggling to assert himself as the man in control, and he did sign our budget check, which we badly needed to survive. Mukunda left for New Vrindaban the next day. While he was gone, devotees from Europe and India called the office to report that the "Krishna killers" story had shown up on their continents. It had truly become a nightmare. To save money for the department, Uddhava, Bhutatma, and I decided to give up the office. Uddhava and I moved to a two-story apartment on the South Coast Highway that had enough room for us to set up the newspaper office in our living room.

"Come on in, Bharata," I said one sunny afternoon, answering a knock at the door. Bharata was the graphic artist who had moved with us from Los Angeles. He was one of those men who always shaved his head, chanted his rounds, and wore the traditional saffron robes. "What can I do for you?" I asked.

"I just came to read your magazines," he said.

"They're right here. You're welcome to them," I shut the door behind him and went back to my desk. Most devotees weren't supposed to read magazines, but the P.R. department didn't always follow that rule.

"Hey, Bharata, old buddy. What's happening?" Uddhava said, coming down the stairs in his baggy white dhoti and Indian shirt. "How are things going?"

"The usual," Bharata said. "I'm getting sick of having to drive to the morning program." He lived alone in an apartment that Mukunda and Bhutatma provided.

"I miss L.A. too," I said, staring into my computer screen. "At least we don't have to drive to that office anymore."

"How can you stand the noise?" Bharata asked.

"You mean the highway? We just keep the windows closed—soundproof glass," Uddhava said.

"We have a nice view of the ocean," I said, glancing out the window to appreciate the broad blue band of Pacific that we could see over the neighbors' roofs.

"Do you want to hear the latest?" Uddhava said. "Someone called me from L.A. today and said Ramesvara quit chanting his rounds. Don't you hate rumors?"

"It's true, isn't it?" Bharata asked.

"Come on, Bharata, Don't you know a rumor when you hear one? Ramesvara has been chanting all his rounds ever since that GBC meeting." Uddhava shook his head in disgust.

"No he hasn't!" Bharata said, his pale skin flushing red. "The L.A. temple board has been watching him, and he doesn't chant. In fact, he has a lot of problems, and it's about time you faced it. Mukunda told me Ramesvara's hanging by a thread and has been for some time."

"Don't pick on our guru," I said. "You're just envious because your guru had so many problems. At least Ramesvara wasn't caught with an arsenal of guns like Hamsadutta."

"Leave my guru out of this," Bharata said. "What we have here is the simple fact that Ramesvara is falling down. You guys are going to have to face it one day, just like I did."

"We don't want to hear this," I said. "You can stay if you want, but just read the magazines, will you?"

"I think I'll go," Bharata said. "But you'll see I was right."

He took a few *Time* magazines and before leaving smiled a childlike smile, perhaps to let us know he wasn't mad at us.

I felt defensive and unhappy that the Governing Body Commission had condemned Ramesvara, but what if he wasn't entirely at fault? In a larger sense, what if ISKCON itself was guilty? Among Ramesvara's sins was a little honesty that kept popping up. He didn't feel like a guru or a *sannyasi*. He could no longer pretend. This was a liability in a world of guru issues and ISKCON politics. It was a world he had helped to create but in which he could no longer live.

❖

The year 1986, the five-hundredth anniversary of Lord Chaitanya, was a year of crisis for ISKCON, and it seemed that everything I'd worked so hard to prop up was crumbling. The only thing that could have made it worse for me would have been a personal hardship, such as a serious disease or the death of a loved one. That came to pass in June, when I called to wish my father a happy sixtieth birthday. He beat around the bush, then said that his doctors had told him he had mesothelioma, a terminal form of lung cancer caused by asbestos. At first the oncologist gave him six months to live but then offered an operation that could prolong his life. After thinking it over carefully, Dad decided to go through with the surgery. I visited him at Cedars-Sinai, a private hospital tucked between West Hollywood and Beverly Hills.

It seemed an endless a maze of hallways decorated with oil paintings and large abstract sculptures. When I finally found the right ward, the nurses stared at me for a moment, probably because I was dressed in a sari, then directed me to my father's room. I pushed the door open and peeked in. He was lying in bed, white sheets pulled up to his chin.

"Dad, how do you feel?"

"Is that Nori?"

"Yes, it's me."

He looked up. "Did you drive all the way up here just to see me?"

I sat down in a chair, and we gazed out the window together.

"Can you see your house from here?" I asked, looking at the view of the Hollywood Hills.

"Hand me my glasses," he said. "It's up there, all right. I can't tell exactly where." He folded the glasses and handed them back to me.

"Did the operation get all the cancer?" I asked.

"It hurt enough," he said. "It better have."

"I'm afraid, Dad. I keep thinking of Betty."

He knew what I meant. In 1982 the vice president of his firm, the spokesperson for the Save the *Delta Queen* campaign, had been diagnosed with cancer and died within two months. It was a loss for my father and also for me, because she had been my friend. I sat there, afraid and unable to comprehend what was happening. Just then a nurse came in and gave me the kind of look nurses give to relatives of terminal patients. "I have to bathe your father now," she said. "Can you wait outside?" I sat on a bench in the hallway, feeling insignificant in a vast universe. I hunched over, quietly counting mantras on my *japa* beads. It wasn't easy for me; all I could do was keep going.

❖

The July paper went to press on schedule. Once it was printed, Mukunda invited everyone in the department over for a critique. Each person had to say something—they liked this or didn't like that—and Navasi, Mukunda's secretary, took issue with the lead story, "Chess Champ Finds Creativity in Krishna Lifestyle." After a former junior chess champion named Jaya Krishna (Jay Whitehead) joined the San Francisco temple, the *San Francisco Examiner* printed a picture of him, dressed in his dhoti and playing in a tournament. Part of the story was that before taking up the faith Jaya Krishna had a "temper tantrum" if he lost a game, throwing "chess pieces onto the floor" with "a host of abusive words not far behind." As a devotee, he had developed peace of mind and near-perfect self-control during a match. Although the anecdotes about chess board manners added to Jaya Krishna's color, we cut these details out because we considered them undesirable, fulfilling a stereotype about the kind of people who join ISKCON.

Navasi, who had seen the original materials, said we had stripped Jaya Krishna of his humanity by making him look too perfect. She urged us to do a more accurate job of reporting, adding that the phony, sanitized character of our paper had bothered her for a long time.

After the meeting broke up Uddhava and I went back to work. We had invoices to write and new subscriptions to process. I was sitting at my computer when he came to my office and leaned against my desk.

"You know, Navasi's right," he said.

"She doesn't know anything," I said, wishing to work rather than chat about the incident.

"It's not truthful," Uddhava said, picking up a copy of the *ISKCON World Review.*

"Hey, I need that," I said.

"What's the point of printing this whitewash?" he asked.

"It's what people want," I said.

Uddhava came from a journalism background, while I had grown up with P.R. I admitted that the *ISKCON World Review* was a P.R. piece. That afternoon Uddhava convinced me it should be otherwise.

When I called Dad to ask him how he was doing, I told him about my revelation. "Up to this point you've been guided by the need to promote ISKCON," he suggested, "when what's really needed is honest dialogue." He was recuperating at home and invited me up for the weekend.

His house on Skylark Lane was built on stilts and set against a steep hillside overlooking West Los Angeles. Visitors often sat on its gracious cantilevered balconies to enjoy the view. Dad and I spent hours outside in the warm

July sunshine, talking about our lives. He told me about the Great Depression, of his parents who had died when he was a child, and how frightening the orphanage had been. His half-brother had taken him in for a time, then on the eve of World War II they had traveled together from Chicago to Bremerton, Washington, to work for the navy. It was in the shipyards that he had been exposed to the asbestos. He told me of the foster family that convinced him to make something of himself and how he went to work for Acme Photos, then took a leave of absence to serve as an army photographer and get his college degree in journalism. When he returned to Acme, he and my mother moved to Minneapolis, where my father became a bureau chief.

After telling his stories, he put a music roll on the player piano and dozed off on the couch. I'd seen my father asleep on the living-room couch of our family home many times. He usually drifted off with a book open across his chest and a reel-to-reel tape playing so loudly that the music could be heard down the block.

I busied myself at my computer until he awakened, then we talked again, this time about ISKCON. The latest news was that the L.A. Times had published a big story by John Dart that told everything about Sulochan, the guru reform movement, and the violence that had resulted. My father commented that every member of ISKCON had a right to know what was going on. I told Dad that our policy at the newspaper was to ignore the New Vrindaban situation until it blew over.

"This has been in every newspaper! You can't ignore it," he said. I'm sure his reaction would have been sharper if he had felt better.

I nodded in agreement. He had an idea for a brief news article to explain ISKCON's predicament, so we sat by his pool and wrote the story, "Former ISKCON Member's Slaying under Investigation." When I telephoned it in, Mukunda and Bhutatma reluctantly said I could print it with some disclaimers and to make sure I mentioned that the alleged murderer and the victims had long been excommunicated.

During our visit, Dad suggested that if I wanted to broach ISKCON's sensitive issues I should interview gurus and Governing Body commissioners, as well as scholars and others who studied the movement. "That way you're reporting what someone else says. An interview is news, not your opinion," he explained. Dad said he would help me if I got started right away. For my fist interview I chose Arnie Weiss, the psychologist who had earned his Ph.D. studying Hare Krishna devotees. Weiss said, "My study had some interesting results. The most prominent was that on the Comrey Personality Scales, both male and female devotees showed a hallmark personality trait. On the average, devotees scored way above the normal range in compulsivity. I don't know of any other group at this point that has been studied, that has such a pronounced measure of compulsivity."

Devotees were close to the norm on all other measures, he added, and compulsivity isn't necessarily bad. It "runs corporate executives," and all people who are "meticulous, highly organized, conscientious and punctual" have a little. His findings were to the point. It was clear to me, at least, that devotees were compulsive. Otherwise how could we live in a highly structured, authoritarian group, wake at four in the morning, chant Hare Krishna on beads for two hours a day, and work seven days a week? I looked forward to publishing Weiss's views. Dad and I wrote an editorial, "Weiss's Psychological Study: Scientific Fact, Not Flattery," which said, "While one may not exactly feel flattered at being called compulsive, the study was designed to be scientific, not complimentary. Despite that slightly negative appellation, devotees are revealed as a tight-knit group of highly self-motivated persons who have adopted a religious lifestyle of their own free will."

It took a lot of discussion, but I convinced Mukunda to let me print the interview. Dad wrote the headline, "Psychological Study: What Makes a Hare Krishna Devotee Tick?" I felt it was a successful presentation because it stirred up some friendly (and not so friendly) discussion about devotee compulsivity.

In August, the Governing Body Commission met in San Diego to discuss deviant gurus. They suspended Bhavananda and gave him a list of guidelines. He was to attend the morning program, shave his head regularly, read Prabhupada's books, and not watch TV. On the list of recommendations, which they expected Bhavananda to sign and follow, was the requirement "do not travel with Bala," his male companion.

The next resolution concerned Kirtanananda. He also received a set of guidelines, and the GBC telephoned him in New Vrindaban to extract his promise to resign if named in indictments for either of the murder cases. Mukunda gave me a press release about Kirtanananda's promise, which I typed and mailed out. The third topic was Ramesvara. The GBC suspended him and formed a committee to monitor his behavior. Rather than wait around for their assessment, Ramesvara left ISKCON for good. He gave a farewell speech to his disciples in L.A. and a separate speech to his peers. He admitted his attachment to the girl and his failure to chant his *japa* but called his break a "change of service" and promised that after working for his parents he would send money to the BBT. The girl stayed to live with her mother on Watseka Avenue and attend public high school.

After Ramesvara left, Uddhava and I went to the L.A. temple to pick up a copy of the speech, which had been taped. I talked things over with my friend Koumadaki, who lived nearby and worked for a law firm in Beverly Hills. She explained that her former boss had made the only decision he could and that she supported it. I understood what he was going through, but still suffered when I joined the ranks of others who had lost their gurus to the GBC turmoil. I was an orphan left in the storm, with only my grandfather Prabhupada to look up to. I kept chanting, so I was still a devotee, Ramesvara or no Ramesvara.

After the temple, Uddhava and I drove downtown to attend a wedding; the bride and groom were both television writers. It was an elegant affair at the downtown L.A. Biltmore, a Spanish Renaissance building facing Pershing Square. During the reception, the bride, Nancy Meyers, gave a humorous speech acknowledging my father as the matchmaker who put her together with the groom, Jon Wilkman. My mother and stepfather had also come from Phoenix for the wedding, and with aunts and cousins added our family took up a whole table in the ballroom. After the dancing started, Terry Pristen, Nancy Meyer's friend from the *L.A. Times,* came over to say hello. She asked me if I planned to stay with ISKCON now that the murder was out in the open. I told her that the overall organization was benign and the brutality was uncharacteristic, considering what Prabhupada had wanted for ISKCON. I said I planned to work within the system to change things.

Terry Pristen smiled compassionately before she walked away. I thought I knew the depths of ISKCON, but I didn't. The murder victim Sulochan and those who believed as he did had said the troubles were symptoms of a spreading cancer of denial. In the P.R. office we wanted to heal ISKCON, but in our minds certain elements were wrecking things for everyone else. We wanted to disassociate ISKCON, but no matter how we tried to pretend, we could not make the problems go away. Some of the supposedly good people were also bad. When Ramesvara fell from grace, I had a dilemma. He was my leader who represented everything ISKCON stood for, but even he could not survive in the toxic system. I was also becoming implicated in ISKCON's karma through my work on the *ISKCON World Review.* I couldn't see it, but somehow the *L.A. Times* reporter knew that I was in a desperate situation.

16

The Budget Axe

Mornings were a good time to chant, as Subhananda had taught me. Rising early to see the deity and meditate helped me put ISKCON's problems out of my mind. Chanting at the Laguna Beach temple was lonely though, because it was always deserted. The dozen or so full-time devotees worked through the morning program tending the deities and preparing the restaurant to open.

One morning in August the desolate restaurant area depressed me, so I threw open the doors to look at the sun making its way over the hills. I chanted outside on the concrete steps as people drove by, beginning their morning Orange County commute. Many of the drivers did a "California slide" through the four-way stop sign on the corner rather than come to a full stop. It was a metaphor for how the P.R. department's problems had started, I thought to myself. If only we had been honest from the beginning, we wouldn't be trapped behind the facade of denial now.

Back inside the temple room, I noticed the only other person chanting was Bharata, our graphic artist who now worked for the restaurant. He had gotten his picture in the *Orange County Register* recently, a great shot that showed him offering obeisances in the temple room. The photo conveyed the spirit of devotion that could only survive in devotees who were innocent of ISKCON's betrayals. The article gave a favorable impression of devotees, despite the murder publicity that seemed to be circulating everywhere else. Maybe the reporter wanted to help us out, or perhaps she didn't even know about the murder. Now, absorbed in his chanting, Bharata paced back and forth on the marble floor where his picture had been taken. After twenty minutes, he sat down next to me to tell me an idea.

"You know, Nandini, Tuesday is Mukunda's twentieth anniversary," he said, his hand still in his bead bag.

"Of what?" I asked.

"Of being a devotee. He was initiated exactly twenty years ago," Bharata said. "I think it would be very nice to have a party."

I agreed because of all the years Mukunda had dedicated to ISKCON. He had faith in the GBC, even though they had disappointed him dozens of times. Mukunda had been out of the country but was scheduled to return to Laguna after a BBT Council meeting in Los Angeles.

On the day of the party, Uddhava and I drove to Laguna Niguel and pulled into Mukunda's apartment parking lot, slowing for the speed bumps. We parked, and Bhutatma pulled up behind us and parked two spaces down. He hopped out and walked briskly toward the building. I called but apparently he didn't hear me.

"What's wrong with Bhutatma?" I asked as we locked up the car. He was dressed in a Hawaiian shirt and bathing trunks, an unusual outfit for a devotee but not unusual for him. Maybe he had been at the beach. We caught up with him and walked to the apartment, where the others were sitting around Mukunda's kitchen table.

"We're all here now?" Bharata asked, poking his head out of the kitchen alcove.

"We're all here," I said, taking a seat with the men.

"Well then, happy anniversary, Mukunda," Bharata said as he brought out a cake with twenty lit candles. Bharata had baked it from scratch. Mukunda obediently blew out the candles, and everyone applauded as Bharata handed Mukunda a big kitchen knife.

While Bharata served the cake, I said, "Let me read about the initiation ceremony," Prabhupada's biography in hand:

Mukunda: I first heard about the initiation just one day before it was to take place. I had been busy with my music and hadn't been attending. I was walking down Second Avenue with one of the prospective initiates, and he mentioned to me that there was going to be something called an initiation ceremony. I asked what it was all about, and he said, "All I know is it means that you accept the spiritual master as God." This was a big surprise to me and I hardly knew how to take it. But I didn't take it completely seriously, and the way it was mentioned to me in such an offhand way, made it seem not very important. He asked me very casually whether I was going to be involved, and I, also being very casual about it, said, "Well, I think I will. Why not? I'll give it a try."

"You've certainly built up your empire since then," Bharata said.

"Thank goodness for Jonestown," Mukunda quipped, but his life-long mission to redeem ISKCON's reputation had become clear long before that tragedy.

I closed the book and laid it on the table. "Tell us what happened at the BBT meetings. How'd it go?"

"I need to meet with you about that later. There are some things we have to go over." He looked as if he had jet lag from traveling. His robes were wrinkled, and he kept chanting whenever there was a lull. I figured that he hadn't had time to do all his rounds.

"We can talk about it now," I said. "Everyone here is part of the department. We all need to know."

"Go ahead, Mukunda," Bhutatma said. "Let's get it over with." He clasped his hands behind his head and tipped his chair back to rest against the wall. Mukunda and Bhutatma had obviously been mulling over the problem for several hours, but now it was up to Mukunda to deliver the bad news.

"Did the BBT cut anyone's budget?" I asked, suspecting that some of Ramesvara's projects would lose their funding.

"Yes, they cut everyone's, including ours."

For a moment there was an incredulous silence. Uddhava and I looked at each other. We looked back at Mukunda.

"It ends in October," he said. "They cut everyone across the board: the artists, the writers, ISKCON-TV. I told them they may not have an *ISKCON World Review,* but they said we would find a way to continue."

"We think the best thing to do now is reduce our overhead," Bhutatma said. He let his chair fall back to the floor and put both hands on the table. He spoke with a rehearsed, almost mechanical tone of voice. "Now we have to raise our own money. Mukunda and I feel that living in Laguna Beach is too expensive. If we move somewhere else, where rents are cheaper, then we can manage much easier." His words pounded in my ears. I wanted him to stop, but he continued.

"Over the months several leaders have made offers—from London and the Bay Area, and I think our best move would be North Carolina. They have a geodesic dome temple, and Bir Krishna Swami wants to help us out. He offered to let us all live on the property or we can rent apartments nearby for much less than we pay here. You could do the *ISKCON World Review* there."

"Wait a minute," I said. "We can't move the paper to North Carolina." Moving to Laguna Beach had been bad enough.

"If you have determination, nothing can stop your service," Bhutatma said. "I certainly don't intend to give up my service to Prabhupada just because of something like this."

"But the paper," I said, almost in tears. "It would be impossible."

"Impossible is a word in a fool's dictionary," Mukunda said. He always said that, because Prabhupada had once said it to him.

"Try to think in a practical way," Bhutatma said. "Keep an open mind. North Carolina might be a good solution."

"Uddhava, can you explain it to him?" I walked out of the room, down the hall to one of the bedrooms, and shut the door. I couldn't believe it: North Carolina? My body felt numb, and I wanted to disappear. I dropped to the floor but felt as if I were falling into an abyss. Nowhere to go. No more guru. No more department. No more budget. Only cover-up and denial. I picked a book from the mismatched volumes of Prabhupada's books on a shelf and read for what seemed like hours. Then Uddhava knocked on the door.

"Nandini, it's all over," he said. "We're going." He stood in the doorway, arms hanging at his side, his eyes lowered. We walked out, leaving the others at the party without saying goodbye. Bhutatma had the money to pay our September rent, but we had some tough decisions to make.

Mukunda came over the next day, and we talked for two hours about the purpose of our department. We all conceded that the budget cut was inevitable. We had seen it coming for a few months because of the chaotic situation in ISKCON and the financial instability of the BBT. Subhananda, as a BBT writer, also lost his budget, Mukunda reminded me. Mukunda asked us not to be angry at Bhutatma, because we were all in it together, and he confided what happened in L.A. after the BBT council meeting. Besides slashing the BBT budget, several gurus took it upon themselves to stop all corrupt forms of *sankirtan* in the L.A. community. They gave special classes denouncing the pick and warning *sankirtan* devotees that they would go to hell if they continued to sell stickers, paintings, and candles in the name of *sankirtan*. The gurus' intentions were good, but the changes they proposed were too severe. Morale in the L.A. community was low; their crusade almost undermined its financial base, as well.

After this, in a completely unanticipated episode, Bhagavan traveled to Colorado to marry one of his godsisters. He sent a five-page fax to his zonal leaders in Europe, informing them that he would not be coming back. He said, "I will keep in touch with you, perhaps through Tamal Krishna Maharaja, but I beg you to allow me some time to myself. So please don't come rushing over with another emergency session. . . . Thank you all for your unmotivated concern and dedication. You might want to make this letter available to the devotees. One day soon, I hope, I can be that person you are all expecting."

I worried that the movement would crash without Ramesvara and Bhagavan, and I was angry to see the Governing Body Commission in such upheaval. The storms had grown cataclysmic. Mukunda still hoped for GBC unity and guru reform, but old leaders were becoming scapegoats while the underlying problems remained unsolved. Uddhava and I appreciated Mukunda's sincerity, but, instead of going to North Carolina we talked for the first time about leaving ISKCON. I knew that Mukunda would continue with his GBC duties out of a sense of dedication, even without a budget, but I wondered whether the *ISKCON World Review* would survive. To the reformers it represented the old style of glorifying gurus, so it may not even be welcomed in a reformed ISKCON.

Living directly under the GBC turmoil was frightening. I could foresee that Kirtanananda and Bhavananda would be the next gurus to go. Bhavananda had signed a promise not to give initiations during his suspension, but aspiring disciples still wanted to take their vows. By performing an initiation ceremony against the Governing Body Commission's orders, Bhavananda sealed his fate. It was only a matter of time until they expelled him.

I wanted to talk to Dad, because if he agreed with our perception that ISKCON was on the brink of self-destruction then we did need to get out. I hoped he might offer Uddhava a job at his studio. When I called to tell him about the budget cut, he invited us to come right over.

We met Dad at his house in the evening and sat around the round wooden coffee table in his living-room. First, Uddhava and I told him what we thought was happening and why we worried that ISKCON could collapse.

"What are your immediate plans?" he asked in his usual level-headed way.

"We don't know," Uddhava said.

"We're thinking of leaving," I said.

"If you two leave, what will you do instead?" Dad asked. He sat comfortably on his couch, looking stern.

"On the way up here, we thought of different things," I said. "I'd like to go back to school for a master's degree."

"That's fine, but graduate school is expensive. Shouldn't both of you work?"

"I didn't think of that," I said. I realized that I had no references and little chance of landing a job with as much responsibility as the one I already had.

"Your typing skills are good, aren't they?" Dad asked, looking at me. "You could work at a temp agency until you find an office you like. Politics run high in the material world, too."

"I don't want to work in an office," I said. I couldn't imagine turning in my saris for business clothes. I sensed that my father wouldn't offer Uddhava a job, so I didn't want to introduce that topic. Blaming Mukunda and running away seemed like the easy way out of the dilemma, but actually it would be more difficult than staying. Although I could have handled the work of a reporter and Uddhava had the ability to work in my father's studio, we would have had trouble fitting in, and Dad knew it. As Hare Krishnas, we had gone a long way toward separating ourselves from the outside world. Our clothing, hairstyles, language, diet, and convictions were out of step with the rest of society. My mind filled with horror tales of devotees who had left ISKCON, only to be bashed against the rocky shore of material existence with no position in society.

"Another alternative would be to start your own business," Dad said. "You both have graphics skills, right? You already have all the equipment." He paused for a moment to smile at us. "I want to tell you my lily pad theory. It goes like this: a smart frog can get across the pond without getting its feet wet. You have to do what the frogs do: put your front legs on the next lily pad before you jump. You have to know where you're going. Starting your own business could be your next lily pad."

A gentle calm descended as we considered Dad's theory. He didn't want us to leave ISKCON and become dependent on him, nor did he advise me to leave completely. Perhaps he hoped I would realize that there was something left to salvage. After talking things over, Uddhava and I decided to find a way to stay in print and ride out the turmoil. The newspaper was a source of strength and faith to many sincere devotees. We would stick with ISKCON for better or worse and try to make the paper honest.

The next morning, our landlord agreed to apply our security deposit to the rent; we could stay until October 31. Uddhava talked to Agnidev, the Laguna temple president, who also did what he could to help. He offered space in the ashram if Uddhava would take over as temple treasurer. We felt it was

Krishna's divine intervention that the answers came so easily after we decided to continue our service. The paper could survive financially as well, because advertising and subscription sales still covered printing and mailing costs. We had depended on the BBT only for our rent but that would be covered by Uddhava's work for the Laguna Beach temple.

Shortly after that, John Dart, the *Los Angeles Times* religion editor, called the P.R. office to ask why two of ISKCON's most prominent leaders—Ramesvara and Bhagavan—had suddenly gone away. Just three months before, when Terry Pristen called, I was willing to deny the problem. This time I told Dart everything I knew and provided names and telephone numbers of people who could say more. The story, headed "Shake-Up Involves L.A. Leader: Two Krishna Gurus Granted Leaves amid Controversy," ran on the front page of the *Times* Metro section, along with a photo of Ramesvara that I supplied. The article quoted BBT accountant Mahendra as saying that Ramesvara "couldn't function in our traditional understanding of the renunciative role—he wanted to help with kids and help with business and be busy all the time. His chanting practice was in question for many years." Dart attributed my quotes to "a Southern California public affairs spokesman for the movement who wishes to remain anonymous," but Bhutatma easily guessed my identity.

That winter Dad and I talked about every aspect of ISKCON and my involvement in it. We determined that if I were to stay, he and I could use the *ISKCON World Review* to address the organization's sensitive issues. He believed that doing so would be healing for ourselves and for the organization. I trusted my father's judgment; if any editor could address ISKCON's issues tactfully, it would be he.

From October to the end of the year the paper carried monthly interviews with gurus. My interview for November, "ISKCON Due for Reform," was with one of the reform gurus, Caru. He felt positive about ISKCON's future now that some of the most dominating old figures were gone. He said, "Elitism in ISKCON is dying a natural death, and therefore I'm optimistic." Rather than a blow to ISKCON, he called the demise of old gurus a "transition." My editorial, "Healthy Growth Cited for Hare Krishna Movement," written with Arnie Weiss and my father, said, "Most of the changes involve the Governing Body Commission and the question of guruship by disciples of Srila Prabhupada. . . . Although there have been some problems in ISKCON over the past nine years, they become diminished as we turn toward the future.

New leaders, new ideas, open communications, and promising plans to increase the international solidarity of the movement are emerging."

To close out 1986, Mukunda interviewed Satsvarupa, one guru out of the original eleven who was the most vocal about reducing guru worship. He had stopped guru *arotik* in his zone, encouraged reform gurus to make disciples in his East Coast territory, and had written a book entitled *Guru Reform Notebook*. Satsvarupa offered an apology to disciples of Prabhupada who had been offended during the years of strife. Not all gurus agreed with Satsvarupa's conclusions, but we presented the interview as evidence of a good future for ISKCON.

In December, the temple presidents from Ramesvara's former zone formed a coalition called the Western Zonal Council and put the word out that they didn't want any gurus entering the zone, which they intended to manage without a guru administrator until the next Mayapur meeting. My dad said we should definitely include that news, and, with Mukunda's approval, I mentioned it in an article about the Governing Body Commission.

Other news that month concerned the North American Governing Body Commission's proposal and unanimous approval of a plan to "reconfirm" itself. Members wanted to hold hearings at the 1987 Mayapur meeting, where all Governing Body commissioners would submit themselves to an electoral assembly of fifty devotees for a vote of confidence. The commissioners would receive a "report card" and have to pass a committee vote to keep their positions. The North American commission hoped the exercise would clear up any doubts about GBC integrity.

My cynicism had grown to the point that I considered the reconfirmation a whitewash, but the article I wrote dutifully explained what the North American GBC hoped it would accomplish. For our editorial that month, Dad and I wrote "ISKCON Newspaper Expands Coverage":

> In recent months we have reported, with increasing frequency, news which at one time would have been thought inappropriate and too controversial. However, a newspaper's primary duty is to report the news, and we may define news as events that interest and concern our readers. . . .
>
> We hope our expanded editorial policy will strengthen communications, provide a vital forum for the exchange of important information, and present a more accurate, realistic picture of ISKCON to the public at large.

Some Governing Body commissioners didn't like our editorial very much, nor the idea of expanded coverage during their vulnerable period. Soon after the issue came out, the Western Zonal Council passed a resolution that asked us to "publish only the good news, suitable for congregational members." The resolution suggested that sensitive news could appear in an insert meant only for insiders.

Most often, Mukunda found himself in the awkward position of promising to rein us in, even though he admittedly believed in more openness. He usually gravitated back to the Governing Body Commission's position of cover-up, so a final conflict was inevitable. In a way, I was asking for it.

17

The *ISKCON World Review* Crosses the Line

When the December issue came back from the printer, I drove to Hollywood to bring Dad his copy. We sat and talked about Kirtanananda and the situation in New Vrindaban. Tirtha (Thomas Drescher) had been convicted of the 1983 murder of Chakradhari (Charles St. Denis) and sentenced to life in prison in West Virginia. Next, he faced a federal grand jury indictment and trial in California for Sulochan's murder. The grand jury was building a conspiracy case against Kirtanananda. To make matters worse for the P.R. department, Kirtanananda had gone on a nationwide "Freedom Tour" to vindicate himself. His press releases talked of religious persecution and said the Freedom Tour celebrated the Constitution's bicentennial. New Vrindaban's adept P.R. department had issued a press packet in a gold-stamped folder and landed interviews with Dan Rather, Peter Jennings, Larry King, and Sally Jesse Raphael. Dad pointed out that we could no longer ignore Kirtanananda and suggested that the *ISKCON World Review* also interview him.

When I proposed the idea to Mukunda, he said, "Absolutely not." I decided to do the interview anyway, hoping to change his mind later. December 30 was a cold winter morning. Rain was falling outside, and the ocean roared in the distance. Uddhava and I had given up our spacious apartment and now operated out of a finished attic room in the Laguna Beach temple. It was crowded with office machines and desks but functional.

When I called New Vrindaban at the appointed time they put me through to Kirtanananda right away. "Hare Krishna," Kirtanananda said, eager to proceed. I found out later that people on his side were also recording our conversation.

I drew a deep breath and began, "Other ISKCON gurus are leaning toward reform, less worship. Why do you disagree with that?"

"You cannot change the position of guru," he said. "You either are a guru or you're not a guru. If you are a guru, what is the question of worshiping a guru less?"

"Do you foresee that you will emerge as the world leader of the society for Krishna consciousness?"

"If I can do the work of leading all my disciples and even all my godbrothers, I'll be glad to do it."

"What special qualification do you have to make you a leader among all of your godbrothers?"

"My only qualification is that I have heard from my spiritual master, His Divine Grace Srila Prabhupada, and I am repeating exactly what he said."

"Do you feel that the bad publicity or the federal grand jury investigation will hurt the future of New Vrindaban?"

"Not at all," Kirtanananda said. "Rather it is helping. How else could I be on television ten times in the last two months?"

"But isn't that bad publicity?"

"No publicity is bad."

"This question is on another subject," I said. "The GBC has set up geographic guidelines for different gurus to open temples, but you have opened temples outside your zone. Why is that?"

"That is not an area of proper jurisdiction for the GBC. Every living entity has the charge of Lord Chaitanya to preach Krishna consciousness all over the world. That cannot be changed by GBC, ABC, or XYZ. If the GBC passed a resolution saying it's okay to eat meat, does that make it okay? If your resolution is contrary to the scriptures, it doesn't make any difference who passed it."

"So in other words you disagree with their policies?"

"No one can tell you not to preach Krishna consciousness."

"Do you think there is any hope of your resolving these differences with the other ISKCON leaders?"

"Of course," he said. "If I'm wrong, I've asked them to please come here and show me—show me from the scriptures where I'm wrong. And if I'm not wrong, why are they objecting? If we both accept the scriptures, then why not use the scriptures to resolve it?"

"If the differences continue, and if things are not resolved, do you think you and your followers may eventually split with ISKCON?"

"I can never split away from ISKCON. In fact, one of Prabhupada's godbrothers, Narayan Maharaja, told me, 'You are Mister ISKCON.'"

"Mister ISKCON?"

"Yes, he meant I am Prabhupada's first disciple. I was the first *sannyasi.* I cannot leave ISKCON. I am not leaving ISKCON. ISKCON is leaving me, but I'm not leaving."

After the interview, I checked the tape, labeled it, and set it at the top of my stack of things to do. The sky was still dark, but the rain had stopped. I put on a wool sweater my father had given me for Christmas and stepped out into the open air. The beach was only two blocks away. The boardwalk was steeped in quiet, but waves smashed against the shore with unusual force. I pulled the sweater closer and wondered whether the storms of 1986 were over or if ISKCON's turmoil would continue into the new year.

My father's studio on Santa Monica Boulevard had a sound stage and a wall of special-effects equipment in a glassed-in corridor. He had been in the same office for twenty-two years, conducting business for the former Muzak franchise, the *Delta Queen,* and now his post-production studio. He welcomed me when I came in with the transcribed Kirtanananda interview, and we faced each other across his wooden desk. Dad looked over the interview, holding his hand to his lips as he read. In the minutes of silence I glanced at the *Delta Queen* posters and award plaques decorating his walls. More wooden plaques sat nearby on a credenza, waiting to be displayed. Besides these sudden symbols of appreciation, there was little evidence that my father was dying.

"Are you going to print it?" he asked, looking up.

"I don't think it's going to work out," I said. "Kirtanananda can be a convincing speaker, and Mukunda's afraid that interviewing him could sway some of our readers to his side."

"Kirtanananda's not convincing at all," Dad said. "I think he's very transparent. I think his ego is in the way, and I think that it's appropriate that people will read this and understand."

"Mukunda says Kirtanananda's opinions aren't relevant to ISKCON, but he's been going on TV and that affects ISKCON, doesn't it?"

"His appearances have been embroiling ISKCON in controversy," Dad said. "Kirtanananda obviously understood your question to say, 'Do you feel the publicity is hurting *you?*' Obviously, 'No, look, I'm getting all this free publicity.' His answer is nonresponsive and in effect shows that he isn't dealing with the issue in a logical manner."

Dad spoke slowly, choosing his words carefully, "The thing that bothers me is the violence of his words. Look at the last paragraph, at the clearly stated ego problems he's having. He says he will never split from ISKCON, that one of Prabhupada's godbrothers said, 'You are Mister ISKCON.' It's such an intemperate statement that there isn't anything anyone could say that would more negatively reflect upon his sanity than what he has said himself. It has to be read as the statement of a very conceited man who is out of touch."

Dad read parts of the interview over and said, "The biggest problem is that this holds one of your prominent gurus up to self-ridicule, he's so kooky. It makes ISKCON seem like it's ruled by some pretty cabbage-headed folk. He's crazy, ergo ISKCON's crazy. So in that respect, it could hurt ISKCON if this interview is published as it is. If the GBC thinks it can wipe him out with one stroke, then perhaps it's better to say nothing, but aren't there a lot of people who think he should be a deity?"

"His followers in New Vrindaban."

"All the people there are his followers?"

"Pretty much," I said.

"If you don't publish this, they're going to say he was thrown out without a fair hearing, that the GBC has no right. Conceivably you could have yourself a revolution."

"If we print it do you think that would ease the situation?"

"When you have a controversy, and it's aired in a reasonably public forum, then people are better able to make judgments about the right and wrong of it. They'll be able to see where Kirtanananda's opinions differ, and they'll understand his ego problems."

After paging through the interview again Dad said, "This New Vrindaban crisis is nothing less than what you had every right to expect, and I think it is a crisis. 'I'm Mister ISKCON' and 'I'm not leaving ISKCON' is dynamite, and I'm not sure I'd want to set that one off. But the business about guru worship—if you print his opinion with two or three other gurus' opinions—then you've stirred the controversy in an objective way. You've let Kirtanananda be heard without giving him a platform to scream from, and you've avoided inflammatory statements like 'I'm Mister ISKCON.'"

He considered for a moment then added, "Here's what's relevant: are you serving the readers or are you serving the ownership of the movement? That's a tough question. Not one I'm qualified to answer. I've been promoting the concept that by being a newspaper, by giving both sides of a controversy, your publication gains a great deal of credibility, you get attention, you get readership, you become a lively, important part of the movement. Guru worship has become a relatively important subject. If the GBC decides to change it, then it's all the more important that the views have been aired, because then it's obvious why the changes were made."

Dad straightened out the pages and tapped them on his desk, then said, "The more important you become as a publication, the more people will try to influence what you print. It gets back to the argument of whether you're a newspaper or a house organ. As a mouthpiece for ISKCON they tell you who to interview and when you do the interview you gotta leave this out and put that in, and it's never going to stop. There's no end to it. Most house organs, as a consequence, wind up saying 'Screw it, I'll ask the boss what he wants in the paper.'"

"Just ask them what they want and then print it," I said, recalling the Western Zonal Council's advice to us.

"It's basically a matter of becoming a mouthpiece and a mailing house," Dad said.

"Hype the good things like we used to," I said.

"It becomes advertising, it becomes propaganda," Dad said. "By the way, I feel strongly enough about the theoretical part of this that if Mukunda feels it would really be against the movement's best interest to publish any of this, then I would like at least an opportunity to express my opinion."

By the time I left it was getting dark, and Dad's Cadillac was the only car left in the parking lot. During the one-hour drive to Laguna Beach I admitted to myself that the Governing Body Commission didn't want the *ISKCON World Review* discussing their problems, particularly New Vrindaban.

Six days after I interviewed Kirtanananda, a team of fifty FBI agents and West Virginia state troopers raided New Vrindaban, breaking down doors and seizing accounting records, computers, and cash. They were looking for evidence of copyright infringement, racketeering, and conspiracy to sell millions of caps, T-shirts, and stickers bearing pirated Peanuts characters and NFL logos. Kirtanananda was incredulous when authorities raided his community, claiming that as a nonprofit corporation New Vrindaban was not bound by copyright laws.

On the night of the FBI raid, state police and county officers exhumed St. Denis's remains at New Vrindaban. News reporters were there; segments on NBC's *A Current Affair* and CBS's *West 57th Street* showed police digging up the skeleton. St. Denis had been battered with a hammer, as his skull, pulled from the mud, clearly showed. Daniel Reid, another suspect in the slaying, had pleaded guilty and led officials to the grave site.

I didn't know about events in New Vrindaban, but on the same day as the raid I had an appointment to interview Larry Shinn, the university dean who had spoken on ISKCON's behalf to the media. Shinn had just finished writing a scholarly book called *The Dark Lord: Images of the Hare Krishnas in America.* It was my second interview with an outside observer, and during our two-hour discussion I went down my list of questions and asked Shinn, "Would you say there's a 'crisis of leadership' in ISKCON?" He replied:

Well there's no doubt that there is. Most people of the general public don't see it up close as I have, but I would say it is probably the most severe challenge that ISKCON has had to face since the death of Prabhupada. In my book, *The Dark Lord,* I argue that Prabhupada basically had two kinds of authority. On the one hand he had what is called "traditional authority"; the hereditary authority. But he also had what is called "charismatic authority." That is authority that stems from his personal qualities, not just an inherited status. It was Prabhupada's personal piety that gave him the real authority. He exhibited complete command of the scriptures, an unusual depth of realization, and an outstanding personal example because he actually lived what he taught.

When he died in 1977, the idea that his disciples could be named as his successors was fairly easy; a traditional transfer of authority. Although there's been some debate about that, too. What's difficult, or rather impossible, is to transfer the personal piety—the charismatic authority. It was literally not possible for Prabhupada to give each of his eleven named successors his own devotion to Krishna, his own personal piety, his scriptural knowledge, his ability to interpret the scriptures. It seems that the crisis in leadership emerged almost immediately after Prabhupada's death, and had its origin in the misunderstanding of the transmission of authority that took place at that time.

One of the things ISKCON is struggling with is how to maintain a singular vision in a diversified community. In an organization as far-flung as ISKCON, there is a great tendency for schism to occur once the founder is gone. If the current attempts to reform the position of the guru in ISKCON are accepted by some and denied by others, then what you have is a fragmented institution. That's exactly what happened in the Reformation. The Catholic Church persisted, while Luther and his followers broke off. Now, after only four hundred or five hundred years, we have well over two hundred denominations of what began as a single protest movement. That's what I fear for ISKCON.

❖

When I showed Shinn's interview to Mukunda, he only glanced at it before telling me I couldn't run it. I suspect it bothered him because it went to the core of the Governing Body commissioners' issues. In the continuing strife, several more leaders had fallen away. One went back to school, another left with his followers to form yet another splinter group, and others joined monasteries in India run by Prabhupada's godbrothers.

As we put together the issue that month, a GBC member unexpectedly showed up at our office. Panchadravida was not one of the original eleven gurus, but he had been appointed a few years before the guru reform movement. Uddhava greeted him at the door, and we all paid obeisances to each other. Panchadravida, about thirty-five, was a short, swarthy man with black hair and always dressed in Hare Krishna robes. He was the guru for much of Latin America, and people in his zone called him "Pancho Swami." The usually jolly Panchadravida seemed distraught.

"I want to do an interview for the *ISKCON World Review,*" he said. "I'm leaving for India tomorrow. I have to do it now."

Uddhava invited him in and got out the cassette recorder. They sat on the couch.

"I read the interview with Satsvarupa and agree with it," the guru said. "I want to apologize to the devotees for what I consider was a great injustice perpetrated over the last nine years." He sounded tired yet frantic. "As a GBC and a guru I can't absolve myself of responsibility for many of the injustices that devotees have experienced."

"Could you elaborate?" Uddhava asked.

"What I feel," Panchadravida continued, "is that for the last nine years, ISKCON underwent a shift from being a very scientific and scripturally presented spiritual movement to a personality cult. The GBC, which was meant to be a group that would oversee the spiritual development of the society, became needlessly involved in so many details of administration, with the end result that it doesn't even administer properly; doesn't even administer to the level of what I would call a 'basic small-town administrative organization.' In other words, it doesn't seem to be the GBC's calling to manage ISKCON."

"How do you feel about the decision to reconfirm the GBC?"

"I think it's certainly a positive move, but it doesn't go far enough. The entire GBC itself should resign because it has served detrimentally for the last nine years. Anyone involved with so much of the politics that went on shouldn't be in that position in the future. We need an entirely new GBC without any of the former members."

"Hmm," Uddhava said. "Pretty radical."

"One cannot know about everything that goes on behind the scenes, right? And therefore the godbrothers may choose an individual to be reconfirmed who is actually implicated in a lot of the things that went wrong in the society. Rather than run that risk, I think it would be much better to start out with an entirely new group of leaders. We have a lot of godbrothers in this society who are qualified spiritually. I don't see where they'll commit the same mistakes that we did. But the main thing I want to tell the readers, especially my godbrothers, is to offer my sincere apologies. I've been as much involved in this as anyone, in so many things that have gone on. I feel the whole position established by the gurus over the last nine years is a complete deviation from the philosophy that Prabhupada presents in his books." Panchadravida stared at Uddhava for a moment.

"So you're in agreement with Satsvarupa?"

Panchadravida glanced down. "Yes, but Satsvarupa expresses very conservative feelings on the issue. I respect that it's a good way of preserving peace within the society, but we have completely restructured the society in violation of the teachings in Prabhupada's books. We have to take some very positive action—and quickly—to keep this movement from deviating from what Prabhupada intended."

"I certainly hope there are some major changes," Uddhava said.

"Satsvarupa's apologies are very nice. But I've heard other individuals say that there's not even a need to apologize, which indicates that they don't recognize there's something wrong. Instead of allowing this to develop into a personality cult, we should have maintained the most humble position possible. A Vaishnava is supposed to be austere, humble, tolerant and kind. I don't really see that we're trying to exemplify those qualities as a society.

"Although there are individuals who are spiritually advanced in one or more qualities, we haven't demanded the same of the leadership. Rather, we established elaborate worship of ordinary persons. We've worshiped people who are more astute politically than spiritually. That creates the impression that Prabhupada was on that level also, whereas before the new gurus we understood that Prabhupada should be worshiped because he's a pure devotee. By establishing that kind of worship for persons who aren't pure, we diminish Prabhupada's position. That has created a fertile ground for the falldowns we've seen."

After the interview Panchadravida flew to India and the shelter of Sridhar Swami's temple.

18

Six Months Out of Print

In an editorial meeting with my father, Uddhava suggested that we print a stinging statement of solidarity with Panchadravida, announce our resignation, and then go out of print. Dad warned against burning our bridges and said that doing so would destroy whatever good we had already accomplished. Instead, he encouraged us to do the honorable thing: follow the Western Zonal Council's advice to produce two separate publications and make both of them the best we could. One would be all the good news, suitable for congregational members; the other would be interviews, editorials, and letters on the guru issue. If we still felt like resigning, we could do it quietly after the double issue came out. Back in Laguna Beach, we prepared layouts of both versions in time for the editorial meeting with Mukunda.

Although we were supposed to meet in the afternoon, it was dark by the time Mukunda arrived at our tiny attic workshop. He looked like he had a headache, because he kept squinting his eyes. His voice was quiet and restrained, almost a whisper. He took the flats and sat on the couch, flipping through the pages. When he got to the supplement, he noticed the first interview.

"I thought I told you not to interview Kirtanananda," Mukunda said. "He's going to use this against us."

"But Mukunda, it's in the internal supplement. No one's going to see it except devotees. Please read it."

"I don't need to read it. I know what he says."

"But it's a great interview," I protested. "Just read it. It reveals how wacky he is. What's wrong with that?"

"I told you not to do it. That's what's wrong with it!"

"Well I did it," I said.

Mukunda held the pages in his lap with one hand and rubbed the side of his head with the other. I knew he suffered from migraines.

Uddhava sat at his desk, and I sat at mine in the cluttered room, which looked like a used office furniture store. We watched quietly as Mukunda read Panchadravida's interview. After a few minutes he put the pages down and said, "I can't go along with this."

"But that's what we want to print," Uddhava said. He pushed back from his desk and walked to where I was seated.

"I can't let you, that's all," Mukunda said.

"Why not?" Uddhava asked, standing beside me and looking Mukunda in the eyes. "Does everything we print have to speak for the GBC? Why can't we print Panchadravida's opinion?"

"I just don't want to make this a forum for deviants. That guy is crazy. He blooped, you know."

"If we can't print this, then we're not going to print anything," Uddhava said. "We want the paper to be objective."

"If that's the way you feel, then fine. I'll get someone else to do the newspaper. I guess there's nothing else to talk about."

Mukunda walked out the door, and I realized that we had just quit the newspaper business. I regretted the argument, because without the prospect of a next issue I suddenly felt powerless in a world that could turn against me. Uddhava assured me that things would work out for the best and that we would find another service. He was genuinely relieved to be rid of the paper, which had been his idea in the first place, but I wasn't ready to let it go. I pulled myself together and called Mukunda. He agreed to talk about it in a few days.

When Dad found out that Mukunda was all too willing to let us go, he said, "The lesson here is: don't make ultimatums." He had made the same mistake twice, once at Capitol Records and once on the *Delta Queen*. He suggested that it would help to have a written editorial policy as a contract of checks and balances before we offered to start again.

Mukunda wanted us back and agreed to work out a new editorial policy. Our final statement said that interviews, editorials, and letters to the editor would be printed, along with unbiased coverage of the news. Our goals were to unify and strengthen ISKCON by providing a forum for opinion and fact.

We agreed that the paper would cover unpleasant and controversial issues. According to the policy, the *ISKCON World Review* would be a newspaper, a friendly newspaper but, as my father had hoped, definitely more than a house organ. As part of the deal, Uddhava and I agreed to forego the "inside edition" interviews. As another compromise, I agreed to bump Larry Shinn's outside-observer interview to a future issue and find something else for the front page. We published the paper with no controversial articles, then Mukunda left for the Governing Body Commission meeting in Mayapur. Uddhava and I checked out of the ashram, rented a nearby apartment, and started our desktop publishing business. We didn't have enough income to print a "next issue," so we put newspaper production on hold.

I only had one friend at the temple who could overlook rumors that the *ISKCON World Review* had gone out of print due to an altercation with Mukunda. People knew the paper had become radical and that it touched on many of the issues they were trained to deny. I felt like a complete fringie being out of print and outside the temple, and I followed GBC events from afar. I wasn't aware that on March 15 (the Ides of March, that dangerous day for all politicians) Kirtanananda had sent a ten-page telex to Mayapur. In a cover letter Kirtanananda apologized for having to miss the meeting but said he was "called to the White House" to talk about "the harassment of our devotees" by federal and state investigations of New Vrindaban. He did have an appointment at the Old Executive Office Building three days later, and *The New York Times* printed a story headed "Guru, Focus of Investigations, Meets Reagan Aide." On March 16, the Governing Body Commission stripped Kirtanananda, in absentia, of all rights, privileges, and powers in ISKCON and issued a statement to the worldwide temples. *The New York Times* picked up Mukunda's press release and added the information to their article. In the morning program back in New Vrindaban, residents declared the GBC resolutions null and void.

Kirtanananda rejected Indian clothes after his expulsion, asking his followers to wear Christian robes as he had done in New York twenty years before. He added a statue of Jesus to the New Vrindaban altar and had devotees sing the Sanskrit prayers of the morning program in English. As winter fell in West Virginia, a group of disciples produced a recording and songbook of Christmas carols, with the words changed to glorify their own faith. Kirtanananda also initiated several women as *sannyasis* and had them shave their heads and wear monks' robes. This was unheard of in ISKCON. Somehow, the GBC thought it could easily disassociate itself from New Vrinda-ban. They didn't realize the expulsion just added fuel to media rumors that ISKCON was about to self-destruct.

While Governing Body commissioners were still in Mayapur, *Rolling Stone* magazine published "Dial Om for Murder: The Case of the Krishna Killers" by John Hubner and Lindsey Gruson. Gruson had reported on ISKCON for *The New York Times,* and Hubner, a Bay Area reporter, followed ISKCON news from California. The *Rolling Stone* article was a true-crime telling of ISKCON's already well known murders, drug busts, and gun raids. With an audience of more than a million readers and syndicated versions of the arti-cle cropping up in other publications, "Dial Om for Murder" was everywhere. Another tough break for the GBC was that a reputable U.S. publisher offered Hubner and Gruson a contract for a book-length version of the story.

Every day for the first half of 1987 I thought about starting the *ISKCON World Review* again. We received letters—sometimes several a day—asking what had happened to the paper. I didn't want to leave our readers hanging, but we kept the publication suspended for four months while we ran our typeset-ting business. Our primary customer was the *Orange County Business Line.* It was the official newspaper of the Orange County Chamber of Commerce, just as *ISKCON World Review* was the official newspaper of ISKCON. It was just like producing the *ISKCON World Review,* but a lot less work. Even though it had more pages, we didn't write it or have to worry about what was printed. Uddhava had gotten us the job through a friend at the temple. The publisher wasn't a devotee but had enough curiosity to hire us when Uddhava walked into his Garden Grove office dressed in full Hare Krishna regalia. The job paid well, and I wanted to use the profits from desktop publishing to revive the *ISKCON World Review,* but Dad advised us to wait until someone from ISKCON offered to finance it. That way we would be sure it was some-thing the organization welcomed.

Meanwhile, Mukunda moved to San Diego, marking the end of the old P.R. office. Rather than follow Mukunda, Uddhava and I moved back to L.A., two blocks from Watseka Avenue. I wanted to be near Dad, and he gave me the money to move and get settled. There was not much time left; his cancer treatments were wearing him down. He already attended a cancer support group in Santa Monica and then, when I moved back, I convinced him to begin seeing Arnie Weiss. The two men were peers, and in Weiss Dad finally found someone to whom he could talk about his internal life. He still held his sadness from Betty Blake's sudden death five years earlier, but Arnie helped him use that pain to inspire his own spiritual search. Within a few months my dad openly discussed the possibilities of God and the eternality of the soul, concepts that he and I had never shared before. He described his beliefs as a combination of Christian, Jewish, Buddhist, and Hindu thought because he had been exposed to all four faiths in his life.

My father's spirits lifted. He saw something in life that he'd never seen before and said that he wanted to spend whatever time remained just visiting with people to share love. Life was happy, at least for the present. In June, just around Dad's birthday, the money came through to start up the *ISKCON World Review* again. Anuttama, the Denver temple president, pledged to give us $2,000 a month. Over the years Anuttama had developed an interest in public relations issues and allied himself with Mukunda. He was satisfied with the new editorial policy and expanded coverage, so he provided our budget through the BBT, along with his usual monthly donation.

Living back in L.A., Uddhava and I met our deadlines each month through the rest of 1987 and all through 1988. We published fifteen interviews, eight with Governing Body commissioners. Subscriptions and ad sales picked up, and we gradually reduced the amount of money we needed from the Denver temple. We ran our desktop publishing company, with the *ISKCON World Review* as our main customer. Mukunda allowed my interview with Larry Shinn one month, and the next month he interviewed Ravindra Svarupa, the man who had written the essay that sparked guru reform. In my editorial I suggested that Ravindra Svarupa's promotion to the Governing Body Commission was a "sign of renewal in ISKCON," meaning, of course, that guru reform could return the spirit of Prabhupada. As a further indication of guru reform's impact, Ravindra Svarupa was chosen to be GBC chair for 1988.

In each issue we printed news of the campaign to free the Soviet Hare Krishnas. Petition and letter-writing efforts were in full swing; *gurukula* students from Australia had a hit song, "Dear Mr. Gorbachev: Please Let Our Friends Go." The teenage "Krishna Kids" traveled around the world to draw attention to the cause and promote their EMI record *Listen to the Children*. In December 1987, during the superpower summit in Malta, Amnesty International secured freedom for Ananta-santi, the first Soviet Hare Krishna, along with other prisoners of conscience. The Soviets later freed all the devotees and allowed ISKCON to register as a state-approved religion. It didn't seem possible, but that was our front-page one month.

Much to everyone's dismay the guru issue continued and so did commissioners' grumblings about expanded coverage in the *ISKCON World Review*. A friend told us he saw guru Hridayananda on the sidewalk, waving the paper and screaming, "How can they print this stuff?!" Another friend over-heard the same man tell a meeting of the BBT council, "The worst thing about this paper is that it's written by a woman." Badri-narayan, the head of the Western Zonal Council, was known to say, "*ISKCON World Review:* All the news that's fit to print, and a lot that ain't."

Badri-narayan complained to Mukunda that devotees in his temple were afraid to let outsiders see the paper. His life membership department and restaurant canceled their orders, he said, because the paper raised too many doubts and questions. Badri-narayan said that the paper should be a "preach-ing tool" and present the "happy news" because, "After all the upheaval and turmoil we've been through, a little steady encouraging news is a great re-lief." He added, "I guarantee you this is what the vast majority of us want."

Badri-narayan wanted Mukunda to print certain stories but not others. It was the blessed end of all house organs, just as my father had predicted. I don't know how many commissioners sided with Badri-narayan, but Muku-nda consistently tried to tone us down. I pushed for an obituary when the expelled guru Jayatirtha was murdered in 1987. One of his followers stabbed and decapitated him in the London hardware store where he worked. Police arrested the killer, whom they found at the scene of the crime, lost in a psy-chotic state and holding the guru's head in his lap. I thought our paper should at least take note of the death because Jayatirtha had been one of the early founding members of ISKCON and an early supporter of the *ISKCON World Review.* Mukunda would not allow the obituary, however.

Another news story we didn't report was when the BBT accountant in L.A. resigned after his bookkeeper accused him of embezzlement. When he stepped down, she left her job on Watseka Avenue to join a convent. The BBT Council hired Uddhava as an interim manager. Part of his job was to search the files for possible abuses, and he reported abundant evidence of waste and mismanagement. He and I found it disillusioning, considering how Rames-vara had always put so much emphasis on the BBT motto "purity is the force." Uddhava's findings were also depressing for the GBC because they were supposed to have been in control through a subcommittee of trustees. Uddhava concluded that there was no way to tell whether money was miss-ing; the accused devotee said his wealth came from an inheritance and wise investment strategy. Everyone parted on cordial terms.

I wanted to address the BBT's dysfunction in an *ISKCON World Review* interview, and Hari-vilas, a new Governing Body commissioner for the Bay Area, agreed to talk. He commented that people "with mixed motives put economic development in the foreground and compromised the spiritual vocation. When Prabhupada was present he was protecting us from just that."

A few weeks after we published the interview, the BBT council partially reinstated Mukunda's budget. I took it as a good sign for our paper and for reviving the department. One of Uddhava's duties at the BBT was to issue checks. He made sure that Mukunda's went out promptly on the first of each month.

Ramesvara kept in touch with the BBT and renewed his promise to send millions when he wrote an open letter to his disciples in March 1987. I never believed it but understood his need to leave. One day while I was in the BBT office, Ramesvara called, and I talked to him. He sounded angry when he asked how things were going and why he had not been receiving the *ISKCON World Review.* I had hoped that someday he would apologize and come to peace with the role he had played in ISKCON. After that telephone call, I wondered if he would ever change. I didn't blame him, but rather the organization. There were insurmountable walls between "insiders" and "outsiders." Gurus, especially, found little gray area once they were outside.

My desk in the newspaper office was full of good news and controversial issues to write about. Because I thought I had some control over the situation, I nearly forgot that many people took "Hare Krishna" to mean two things: "cult" and "airport solicitation." The new book by the "Dial Om for Murder" reporters would play upon the public's deepest fears, tying together the two New Vrindaban murders, the Berkeley gun episode, and the Laguna Beach drug ring to portray ISKCON as a cult run by criminals. The authors were racing to get the volume out in time for the holiday season; it was up to Mukunda and GBC chair Ravindra Svarupa to soften its impending blow. Both gave interviews to John Hubner, the San Jose reporter, and Mukunda agreed to give him photos from the BBT and *ISKCON World Review* archives. When Hubner came to Watseka Avenue, Uddhava took care of the matter. After going through the archives, the author invited both of us to lunch at the temple restaurant. We talked about his book and the role of journalism in a democracy. After our meal, he drove us to the spot where Sulochan had been killed, about a mile from the temple.

Visiting the murder scene made me reflect on the years of public and private crises I had faced in ISKCON. Up to that moment, I believed that the organization still represented Prabhupada and that ISKCON, after the problems were fixed, would fulfill its spiritual mission. Seeing the place where Sulochan died changed that view. My allegiance as a member waned while my need to scrutinize the GBC grew stronger. I still chanted and attended the morning program, but I excused myself from Bhagavatam class if I disagreed with the speaker's political views. Some devotees admitted that mistakes had been made, but not by their guru or their zone. Others, such as

Panchadravida, believed that all Governing Body commissioners needed to apologize publicly and step down.

When *Monkey on a Stick* came out, a large crop of potential readers learned of the book through a half-page ad in *Time* magazine. The ad, prominently placed next to the contents on page two, started, "Drugs, perversion, child abuse, murder—ALL IN THE NAME OF RELIGION. Now see them as they *really* are—in a terrifying new book about a cult that practiced love, simplicity and devotion, while its leaders became obsessed with money, power and control." The book's title referred to a cruel practice among Indian farmers of impaling a crop-raiding monkey and setting it out like a scarecrow to warn its fellows away. Prabhupada had told of the practice. He could not have foreseen that his organization would become a field in which one of his own disciples would be killed for pointing out corruption.

The book made it onto *The New York Times* bestseller list. The *Times*'s book review, "Not What Krishna Had in Mind" by Anne Fadiman, lamented that the genuine spiritual teacher, Prabhupada, was betrayed by a band of followers who gradually "descend back into *maya*, and in so doing, involve ISKCON . . . in a variety of activities that were eminently bustible by the fuzz." R. Z. Sheppard's review in *Time* magazine was headlined "Good Hustle, Bad Karma." Apart from the cops-and-robbers dialogue Sheppard and Fadiman complained of, the events portrayed in *Monkey on a Stick* were true enough. With the *Time* ad and the book reviews on the stands, I felt self-conscious wearing a sari. In a health food store on Venice Boulevard one day a man shouted "Hare Krishna" to me. "What do you mean by that?" I snapped back. The incident made me realize how defensive I had become. I bought some jeans at a nearby store the next day because I knew that I would not fit into the organization much longer.

19

Women's Lesser Intelligence

As the spring of 1988 turned into summer, an ad hoc committee of East Coast devotees planned a conference at the Towaco, New Jersey, temple to examine ISKCON's issues. By that time, more temples were reducing guru worship, especially on the East and West Coasts, and Towaco had been the site of the temple presidents meeting that originally led to guru reform. Sponsoring another conference there, now that guru reform was taking place, attracted much favorable attention. The organizers ran an ad in the *ISKCON World Review* to invite people to present papers on any subject, including the role of women.

My experience of that role had convinced me of the need for reform. As a joke, I had once drawn a series of cartoons on the subject. In one, a woman wearing a dunce cap sits facing the corner. The headline reads, "What is the place of women in ISKCON?" Some of the men around the office thought it was funny, but I didn't dare show it to anyone else. Outside the department no one knew who I was, and I dared not joke about my inferior status. Any other Governing Body commissioner wouldn't have let a woman write the organization's newspaper, but Mukunda appreciated my service. He had once given me the ISKCON compliment: "If you were a man, you would have climbed a lot higher in the organization by now." I was glad to be a woman. Being an ISKCON bigwig was no longer my idea of fun. I wrote a speech about the place of women and planned a trip to Towaco.

After spending the night at the women's ashram of the Brooklyn temple, I rode to the conference in a van full of women. The New Jersey temple was a grand old country house built on a grassy hillside. The parlor was crowded with Governing Body commissioners, *sannyasis,* and temple presidents when we arrived, so the women went outside to sit in a garden and wait. I didn't know Subhananda would be there, but he walked up and greeted me. He was dressed in jeans and an Indian shirt, and his hair was shoulder length. He was earning his master's degree at Harvard Divinity School and said that his presentation that day would explain why he had chosen to leave ISKCON.

When the conference convened, all the women sat in the last two rows of chairs. I wanted to sit closer to the front, with the men who would be presenting their papers, but didn't know whether I would be accepted. Unable to decide and feeling tired from being on an airplane the night before, I napped in the van. When I came back at lunchtime I met the other devotee scheduled to present a paper on women's place in ISKCON. Urmila, a slim, dark-haired woman about my age, was headmistress of the Detroit *gurukula.*

The conference reconvened and went on all afternoon, with men presenting papers until 4:30. The women's issue was last on the agenda, and the moderator called Urmila to give her paper before me. She started reading on page one of sixteen densely typeset pages. I glanced at my watch and felt nervous. The first page was something about "misguided feminists," and under the heading "Woman's Basic Duty" Urmila read, "If a husband situated in the mode of goodness can control his wife, who is in passion and ignorance, the woman is benefited. Forgetting her natural inclination for passion and ignorance, the woman becomes obedient and faithful to her husband, who is situated in goodness. . . . Although the female body is a symptom of lesser intelligence, by serving her husband she becomes his good intelligence. What a wonderfully easy method of elevation."

According to Urmila, women had no standing in the *varna-ashrama* system. She read, "It should also be noted that women are classified among the *sudras* because without serving a man and thereby coming to the platform of goodness, she remains in the modes of passion and ignorance. We can conclude that this is woman's basic duty: serve a man and depend on his protection. Don't be independent." It clashed with my understanding that Prabhupada had initiated men and women as *brahmanas,* or teachers of the highest class.

Urmila finished by thanking all the men present and naming those who had helped with her research over the years. A few comments and some friendly discussion followed. When she stepped down to take her seat, most of the men applauded.

Next it was my turn to speak. I had studied the same scriptures as Urmila, but my conclusion was that gender didn't affect one's abilities. I felt torn and wanted to run from the room and from the organization, but I walked to the podium and read my speech, which was about six minutes long. I started out:

> In a patriarchal, male-dominated society, women are looked upon as less intelligent. They stand in the back; don't get involved. But what you get is a limited, single-dimensional society. Men are usually thought to be objective, intellectual and analytical. This system denies the sympathetic viewpoint necessary to round out the whole. . . . Our ISKCON society has had to face a lot of problems. Even though it's not pleasant to talk about, we all know what they are. Many of these problems can be solved if we just communicate better. The qualities of understanding and sensitivity—the feminine qualities—are missing. That may be because women are expected to take a subordinate role instead of participating in the process.

I recommended that women give Bhagavatam class and that the GBC reconsider its position on women gurus. After all, Chaitanya's movement had women gurus in the fifteenth century, and there have been other women gurus in Vaishnava history. When I finished reading I expected the conference to end right there. But there were questions. One of the *sannyasis* addressed me, saying, "You seem happy in your service, and Urmila seems perfectly content. What is it you're complaining about?"

I didn't know how to answer, but then a woman in the back row stood up, shaking with self-consciousness. "I joined the New York temple in 1968 and have been chanting sixteen rounds a day ever since," she said. "I've tried to do everything my authorities asked. I'm so fed up with the way I'm treated that I could cry. The women have the worst rooms in the building, and the plumbing is breaking down. When I told the temple president our shower was broken, he said to use a bucket. We never have a place to chant because the men won't let us in the temple room during *japa* time. Sometimes I think ISKCON is only for men and I'm just in the way. How can I make any contribution?"

When she sat down the room was silent a bit too long.

"Wouldn't that discourage a new woman who was about to join a temple and dedicate her life to Krishna?" someone shouted.

"ISKCON is supposed to protect women, but it doesn't sound like that's happening," Ravindra Svarupa said. The GBC chair had a cast on his leg, which he rested on a cushioned footstool all day. His observation seemed accurate, but maybe my dad was right. The male leaders weren't interested in improving women's lot in ISKCON. They liked the patriarchal system because they were part of it.

At seven o'clock the moderator called the discussion to a close by announcing that the next day, Sunday, would be the Manhattan Ratha-yatra, and people had to be going back to New York. Nothing about the clashing presentations was resolved, however, and some men continued arguing in the front hall. Subhananda cursed a stubborn *sannyasi,* saying, "You should spend one day as a woman in ISKCON. Then you'll find out how bad it really is."

The next day at the festival, Subhananda complained that he had heard so many horror stories from women in ISKCON that he wanted to write a book on the topic. When I returned to California I told my husband and father of the argument that followed my paper and the cold feeling I experienced from the men, as well as the women, for opening the wounds. I decided to put my thoughts down in an editorial for the *ISKCON World Review,* hoping that would clarify where I stood.

During the next editorial meeting, Mukunda refused to let me print my editorial or even a letter to the editor I had received on the subject of women gurus. He said that he knew that his censorship violated editorial policy, but he'd felt obligated to get the Governing Body Commission's blessings for that policy. He insisted that we either seek the GBC's approval or stop publishing controversy.

Mark Twain once wrote, "The editor of a newspaper cannot be independent, but must work with one hand tied behind him by party and patrons and be content to utter only half or two-thirds of his mind." That described my situation. Later, discussing Mukunda's demand, my father agreed that it would be virtual suicide to ask the GBC's approval, which would probably be withheld. He suggested that we keep interviewing commissioners one by one and wait for them to bring up their complaints to us. But Mukunda stubbornly insisted that either Uddhava or I go to the next American GBC meeting.

Uddhava said that trying to get through to the GBC was "like trying to drill through titanium." He'd had his fill of the fight for ISKCON glasnost, although he still supported my efforts to have the editorial policy approved. I agreed to go to the October GBC meeting in Dallas because I believed that the conflict could be resolved with honest communication.

I flew to Dallas on September 29 and spent the day visiting with devotees. Some women asked if I was in town to cover the GBC meeting, and I said, "No, I'm here to defend our editorial policy." They couldn't understand the problem because they read the *ISKCON World Review* in the belief that it was already the official word. My struggle for independence was difficult to explain, so I dropped it.

The next day I went to the GBC meeting and read my speech to twenty commissioners seated around a conference table. They were all dressed in devotional robes; some (like Mukunda) had shaved heads, whereas others had conventional, short hairstyles. I recognized each of them, although not all of them knew me. My ally was Hari-vilas, the Governing Body commissioner whom I had interviewed about abuses in the BBT. He was a guru reform advocate who had been forced out of France during the gurus' early reign.

I may have been the first woman to ever address the GBC. It was like speaking at a board meeting of the Bohemian Club, only more so. They politely listened to my ten-minute speech, which included comments from a subscribers' survey we had done: "Don't be afraid to discuss ISKCON's shortcomings and problems"; "The controversies are most important to be reported"; "Have more input from leaders. Report on GBC meetings. I think *IWR* is an important forum for ISKCON"; "Balanced reporting. Print stories about the emotional realizations of the movement"; "*IWR* should concentrate on problems faced by ISKCON, and their solutions"; and, "The newspaper is helping to keep devotees. I will continue to support its efforts and policies."

I made a case for printing a review of *Monkey on a Stick*, repeating what my father had told me days before: "The book may very well become a best seller. But if we fail to acknowledge its existence, that is the surest way to convince our readers that the movement is in trouble. The same can be said about other controversial issues we face."

I looked around the room at the long-faced Hare Krishna leaders and felt hopeful because of the attentive way they had listened. They discussed the newspaper for twenty-five minutes, then voted to form a committee. Mukunda nominated our critic Badri-narayan, but I vetoed the idea. We ended up with Ravindra Svarupa and Hari-vilas. I walked out feeling confident that I had gotten what I came for. Ravindra Svarupa was the current GBC chair, so if I wanted to know the GBC's position on something, I could ask him. Hari-vilas was also a good choice; perhaps he would write guest editorials. They could even share responsibility for a monthly GBC column. Shaking with excitement, I called Uddhava to tell him the good news.

That evening I drafted an article called, "GBC-IWR Editorial Board Formed." Quoting from my speech, I implied that the North American Governing Body Commission had acknowledged the need for an open forum in *ISKCON World Review*. I couldn't have been more mistaken. The advisory board was meant to narrow our editorial content, not expand it.

20

Moving On

The lead story for the November issue was the *Monkey on a Stick* book review. My father suggested the headline, "'Monkey' Book Unfair to Hare Krishna Movement" and wrote the lead paragraph: "A new book, now at the bookstores, deals harshly with the International Society for Krishna Consciousness (ISKCON), painting a picture of worldwide crime and corruption." Our editorial, "New Book Slights Movement, Sincere Devotees," argued that many devotees were not even aware of the illegal activities described in *Monkey on a Stick*.

My interview that month was with Drista, headmaster of the Dallas *gurukula*, the very location that had once been so controversial. I asked Drista, "At one time teachers tried to keep parents from seeing their children. How has that changed now?" He explained that after being closed down for many years, the *gurukula* had reopened with new management and policies. He showed me the schoolhouse and pointed out that the children had toys and lived with their parents. I asked how he felt about children going to college, and he said, "We think it's great, we encourage it." He added that the school used a creationist curriculum developed by Christians, which prepared students for college. He spoke enthusiastically and said he was proud that many of his graduates had gone on to a local junior college and one had even received a scholarship to a four-year school.

Mukunda and Ravindra Svarupa approved my *Monkey on a Stick* articles but changed the question about the old *gurukula* to say, "What is the relationship between parents, children and the school?" It seemed a cowardly sidestep of the issue I had intended to address. They also changed Drista's positive response about college to read, "Prabhupada didn't encourage it, but we feel it can be worthwhile." I wondered why the topic was so sensitive. Perhaps because many valuable members had, like Subhananda, left to pursue degrees. Up until then I trusted the editorial board, but now I felt betrayed because they had unfairly censored my writing, even before the first meeting. I wanted to argue for fair play, so I confronted Ravindra Svarupa on the telephone.

He reacted with force, warning me not to be a "crusading, expose, get-all-the-dirt-out journalist" in the official ISKCON publication. He called ISKCON a "hierarchical society" that didn't allow women (or anyone) to act independently. "Just like the Vatican," he said, "they have their official newspaper," and he added that there were some things he would like to "see buried." In my view, if the GBC advisory board had a problem about the content of an interview, they were welcome to write an editorial, not change the interview. Ravindra Svarupa and Mukunda had even called Drista to get his approval for the changes. I felt this was even more dishonorable, because a simple *gurukula* teacher could hardly say no to the GBC chair and minister of public affairs.

After a bit more discussion Ravindra Svarupa finally agreed to let the question read, "In the old days, the school discouraged parental involvement. What's your philosophy now?" It was a victory, but he wouldn't budge on the question about going to college. Ravindra Svarupa, a doctor of philosophy, said Prabhupada just wouldn't have liked it if the official newspaper seemed to advocate college.

I was especially disappointed to learn that the editors had spiked my story, "GBC-IWR Editorial Board Formed." When I asked Ravindra Svarupa about it, he said, "Your article presents your opinion from your own point of view, but I just don't see that any particular point of view came out in that meeting where we decided, 'Yeah it's going to be like this.'"

"All right," I said. I realized it was true. The Governing Body commissioners at the meeting didn't support my policy, they formed a committee to discuss it. I was fooling myself to think otherwise.

"That's my reason," he said.

"Okay, well, we'll see how it goes, if we can all work together," I said. "Maybe you and Mukunda would like to do the paper yourselves. Then you can have it any way you want."

"Oh, don't get the wrong idea," he said. "I don't want to discourage you in your service."

I paused.

"We're still going to have a meeting soon?" he asked.

"Yes, soon," I said. The meeting was scheduled to coincide with the *Geroge v. ISKCON* appeal, when commissioners would be in San Diego.

That evening I told Uddhava all that had happened, and he said, "Let's get out of this." I talked things over with my father, other relatives, and friends. Koumadaki agreed that changing an interview to suit a political position was wrong. Subhananda, who happened to be visiting, assured me that there would be life after the *ISKCON World Review*. Uddhava and I wrote our resignation to bring to San Diego.

On the day of the meeting we knocked on Mukunda's apartment door. His assistant let us in, then we waited a long time. Finally, Ravindra Svarupa and Hari-vilas joined us, and we formed a circle in Mukunda's living room. I sat on the couch, Uddhava sat in a rocking chair, Hari-vilas sat in a round "papa-san" chair, Ravindra Svarupa took a kitchen chair, and Mukunda sat on the floor.

"Let's start by making an agenda," Mukunda said. "Why not start by going over the last issue? Let me write that down." He scribbled it on a legal pad.

"We want to talk about the editorial policy," I said.

"Okay. Editorial policy," he said, writing down those words.

"I think I can save a lot of time," Uddhava said. "Let me just explain that we came here to resign."

"Okay," Mukunda said without flinching. "Can we put that under the heading 'editorial policy'?" He started to write again.

Uddhava and I looked at each other.

Hari-vilas spoke up. "Mukunda, Uddhava just told you he wants to resign. We better talk about this, seriously."

"I've already talked to them about it," Mukunda said. He put his pen down and reflected for a moment.

Uddhava spoke again. "Nandini and I have been trying for years to come to an understanding about the editorial policy. Maybe we alienated ourselves by ignoring criticism from the GBC and others. But now we've decided to stop forcing our writing on people. We're ready to quit."

"You can't just do that," Ravindra Svarupa said.

Everyone argued at once, but no one listened to each other.

"Everything has an apparent cause and a subtle cause," Hari-vilas said, commanding silence with his esoteric philosophical point. "Maybe Nandini's disagreement with Ravindra Svarupa was the apparent cause, but I think it goes deeper than that." He paused for a moment to see if everyone was with him, then continued. "Uddhava and Nandini's decision has come from months of frustration. Uddhava, you said before that you alienated yourselves by ignoring feedback from the GBC, so that contributed to the problem. As I see it, Ravindra Svarupa was just a catalyst for something that was developing for a long time."

"I agree," Uddhava said, finally.

"Okay, then," Hari-vilas continued, "we have a lack of communication. There's no reason to be mad at Ravindra Svarupa. Simply, Uddhava and Nandini feel they can't do the *ISKCON World Review* the way they want anymore, so they're resigning. Maybe it was meant to be, and I think we all appreciate their service. Perhaps they could do another issue or two until Mukunda can find someone else to take over."

Hari-vilas was seated on a wicker chair the shape of an inverted umbrella, with blue paisley cushions. He reminded me of the caterpillar in *Alice's Adventures in Wonderland*. He got us to agree to produce three more issues without controversial content, then turned to Mukunda, "The newspaper has gone on for eight years already. I think that's remarkable in itself. You started the paper, didn't you Mukunda?"

"With a little help from my friends," Mukunda replied.

"Uddhava ran it all those years, right? It's like the Hindu trinity of Brahma, Vishnu, and Shiva. Brahma is the creator, so that's like Mukunda. Vishnu's the maintainer, so that's like Uddhava. And Shiva's the destroyer. Nandini? Nandini, are you the destroyer?"

Hari-vilas smiled at me, and I raised my arms over my head and made a face to look like an ominous destroyer. I guess I startled Hari-vilas, because the chair tipped over and spilled him onto the floor. Everyone was surprised, and there was a moment of hilarious laughter.

"I don't know what happened," Hari-vilas said, getting to his feet. He brushed himself a few times and straightened his robes. Then he set the chair up and hopped back into it.

We all looked around at each other. There was a sad silence as everyone realized that the resignation had been accepted. Uddhava vaguely smiled. Mukunda, who was sitting on his hands, stared at the floor. I felt sorry, and it was all I could do to keep from changing my mind.

When I told my dad about the resignation, he was relieved that they'd let us go peacefully. I was also glad. I didn't know how I could do the paper without my father's help, and now I would not have to. I just hoped he would live a little longer. It had been a year since he started to work with Arnie Weiss, exploring his spiritual interior and learning about the power of forgiveness.

He found peace in God and the faith that his soul would continue after death. Despite the inconvenience and pain of his cancer, he said the last year had been his happiest and that working on the *ISKCON World Review* had kept him going. He asked for a Dixieland funeral so people wouldn't be sad after he died. He called upon musicians from his days with the *Delta Queen* to play at his funeral—and at a few parties in the meantime. They played at a professional dinner given in Dad's honor in Universal City. The evening was a success, and Dad, the master of ceremonies, invited friends to stand up and tell memories of their time together. Although he later commented that it was awkward to have a roast for someone who was about to die rather than retire, the mood of the party mirrored my dad's optimistic and accepting attitude about death.

In the final days, Arnie Weiss helped everyone in the family say the things that we needed to say. Dad questioned me about what I would do after leaving ISKCON. I told him that I wanted to write a book, and he agreed that it was a project worth doing. He also gave me permission to spread his ashes at a holy place in India, according to Hindu custom. He spent New Year's Day visiting with relatives, then the next day announced that he had completed all his work here. The pain started in his chest at 10:30 P.M., and my brother stayed up with him all night. When I took over at 4 A.M., Dad asked me to tell him stories about God, and I did so throughout the morning, then I called his friends to come say goodbye. Dad greeted visitors from his director's chair, half-conscious and lungs filling with fluid. The doctor checked his breathing with a stethoscope and said, "Today's the day, Bill. Just let go." Some old friends stopped by with their three-week-old son. Dad reached out to shake the baby's fingers, a meeting of one just leaving and one just coming into the world. My father died consciously and peacefully that night, surrounded by people who loved him.

I had known Hare Krishnas exactly eleven years. Dad fought his cancer two and a half years, just long enough to see me move away from the temple and put away my saris. The timing had to be more than just a coincidence. I remember the last few years as though he and I were engaged in a complex chess match. Dad knew what he was doing when he encouraged me to write about issues the leaders wanted to forget. He knew the power of words.

I published an obituary for my father in the last issue, then passed the *ISKCON World Review* on to capable, less audacious hands. Uddhava and I took my father's ashes to South India, where we met a Vaishnava priest at a remote temple on an island in the Bay of Bengal. Sanjeevi, the priest, led a sunrise ceremony, reciting prayers in Sanskrit and his native Tamil. We walked from shore until we were shoulder deep in the warm, embracing water. Sanjeevi held the metal urn and told us to take handfuls of ashes, go underwater, and release them. The ashes bloomed like white fans in the gently rocking stillness. As we walked to shore, the priest told me that my father's soul would rest there until deciding on a direction. To the east, thousands of migrating flamingos chattered in the sandbars; to the north was a Shiva temple, to the west was a Rama temple, and to the south, the island of Sri Lanka. I bid my father's soul goodbye and good luck.

Sanjeevi was not a member of ISKCON, but he had met some German Hare Krishnas the previous year. I tried to tell him of my experience in the organization and my father's part in it, but it seemed irrelevant in that distant, spiritual land. Sanjeevi lived a humble life of service among the fishermen and their families, tending the Rama temple and greeting pilgrims who came on government tour buses. His devotional life was the utopia I had hoped to find when I became a Hare Krishna devotee. My expectations had been so great.

After returning from India, Uddhava and I moved to Oregon, far from the nearest temple. Within a few years I had earned my master's degree and gotten a job counseling teenagers. Uddhava became executive editor of a weekly newspaper, and I wrote for him as a freelance reporter. These were our first "real" jobs in a long time.

The ISKCON I joined was exuberant, joyful, and confident. The ISKCON I left was scarred with scandal, enmity, and disgrace. When I consider that difference, I cry. The events I witnessed left an indelible mark on my soul; I had no idea of the troubles that would come to pass. Prabhupada's death brought sudden changes and a decade of confusion, which was much more tumultuous than any of us realized at the time. Many people's lives were affected. Perhaps qualified gurus would have emerged through a natural process if the GBC had not tried to enforce the rule of eleven men. Some of the eleven are still gurus; their dignity survived the storms.

The lack of accountability between leaders and followers was ISKCON's greatest weakness. The organization couldn't take responsibility for the deviant acts of a few (like Ujjvala's assault on Charles Manson), however the followers were also frustrated in controlling the deviations of certain leaders. The rigid patriarchal structure ultimately lacked flexibility. "Prabhupada said" was a phrase that could cast a notion in stone and defy anyone who tried to raise an alternate opinion.

ISKCON's second failure was its isolation and faltering honesty with the outside world. The taste for easy money corrupted some zones more than others as a feeling of invincibility spread like cancer. ISKCON's integrity was tarnished, and it has become even more of a challenge for the organization to pursue its evangelical mission. How will devotees and the rest of the material world ever get along? There will never be a perfect consensus in morality or religion, only conscious practice of tolerance and understanding.

Prabhupada wanted a unified, worldwide ISKCON. At times I have doubted whether that was possible, but I do have hope. I've been many things in my life but being a former ISKCON devotee is a big part of my identity. Some of my friends are (or were) Hare Krishnas, and whenever two or more former full-timers get together, talk always turns to our ISKCON memories. As a friend once said, visits can start to sound like ISKCON-Anon twelve-step meetings, with everyone telling their ISKCON "war stories."

Like many former members, I still hold the philosophy, the rituals, and my relationship with Krishna as sacred. There is something wonderful about chanting in a big congregation, so I occasionally visit the L.A. temple for a *kirtan*. I regret that the problems nearly eclipsed the good things about Krishna consciousness. Prabhupada delivered Lord Chaitanya's message that Krishna is God, adding spirit to the scholarly understanding of the Vaishnava religion. I admire Prabhupada. He spoke about Krishna on every page of his books, in every lecture he gave, and in the way he lived and breathed. His teachings about vegetarianism have influenced thousands—perhaps millions—to live more wholesome lives. Reincarnation, karma, and meditation have become household words all over the United States, due in part to the BBT books that turn up everywhere. The fact that his disciples fell short no longer diminishes his position in my mind. Were it not for Prabhupada's courage and sacrifice in coming to the United States in 1965, many more lives would have been wasted on drugs and fruitless searching.

Appendix

❖

Status of People and Things
in This Volume

From the P.R. Office. Uddhava and Nandini live outside ISKCON and have no roles in the organization. Mukunda, still a *sannyasi,* guru, Governing Body commissioner, and minister of public affairs, heads ISKCON Communications, based in Potomac, Maryland. The *ISKCON World Review* is published six times a year at ISKCON's rural community in Alachua, Florida. Bhutatma lives outside the temple and is still a devotee. Bharata continues as a graphic artist, based at the L.A. temple. Subhananda is no longer an ISKCON member.

The Eleven Gurus. Only two (Jayapataka and Harikesh) remain in their status as gurus, *sannyasis,* and Governing Body Commission members. Jayatirtha was murdered by a disciple in 1987. Kirtanananda (who has legally changed his name to Bhaktipada Swami) lives in New York, under house arrest and awaiting various appeals. The West Virginia real estate is tentatively in the hands of the main ISKCON branch. Hamsadutta married and settled in Geyserville, California. In 1992 he asked the Governing Body Commission to let him come back but felt discouraged at their unfriendly response. He has since established an alternative Krishna organization and initiates disciples. Hridayananda, Tamal Krishna, and Satsvarupa resigned from the GBC but continue as gurus and *sannyasis.* Hridayananda earned his Th.D. at Harvard University, Tamal Krishna is earning a doctorate in Texas, and Satsvarupa writes books for his disciples. Ramesvara, Bhavananda, and Bhagavan live private lives outside and have made no public statements about the organization.

❖

Notes

Foreword

xiv Michael Novak, *Ascent of the Mountain, Flight of the Dove* (New York: Harper and Row, 1978), 156.

Chapter 1 / ISKCON: The Krishnas' International Society

4 The Save the *Delta Queen* campaign is documented in Muster, *The Story of the* Delta Queen; also see Keating, *The Legend of the* Delta Queen, 40–47, which describes the 1970 battle in Congress.

4 Timothy Leary and Richard Alpert explain some of their views in the Foreword they wrote for Watts, *The Joyous Cosmology.*

6 An obituary for Srila Prabhupada appeared in the *Los Angeles Times;* see also Perry, "Hare Krishna Founder Dies," and Spane, "Death of a Spiritual Master."

7 *Back to Godhead* published a selection from Subhananda's journal, see Subhananda, "A Pilgrimage Journal."

9 Prabhupada's exchange with Ginsberg appears in Bhaktivedanta and Ginsberg, "A. C. Bhaktivedanta Swami and Allen Ginsberg: Conversations," 8.

Chapter 2 / Unexpected Requirements

17 Information about the Garden Court Apartment Hotel is from Parker, *L.A.*

21 Srila Prabhupada met Bhaktisiddhanta in 1922, first visited Vrindavana in 1925, took initiation in 1932, and took *sannyas* initiation in 1959 (from a godbrother) while living in Vrindavana as a mendicant from 1956 through 1965, the year he came to the United States. For more about Prabhupada's life in India, see Brooks, *The Hare Krishnas in India,* 72–76; Knott, *My Sweet Lord,* 27–29; Shinn, *The Dark Lord,* 34–39; and the writings of Satsvarupa and Hayagriva.

Chapter 3 / Going Solo into ISKCON

23 For more on Lord Chaitanya, see the writings of Bhaktivedanta Swami; see also Kapoor (a disciple of Bhaktisiddhanta in the Gaudiya-math), *The Philosophy and Religion of Sri Chaitanya.*

24 Prabhupada's 1935 conversation with his guru is described in Satsvarupa, *Prabhupada: He Built a House in Which the Whole World Can Live,* xx.

26 More information on the mantra rock dance can be found in Brooks, *The Hare Krishnas in India* (the statement that Prabhupada was a "cult hero" to the hippies is on 79–80); the writings of Hayagriva (see "The Hare Krishna Explosion," 30, for Leary's "it's a beautiful night"); and Satsvarupa, *Prabhupada.*

26 The interaction between the Beatles and ISKCON is documented in Giuliano, *Dark Horse,* 85–115. See also Hayagriva, *The Hare Krishna Explosion.*

26 Mukunda's quote about the devotees' success in Europe after meeting the Beatles appears in the booklet accompanying EMI's 1993 compact disc reissue of *The Radha-Krsna Temple* recording, produced by George Harrison and published by Apple Records.

26 The 1976 resolution about P.R. appeared in Governing Body Commission, "Final Resolutions Passed by the GBC and Approved by His Divine Grace A. C. Bhaktivedanta Swami Prabhupada, at the Mayapur Meetings, Gour Purnima, 1976," item 20, 6.

The following year the GBC passed another P.R. resolution: "Resolved: (a) Each Temple President will instruct the devotees that as each devotee approaches people in any way, he is acting as a public relations representative for Srila Prabhupada; (b) At least one day a week there must be chanting and food distribution in public performed by each Temple; (c) Balavanta Prabhu, who is P.R. Minister for the U.S., will be editor for a monthly newsletter to ISKCON, reporting on public relations programs to be executed, including "do and don't" policies; and (d) Every temple will start a program of sending a monthly *Back to Godhead* and letter from a devotee to his parents if his parents are at least approachable. (Secretary's note: When we read this item to Srila Prabhupada, he exclaimed, 'That is a very good idea')." In Governing Body Commission, "GBC Meetings: March 1–4, 1977, Mayapur Chandrodaya Mandir," 4.

27 Positive news articles in the P.R. files include Dart, "Two Hundred Scholars"; and Nordheimer, "Young Ascetics." Articles on ISKCON's early troubles include Harris, "Hashish Oil Ring Smashed"; Herskowitz, "When Country Meets Krishnas"; Johnson, "Children of a Harsh Bliss"; King, "Kirshna Arms Caches Draw Police" and "Religious Panhandlers Stirring Anger"; Lindsey, "California Slaying Case"; Maxwell, "Eleven Linked" and "Mystics and Mobsters"; Paskevich, "Bovan Case"; and Schumach, "Judge Dismisses Charges."

28 All information about the Chicago press conference with Prabhupada came from Public Relations Center, Inc., *Public Relations Report for International Society for Krishna Consciousness;* pages 4–17 cover the July 9 Sheraton-Chicago Hotel press conference. According to the P.R. firm, "A combined audience of more than *1.5 million* Chicago area residents read reports of the Swami's conference" (4, emphasis in original). The 125-page report documents the company's equivocal campaign for ISKCON Chicago throughout 1975. Constantine's "It's *Men* as in '*Men*tal'" appeared in the *Chicago Sun-Times* on July 10, 1975. The evening newscast was broadcast on WMAQ-TV on July 10, 1975. A transcript appeared on page 9 of the Public Relations Center folio.

32 A manual for new devotees was compiled and used throughout Ramesvara's zone. See Danavir, *Bhakta Program Manual.* Women based their discipline on this manual as well.

Chapter 4 / My Zonal Guru

36 The change-up technique has been described in many articles, including Mankin, "Chanting for Dollars," and Anderson, "Two Years in the Hare Krishna Temple."

37– The GBC resolution about women's *sankirtan* comes from the 1977 GBC
38 Resolutions, item 22, 6. The next year, a resolution called for a committee to "correct difficulties regarding women's [*sankirtan*] in Berkeley and Los Angeles within three months' time." Another committee was to deal with the New Vrindaban women's party. See Governing Body Commission, "GBC Resolutions, March 19, 1978," item 4, 1.

38 The story of Jayananda's sacrifice and recognition from Prabhupada were covered in *Back to Godhead* shortly after his death; see "Condolences"; see also Nandini, "Remembering Jayananda."

Chapter 5 / Jonestown Fallout

50– "Keeping Up with the Joneses," the lead article of the *ISKCON Public Af-*
51 *fairs Newsletter* in 1978, included a sample press release mentioning "Jonestown dog-pack journalism."

51 Ryon's article, "Krishna Sect Deep into Real Estate," appeared on November 26, 1978; the *Time* and *Newsweek* cover stories came out on December 4, 1978.

52 See Subhananda, *A Request to the Media;* quotations are on 2 and 16.

53 For more information on the FROGS, see Clements, "'Clickers' Are Cracking Down."

Chapter 6 / A Spiritual Disneyland

56 Prabhupada's recommendation that Kirtanananda return to Bellevue Hospital appeared in Letter 67-10-12, to Brahmananda, October 16, 1967, in Bhaktivedanta Swami, *Letters from Srila Prabhupada,* 229.

55 The New Vrindaban temple room attack was reported in "Hare Krishna
Ascetic Farm Grows." The incident is also mentioned in Herskowitz, "When
Country Meets Krishnas," Megan, "Krishna and Community," and Kozel,
"Settlement Refutes *Philadelphia Inquirer* Statements."

58 For Indian media coverage of New Vrindaban, see Bhatia, "New Vrindavan
in U.S."

Chapter 7 / Drug Busts, Guns, and Gangsters

63 See Welborn, "Kulik Tied Close to Krishna Boss," for a media report linking drug smugglers with the BBT.

63 For information on the 1977 drug murder, see Lindsey, "California Slaying
Case"; Maxwell, "Eleven Linked to Krishna Cult Indicted" and "Mystics and
Mobsters"; Paskevich, "Bovan Case"; and Warner, "W.Va. Krishnas Study
of Contrasts."

64 Prabhupada's letter to the PDI crew included the statement, "There is no
need to engage in anything dishonest. Krsna has given enough money, now
earn by honest means." See Letter 77-1-34, January 24, 1977, in Bhaktivedanta
Swami, *Letters from Srila Prabhupada*, 3316.

64 For the *Yoga Journal* and *Rolling Stone* obituaries, see Spane, "Death of a
Spiritual Master," and Perry, "Hare Krishna Founder Dies."

65 For information about the 1980 hash bust, see "Hare Krishna Hash Bust";
Candida, "LB Man Gets Fourteen Years"; Harris, "Hashish Oil Ring Smashed";
and "Ex-Krishna Members Convicted."

65 Mukunda's speech at the Krishna hash bust conference was published in
an ISKCON press release on November 7, 1979.

65 *The New York Times* quoted "post-Jonestown dogpack journalism" on June
17, 1980; see "Krishna Sect Denies Policy on Guns."

66 Ramesvara's comments on terrorist groups were published in the *Public
Affairs Newsletter;* see Ramesvara, "Focusing on the Real Issue," 1–2.

67 For information on the Berkeley weapons problems, see Brydolf and
Ramirez, "Hare Krishna Sect Faces Growing Police Scrutiny"; Eastham,
"Hare Krishna Maligned?"; and "Hare Krishna Leader Arrested."

67 The statement about devotees carrying cocaine in their bead bags appeared
in Dorgan, "Hare Krishna, Hare Krishna, Guns 'n' Ammo, Guns 'n' Ammo,"
56.

68 Hamsadutta's lyrics to "Guru, Guru on the Wall" are from the LP *Nice but
Dead* (1978), from Hansa Associates.

69 Bhagavan's statements about the strength of the GBC were published in an
ISKCON press release of May 29, 1980.

69 The 1980 resolution about P.R. appeared in "I.S.K.C.O.N. Governing Body
Commission Manifesto for 494 Caitanya Era (1980–81)," no. 4b, 6.

70 After Hamsadutta's weapons trial in Germany, *Back to Godhead* printed an
article with the following headlines in various type sizes: "Religions Perse-

cution in West Germany, the Trial of the Hare Krishna People. The Raid . . . the Media Barrage . . . the Courtroom Encounter. A Half-Million Dollar Effort to Snuff out the Hare Krishna Movement."

Chapter 8 / Who's Watching the Children?

72– Mukunda, "Krishna Constricts the *Life* Asura [Demon]," includes a discus-
73 sion of the legal negotiations with *Life* magazine.

74 Hridayananda's comments about women were originally made in a March 24 letter to Ramesvara, who turned them over to Mukunda for use in that edition of the newsletter.

74 *The ISKCON World Review* published a photo of the Bombay billboard advertising the *Life* magazine cover. See *ISKCON World Review*, "*Life* Ad Hinges on Krishna's Kids." *ISKCON World Review* reprinted the *Life* letters to the editor in "Readers Rave over *Life* Cover."

74– For media reports mentioned in this chapter see Chriss, "Hare Krishna Sect
75 Children Reared in Isolation"; Sigall, "A Crackpot School"; Lunnen, "Gurukula"; Rothchild and Wolf, *The Children of the Counterculture*, 134–46; and Wax, "Raise Your Hand if You're a Spirit Soul."

76 See Brooks, *The Hare Krishnas in India*, 27–55, for a good discussion of the significance of Vrindavana to Krishna devotees.

Chapter 9 / The Gurus Start World War III

78 The group that split away from the BBT to form an alternative center is described in Rochford, "Factionalism, Group Defection."

80 Facts about Croome Court come from "Croome Court Goes on Offer," and Lines, "Croome and Krishna."

81 Prabhupada's statements about India and Pakistan are from an April 4, 1975, audio cassette recording, "Morning Walk: W.W. III," in the Bhaktivedanta Archives, Sandy Ridge, North Carolina. See also Satsvarupa, "Secretary to a Pure Devotee," and Bhaktivedanta Swami, "Srila Prabhupada Speaks Out on War and Death," 29.

81 In 1974 *Back to Godhead* quoted Prabhupada that "there will be no nuclear war." See Satsvarupa, "Secretary to a Pure Devotee," 28. In 1981, when fears of World War III were heating up, *Back to Godhead* published a quote of Prabhupada saying that since the superpowers had amassed arsenals, "They must use them." See Bhaktivedanta, "Srila Prabhupada Speaks Out on War and Death." See also Balavanta, "Cooling the Nuclear Vesuvius"; Drutakarma, "Exploding the Myth of the Innocent Citizen" and "Surviving the Eighties"; Ramesvara, "Focusing on the Real Issue," "The Hard Rain of Karma," and "'There Cannot Be Peace'"; and Suhotra, "Two Faces of Krishna." See also Brydolf and Ramirez, "Hare Krishna Sect Faces Growing Police Scrutiny"; MacRobert, "The Krishna Question"; and Avery, Quintana, and Knutson, "The Krishna File," 3.

82 The quoted translation of the first offense was published in *The Process of Deity Worship* (Arcana-paddhati), ed. Jayatirtha, 94. The common translation, memorized by most ISKCON members, is, "The first offense is to blaspheme the devotees who have dedicated their lives to propagating the holy name of the Lord."

83 The open letter from Jayatirtha addressed to "All Devotees of Srila Prabhupada's Lotus Feet" was undated, but it appeared in 1982 after his expulsion. The quoted statement is on 5.

83– The guru deviations of 1980 are described in Rochford, *Hare Krishna in Amer-*
84 *ica,* 221–56. Jayatirtha's departure is also described in Knott, *My Sweet Lord.* Resolutions taking away Jayatirtha's responsibilities in ISKCON appeared as a supplement to the 1982 Governing Body Commission resolutions

Chapter 10 / The Storm Within: The Guru Issue

86– For Prabhupada's statement about his disciples becoming gurus, see Letter
87 67-11-2, to Madhusudan, November 2, 1967, in Bhaktivedanta Swami, *Letters from Srila Prabhupada,* 242. Letters criticizing the GBC include Letter 72-4-18, to Hamsadutta, April 11, 1972, and Letter 72-12-28, to Karandhar, Dec. 22, 1972, both in Bhaktivendanta Swami, *Letters from Srila Prabhupada,* 1954, 2184. The GBC opposed the Bhaktivedanta Archives' plans to publish Srila Prabhupada's letters in a five-volume set. In 1982 they passed a resolution stating that "the compilation and the publication of Srila Prabhupada's letter book be cancelled." The Bhaktivedanta Archives published the books in 1987 despite the GBC's resolution.

87 The channeler's comments come from Amogha-lila's writings of mid-August 1979, which were compiled in 1986 by Trivikram. See Amogha-lila, "Writings of mid-August 1979."

87 The second appointment tape was recorded July 8, 1977, and the letter to temple presidents announcing the appointment was dated July 9. On that same date, Tamal Krishna wrote a notice that he titled "To All G.B.C., and Temple Presidents."

88 Ramesvara's statements expressing doubts about his own guruship are from page 30 of Ramesvara and Subhananda, "On the Position of the Initiating Guru in the Western USA Zone."

90 District Attorney Arlo Smith's derogatory comment about *sankirtan* was published in Avery, Quintana, and Knutson, "The Krishna File," part 3, 1.

91 Badri-narayan's comment about soliciting in plain clothes appeared in Gilmon, "'Get Better Response.'"

91 The Bangor art dealer's comments about devotee art sales appeared in Banks, "Krishna Members Accused of Art Swindle."

92 Tamal Krishna's statements about *ritvik* gurus come from a transcript of the "Pyramid House Talks."

92– "The Descending Process of Selecting a Spiritual Master," was distributed
93   along with the 1981 GBC resolutions in March 1981. See also *ISKCON World
      Review* Associate Editors, "GBC 'No New Guru' Vote."

Chapter 11 / P.R. Publications Promote ISKCON

96   Steve Allen came to the P.R. office on August 31, 1981, while he was writing
      Beloved Son. Accounts of his talks with Subhananda, Mukunda, and Rames-
      vara and his tour of Watseka Avenue are on 200–204.

96   Annie Lennox married a German devotee she met through Magic Lotus
      catering. See "Split."

97   See "High Fashion Model" for Satarupa's conversion; see also Angly, "From
      Catwalk to Krishna."

102   *The New York Times* published two articles about Hare Krishnas in the So-
      viet Union. See Shabad, "Hare Krishna Chant," and Schmemann, "Soviet
      Says Hare Krishna."

Chapter 12 / Ramesvara Crashes

108   On September 29, 1995 Lekhasravanti and Bhusaya, whose 1977 wedding
      made national news, attended a White House ceremony to accept the Pres-
      idential Medal of Freedom that was given posthumously to Walter P. Reu-
      ther. See Kunti Dasi, "Clinton Meets Devotees."

108   On the Detroit opening, see Suplee, "The Temple of Tomorrowland"; see
      also "For the Krishnas, a Rebirth."

110   Senesi's quote, "Wow! This organization is really sick," comes from an inter-
      view published by the Christian Research Institute. Senesi further stated,
      "Being involved in the public relations division, I also had access to the clip-
      ping service which received articles from newspapers and magazines from all
      over the world—bad publicity about the movement, about people getting
      busted for smuggling, and the leaders of the temple shooting crowds of Ben-
      galis in Mayapur outside of Calcutta, and all this really bizarre stuff which
      most of the devotees didn't even know was going on, because the leaders se-
      lectively present what they want the devotees to hear, and they discourage
      them from reading any outside literature." See Senesi, "Inside ISKCON," 1.
      Senesi's interview was adapted by Pement in "Hare Krishna Starved My Soul."

111– ISKCON issued a press statement on June 17, 1983, following the *George v.*
12   *ISKCON* verdict.

113   On Hamsadutta's expulsion, see "Kary Will Harry Krishnas No More," and
      Hirsch, "Hare Krishna Cult Excommunicates an 'Eccentric.'" Hamsadut-
      ta's legal name is Hans Kary.

115   For a discussion between Subhananda and Larry Shinn about the biblical
      passage "no one comes to the father but by me," see Gelberg, *Hare Krish-
      na, Hare Krishna.*

115 An excerpt from Roszak, *Unfinished Animal,* mirrors my dilemma on Hollywood Boulevard: "In the lives of young Krishnaites, the entire Western experience (or as much of it as they have acquired since childhood) must simply be switched off and obliterated by unquestioning obedience and rigid imitation of an alien model" (204).

Chapter 13 / The Revolution of Guru Reform

118 Allegations against Harikesh are summarized in a regional secretary's writings of 1985, which include letters to the GBC, the GBC Privilege Committee, "All Authorities in ISKCON," and godbrothers, as well as photocopies of the pendulum reading charts.

120 The photo of the robed Italian monk was published in Gokulananda and Saugita, "Krishna Festivals."

121 See Ravindra Svarupa, "'Under My Order,'" 1, for the quotation from *Caitanya-caritamrta,* 5, on the disintegration of the Gaudiya-math, and Ravindra Svarupa's call to arms, 7.

121 Three gurus were added in 1982: Pancadravida, Bhaktisvarupa Damodara, and Gopala Krishna. See *Back to Godhead* editors, "Hare Krishna Movement Expands Leadership," and *ISKCON World Review* editors, "ISKCON Gets Three New Initiating Gurus." See "The Process for Expanding the Number of Initiating Gurus in ISKCON," an addendum to the 1982 GBC minutes. Four more gÂrus were appointed in 1984, including Bhakti-tirtha, ISKCON's black collegian from Princeton University.

122 The European Continental Assembly published a statement of their intent to overthrow the guru reform movement in their resolutions and mailed copies to each Governing Body commissioner. See Hare Krishna Dasa, "The European Continental Assembly."

123– Dart, "Killing Sparks Federal Probe," describes death threats against Su-
24   lochan. According to the report, reformers numbered approximately three hundred, including about half of the ISKCON leadership. Marshall County assessor Alfred Clark also received death threats after he tried to raise property taxes at New Vrindaban. Ten years after Sulochan's murder his former associates still complained of gurus making death threats. Dart's article first noted their complaints in 1986: "Bryant's fellow dissidents continue to maintain that critics of the sect are in danger. Several followers said in interviews that they have been threatened themselves or have heard certain leaders casually mention violence as a way to deal with internal critics." Dart also characterizes the Governing Body Commission's relationship with the gurus as "still murky."

124 Sulochan's statement about the possible impact of his book appeared in *The Guru Business,* Appendix 22, 16.

124 Information about Sulochan comes from his writings and interviews with his former associates.

125 For information on Kirtananda's attack, see Rouvales, "Krishna Chief Blames 'Crazy Man,'" and Hubner, "Crime and the Krishnas."

125 Triyogi's apology to New Vrindaban President Kuladri was written in January 1986.

126 Remensky, "Krishna Sect Splintering in Top Ranks," was a sidebar to Rouvalis, "Krishna Chief Blames 'Crazy Man.'"

126 For reviews of the *Persuaders,* see Brayfield, "When Rock Was Hard"; Dunbar, "Harbingers of Things to Come"; and Kenny, "New Stars Shine Bright."

Chapter 14 / P.R. Bails Out of L.A.

135– Quotations from Ramesvara's meeting with the two women in the Santa
36 Monica Mall were taken from Rasamanjari and Amrita, "Conversation at Santa Monica Mall," 4, 6.

Chapter 15 / 1986: The Year of Crisis

137 Sulochan's allegations of child abuse, prostitution, and drug trafficking "were widely disregarded" until he was murdered in Los Angeles. Sheriff Donald Bordenkircher, an official investigating the case in West Virginia, said that Sulochan's death "brought instant credibility." See Gruson, "Friction over Krishnas."

138 See Trippett, "Troubled Karma," for a comparison of New Vrindaban to Jim Jones's People's Temple.

138 Six months after Sulochan was killed, his three-year-old son drowned in a pond at New Vrindaban. The death was called an accident; see Hubner, "Temple of Doom," 11.

142 Jaya Krishna Dasa (Jay Whitehead) was recognized by the Federal International des Echeques (FIDE) in 1986. See *ISKCON World Review,* "Jaya Krishna Dasa."

144– Governing Body Commission, "Minutes of North American GBC Meeting
45 (August 18, 19, San Diego)" contained suggestions for Bhavananda (Resolution 1), Kirtanananda (Resolutions 2–5), and Ramesvara (Resolutions 6–7).

145 John and Nancy Wilkman were both nominated for Emmy Awards for their writing in 1988. John won in two categories.

145 The downtown L.A. Biltmore Hotel landmark is described in Parker, *L.A.,* 6–7.

Chapter 16 / The Budget Axe

147– Mukunda's 1966 remembrance is from Satsvarupa, *Prabhupada: He Built a
48 House in Which the Whole World Can Live,* 57–58.

149– Bhagavan's resignation was dated on September 23, 1986.
50

154 The Western Zonal Council resolution about Uddhava and me was passed in November 1986 and delivered to the editors after the December issue was printed.

Chapter 17 / The *ISKCON World Review* Crosses the Line

156– Kirtanananda's interview was recorded on December 30, 1986; Bill Muster's
62   statements about editorial policy were recorded on January 15, 1987; Larry
      Shinn's interview was recorded on January 5, 1987, and published in
      ISKCON World Review in August 1987; and Panchadravida's interview was
      recorded on January 7, 1987.

159   For information about the FBI raid of New Vrindaban and discovery of St.
      Denis's remains, see Smith and Penny, "Possible St. Denis' Remains Are
      Discovered."

Chapter 18 / Six Months Out of Print

165   The *Washington Post* published a special report on New Vrindaban after its
      split from ISKCON; see Ahrens, "West Virginia's Krishnas." See also Fitzger-
      ald, "Female Hare Krishnas Initiated" for information about female *sann-
      yasis* at New Vrindaban. The Cult Awareness Newtwork has also followed
      Kirtananda's legal and spiritual troubles; see "$125 Million Lawsuit Filed
      against Krishna Leader."

168   The letter from Badri-narayan to Mukunda was dated June 28, 1988.

168   See Nandini, "Interview: ISKCON Faces Dilemma," for Hari-vilas's com-
      ments about the health of the BBT.

170   The *Monkey on a Stick* advertisement appeared in *Time* magazine in late
      1988.

170   For reviews of *Monkey on a Stick,* see Fadiman, "Not What Krishna Had in
      Mind," and Sheppard, "Good Hustle, Bad Karma."

Chapter 19 / Women's Lesser Intelligence

171   The ISKCON Current Affairs Seminar took place in Towaco on June 17, 1988.
      See Bhaktarupa Dasa, "Announcing New York's Famous Ratha-yatra Week-
      end."

173   My speech, *"ISKCON World Review:* Story of a Hare Krishna Newspaper,"
      was presented at the North American Governing Body Commission meet-
      ing in Dallas on September 28, 1988.

174   Mark Twain's quote about newspapers from *Life on the Mississippi,* 93.

Chapter 20 / Moving On

177   Ravindra Svarupa's conversation was recorded in October 1988.

Appendix

183   For Hamsadutta's appeal to the GBC and their reply, see Bhurijan, "Letter
      of 'Fourteen Guidelines.'"

Glossary

Arotik	Ceremony of Hindu deity worship (spelled *arati* in Sanskrit)
BBT	Bhaktivedanta Book Trust, ISKCON's publishing division
To bloop	To leave ISKCON
Fringie	A fringe member
Gaudiya-math	ISKCON's predecessor organization in India
GBC	Governing Body Commission, made up of Governing Body commissioners
Guru	Spiritual teacher
Gurukula	School of the guru
ISKCON	Acronym for the International Society for Krishna Consciousness
ISKCON World Review	P.R. department's monthly publication
Japa	Chanting on beads
Kirtan	Chanting with musical accompaniment
Lord Chaitanya	Fifteenth-century incarnation of Krishna (1486–1534)
Mayapur	Chaitanya's birthplace in India, where ISKCON has a temple and cultural center
New Vrindaban	West Virginia community, including Prabhupada's Palace of Gold
Prabhupada	A. C. Bhaktivedanta Swami, founder-*Acharya* (spiritual leader) of ISKCON
Sankirtan	Congregational chanting (in ISKCON refers to book distribution)

Sannyasi	Renounced preacher
Srila Bhaktisiddhanta Sarasvati Thakur	Prabhupada's guru; founder of the Gaudiya-math (1874–1936)
Sripada Bhakti Raksaka Sridhar Maharaja	Disciple of Bhaktisiddhanta; Prabhupada's contemporary (1895–1988)
Vrindavana	Krishna's birthplace in India, where ISKCON has a temple
Vyasasana	Seat of the spiritual master

❖

Bibliography

Ahrens, Frank. "West Virginia's Krishnas." *Washington Post,* September 8, 1991.

Allen, Steve. *Beloved Son: A Story of the Jesus Cults.* New York: Bobbs-Merrill, 1982.

Allen, Tom [Toshan Krishna]. "Official Statement Given by [ISKCON] in Regards to *The New York Times* Article, 'Krishna Arms Caches Draw Police Scrutiny in California,' of June 9, 1980." ISKCON press release. New York, June 11, 1980. Author's collection.

Allen, Tom [Toshan Krishna], and Harold Wilson [Bharata]. "News Release RE: Hare Krishna Probe." ISKCON press release. Berkeley, Calif., April 1, 1980. Author's collection.

Anderson, Wendy. "Two Years in the Hare Krishna Temple." *Glencoe* [Ill.] *News,* June 11, 1981.

Angly, Pat. "From Catwalk to Krishna: The Cover Girl Who Works for Love." *Cleo* [Australia], May 1979, 32–35.

Aversa, Rudy. "She's Singing for Krishna." *Los Angeles Herald Examiner,* February 19, 1977.

Avery, Paul, Joe Quintana, and Peter Knutson. "The Krishna File." *Sacramento Bee,* June 22, 23, 24, 25, 1980.

Balavanta. "Cooling the Nuclear Vesuvius." *Back to Godhead* 13 (June 1978): 27, 34.

Banks, Harold. "Krishna Members Accused of Art Swindle." *Boston Herald,* November 1, 1981.

Bhaktarupa Dasa. "Announcing New York's Famous Ratha-yatra Weekend/ ISKCON Current Affairs Seminar at ISKCON Towaco." Advertisement in *ISKCON World Review* 7 (May 1988): 7.

Bhaktivedanta Swami, A. C. *Bhagavad-gita as It Is.* Revised edition. Vaduz, Lichtenstein: Bhaktivedanta Book Trust, 1983.

————. *Caitanya-caritamrta.* Los Angeles: Bhaktivedanta Book Trust, 1974.

————. *Lennon '69: Search for Liberation.* Los Angeles: Bhaktivedanta Book Trust, 1981.

————. *Letters from Srila Prabhupada.* 5 volumes. Culver City: The Vaishnava Institute, 1987.

————. "Morning Walk: W.W. III." April 4, 1975. Audio cassette recording. Bhaktivedanta Archives, Sandy Ridge, N.C.

————. *Nectar of Devotion.* Los Angeles: Bhaktivedanta Book Trust, 1970.

————. "Prabhupada at New Vrindaban." *Back to Godhead,* no. 29 (1969): 12–15.

————. "Srila Prabhupada Speaks Out on War and Death." *Back to Godhead* 16 (January–February 1981): 29.

————. *Srimad-Bhagavatam.* Los Angeles: Bhaktivedanta Book Trust, 1987.

Bhaktivedanta Swami, A. C., and Allen Ginsberg. "A. C. Bhaktivedanta Swami and Allen Ginsberg: Conversations." Recorded May 11, 12, 14, 1969. *Back to Godhead,* no. 28 (1969): 7–14.

Bhatia, V. P. "New Vrindavan in U.S. a Tourist Draw." *Times of India,* November 10, 1980.

Bhurijan. "Letter of 'Fourteen Guidelines for Welcoming Hansadutta Back to ISKCON.'" In Hansadutta, *Excommunicated Uncommunicated Incommunicado.* Geyserville, Calif.: Nam Hatta World Sankirtan Party, 1993.

Brayfield, Celia. "When Rock Was Hard." *London Times,* January 2, 1986.

Brooks, Charles R. *The Hare Krishnas in India.* Princeton: Princeton University Press, 1989.

Brydolf, Carol, and Raul Ramirez. "Hare Krishna Sect Faces Growing Police Scrutiny." *Oakland* [Calif.] *Tribune,* May 25, 1980.

Back to Godhead Editors. "Condolences" [obituary for Jayananda]. *Back to Godhead* 12 (June 1977): 17.

————. "Hare Krishna Movement Expands Spiritual Leadership." *Back to Godhead* 17 (June 1982): 19.

Came, Barry. "Krishna-by-the-Sea." *Newsweek,* January 30, 1978.

Candida, Frank. "LB Man Gets Fourteen Years for Smuggling Hashish." *Orange County Register,* February 27, 1980.

Chriss, Nicholas C. "Hare Krishna Sect Children Reared in Isolation on Ancient Mysticism." *Los Angeles Times,* September 1, 1974.

Clements, William. "'Clickers' Are Cracking Down on Solicitors in Airport." *New Orleans Times-Picayune,* October 7, 1979.

Constantine, Peggy. "It's *Men* as in '*Mental*': Swami Slams the Second Sex." *Chicago Sun-Times,* July 10, 1975.

Contemporary Vedic Library Series Editorial Board. *Chant and Be Happy: The Power of Mantra Meditation.* Los Angeles: Bhaktivedanta Book Trust, 1983.

————. *Chant and Be Happy, The Story of the Hare Krishna Mantra.* Los Angeles: Bhaktivedanta Book Trust, 1982.

———. *Coming Back: The Science of Reincarnation*. Los Angeles: Bhaktivedanta Book Trust. 1983.

———. *The Higher Taste: A Guide to Gourmet Vegetarian Cooking and a Karma-Free Diet*. Los Angeles: Bhaktivedanta Book Trust, 1983.

"Croome Court Goes on Offer." *Berrow's Worcester* [U.K.] *Journal*, June 7, 1984.

Danavir. *Bhakta Program Manual*. Los Angeles: ISKCON, 1976.

Dart, John. "Killing Sparks Federal Probe of Krishna Sect." *Los Angeles Times*, July 20, 1986.

———. "Shake-up Involves L.A. Leader: Two Krishna Gurus Granted Leaves amid Controversy." *Los Angeles Times*, October 5, 1986.

———. "Two Hundred Scholars Support Hare Krishna." *Los Angeles Times*, November 6, 1976.

Dorgan, Michael. "Hare Krishna, Hare Krishna, Guns 'n' Ammo, Guns 'n' Ammo." *High Times*, no. 65 (January 1981): 56.

Drutakarma. "Exploding the Myth of the Innocent Citizen: East and West, Bad Karma Is Building to a Critical Mass, and Catastrophe." *Back to Godhead* 17 (August 1982): 5–6.

Dunbar, Bob. "Harbingers of Things to Come." *Film and TV Technician*, December 1, 1985.

Eastham, Todd R. "Hare Krishna Maligned?" *Whittier* [Calif.] *Daily News*, September 6, 1980.

Eck, Diana L. "Krishna Consciousness in Historical Perspective." *Back to Godhead* 14 (October 1979): 26–29.

"Ex-Krishna Members Convicted." *Orange County* [Calif.] *Daily Pilot*, January 22, 1980.

Fadiman, Anne. "Not What Krishna Had in Mind." *New York Times Book Review*, November 20, 1988.

Fitzgerald, Sandy. "Female Hare Krishnas Initiated as Swamis." *Wheeling* [W.Va.] *News Register*, November 17, 1987.

"For the Krishnas, a Rebirth in Detroit." *New York Times*, May 26, 1983.

Gadahar Dasa. "Controversial Swami of Hare Krishna Community in West Virginia Begins First Amendment Freedom Tour." New Vrindaban press release, December 1986. Author's collection.

Gelberg, Steven J. [Subhananda], ed. *Hare Krishna, Hare Krishna: Five Distinguished Scholars on the Hare Krishna Movement in the West*. New York: Grove Press, 1983.

Gillmon, Rita. "'Get Better Response': Krishnas Now Solicit in 'Civies.'" *San Diego Union*, August 11, 1978.

Giuliano, Geoffrey. *Dark Horse: The Private Life of George Harrison*. New York: Penguin Books, 1991.

Gokulananda and Sangita. "Krishna Festivals in L.A. and Italy Mark Summer." *ISKCON World Review* 3 (September 1983): 1.

Governing Body Commission. "The Descending Process of Selecting a Spiritual Master: A GBC Committee Report from the Initiating Spiritual Masters."
March 1981. ISKCON document. Author's collection.

———. "Final Resolutions Passed by the GBC and Approved by His Divine
Grace A. C. Bhaktivedanta Swami Prabhupada, at the Mayapur Meetings,
Gour Purnima, 1976." 1976 GBC Resolutions. ISKCON document. Author's
collection.

———. "GBC Meetings: March 1–4, 1977, Mayapur Chandrodaya Mandir." 1977
GBC Resolutions. ISKCON document. Author's collection.

———. "GBC Resolutions, March 19, 1978." 1978 GBC Resolutions. ISKCON
document. Author's collection.

———. "Governing Body Commission Annual Meeting, Sridham Mayapur,
March 5, 1979, Minutes." 1979 GBC Resolutions. ISKCON document. Author's
collection.

———. "I.S.K.C.O.N. Governing Body Commission Manifesto for 496 Caitanya Era (1982–83)." 1982 GBC Resolutions. ISKCON document. Author's collection.

———. "Minutes of GBC Meetings Held at New Vrindaban, Sept 16–20, 1985."
ISKCON document. Author's collection.

———. "Minutes of North American GBC Meeting (August 18, 19, San Diego)."
August 1986. ISKCON document. Author's collection.

———. "The Process for Carrying Out Srila Prabhupada's Desires for Future
Initiations: A Paper Prepared by the GBC in Consultation with Higher Authorities, Mayapur, March 1978." March 1978. ISKCON document. Author's
collection.

———. "The Process for Expanding the Number of Initiating Gurus in
ISKCON." Addendum to 1982 GBC Resolutions. ISKCON document. Author's collection.

———. "Resolutions, March 1987." 1987 GBC Resolutions. ISKCON document.
Author's collection.

Gruson, Lindsey. "Friction over Krishnas in West Virginia's Hills." *New York
Times,* October 1, 1986.

Hansadutta. *Excommunicated Uncommunicated Incommunicado.* Geyserville,
Calif.: Nam Hatta World Sankirtan Party, 1993.

"Hare Krishna Ascetic Farm Grows Despite Complaints in W. Virginia." *Los
Angeles Times,* July 12, 1973.

Hare Krishna Dasa. "The European Assembly: Minutes of the Meeting of Sannyasis, National/Regional Secretaries, Ministers and Temple Presidents of the
International Society for Krishna Consciousness in Europe, held at Krishnaville (Ermenonville) France, November 8, 9, and 10, 1985." November 15,
1985. ISKCON document. Author's collection.

———. "The European Continental Assembly: Minutes of the Meeting of Sannyasis, National/Regional Secretaries, Ministers and Temple Presidents of the

International Society for Krishna Consciousness in Europe, Held at Krishnaville (Ermenonville) France, January 31, February 1 and 2, 1985." ISKCON document. Author's collection.

"Hare Krishna Hash Bust, Eleven Indicted in O.C. Crackdown." *Orange County* [Calif.] *Daily Register,* November 6, 1979, 1.

"Hare Krishna Leader Arrested." *Hayward* [Calif.] *Daily Review,* May 14, 1980.

Harris, John. "Hashish Oil Ring Smashed." *Los Angeles Herald Examiner,* November 6, 1979.

Harrison, Eric. "Crimes among the Krishnas." *Philadelphia Inquirer Sunday Magazine,* April 5, 1987.

Hayagriva. *The Hare Krishna Explosion: The Birth of Krishna Consciousness in America, 1966–1969.* New Vrindaban: Palace Press, 1985.

———. "The Hare Krishna Explosion: The Joyful History of a Dynamic Transcendental Movement." *Back to Godhead,* no. 26 (1969): 26–30.

Herskowitz, Linda. "When Country Meets Krishnas: Sect Stockpiles Weapons in War of Nerves at New West Virginia Home." *Washington Post,* January 5, 1979.

"High Fashion Model Trades Jet Set for Hare Krishna." Religious News Service, February 21, 1980.

Hirsch, Rick. "Hare Krishna Cult Excommunicates an 'Eccentric' Founding Father." *Miami Herald,* July 10, 1983.

Hubner, John. "Crime and the Krishnas: How the Krishnas Turned Bad." *San Jose Mercury News West Magazine,* June 21, 1987, 6–13.

———. "Crime and the Krishnas: The Temple of Doom." *San Jose Mercury News West Magazine,* June 28, 1987, 6–13.

Hubner, John, and Lindsey Gruson. "Dial Om for Murder." *Rolling Stone,* April 9, 1987, 53–58, 78–82.

Hubner, John, and Lindsey Gruson. *Monkey on a Stick: Murder, Madness, and the Hare Krishnas.* San Diego: Harcourt Brace Jovanovich, 1988.

ISKCON Temple Presidents. "Minutes of the ISKCON North American Temple Presidents Meeting." November 1984. ISKCON document. Author's collection.

———. "Minutes of the North American Temple Presidents, Regional Secretaries, and Sannyasis Meeting Held at New Vrindaban on August 19–20, 1985." ISKCON document. Author's collection.

ISKCON World Review Associate Editors. [Nandini.] "Ananta Santi's Freedom Announced at U.S.-Soviet Summit." *ISKCON World Review* 7 (January 1988): 1.

———. [Nandini.] "Book Review: Scholar's Work Assails Cult Stereotype." Review of *The Dark Lord* by Larry Shinn. *ISKCON World Review* 7 (October 1987): 6.

———. [Nandina and Uddhava.] "Chess Champ Finds Creativity in Krishna Lifestyle; Accomplished Chess Competitor Leads Life as a Hare Krishna Devotee." *ISKCON World Review* 6 (July 1986): 8–9.

———. [Nandini.] "Devotee Vowed to Fast until Her Fiance Released." *ISKCON World Review* 5 (December 1985): 8–9.

———. "Ecstatic Ratha-yatra Liberates New York City." *ISKCON World Review* 3 (November 1983): 1.

———. [Nandini.] "Editorial: 'Monkey' Book Unfair to Hare Krishna Movement." *ISKCON World Review* 8 (November 1988): 1.

———. [Nandini and Bill Muster.] "Former ISKCON Member's Slaying under Investigation." *ISKCON World Review* 6 (August 1986): 3.

———. [Nandini.] "Friendly Critic's View of ISKCON." *ISKCON World Review* 7 (August 1987): 1, 6.

———. [Nandini.] "GBC Meeting Raises Vital Issues for ISKCON." *ISKCON World Review* 6 (December 1986): 5.

———. "GBC 'No New Guru' Vote Based on Committee Report." *ISKCON World Review* 1 (June 1981): 16.

———. [Nandini and Uddhava.] "Hare Krishna Devotee Elected." *ISKCON World Review* 4 (April 1985): 1.

———. [Nandini.] "Hare Krishna Movement Wins Legal Status in Soviet Russia." *ISKCON World Review* 7 (December 1987): 1.

———. [Nandini.] "High Court Judge Arranges Meeting: ISKCON Leader Hosted by Zambian President Kaunda." *ISKCON World Review* 5 (September 1985): 8–9.

———. [Nandini.] "In Memory [of Sridhar Swami]." *ISKCON World Review* 7 (October 1987): 3.

———. [Nandini.] "Interview: ISKCON Faces Dilemma of Devotee Lifestyle." *ISKCON World Review* 7 (March 1988): 1.

———. "ISKCON Gets Three New Initiating Gurus." *ISKCON World Review* 1 (February–May 1982): 3.

———. [Nandini.] "ISKCON Newspaper Expands Coverage." *ISKCON World Review* 6 (December 1986): 2.

———. [Nandini.] "*IWR* Announces New Editorial Policy." *ISKCON World Review* 7 (July 1987): 2.

———. [Nandini.] "IWR Interview: Gurukula Today in Dallas." *ISKCON World Review* 8 (November 1988): 2, 6–7.

———. [Nandini.] "Jaya Krishna Dasa Awarded International Chess Masters Title." *ISKCON World Review* 6 (January–February 1987): 7.

———. "*Life* Ad Hinges on Krishna's Kids." *ISKCON World Review* 1 (January 1982): 2.

———. [Nandini.] "Mauritius: The First Vedic Country?" *ISKCON World Review* 2 (September 1982): 2.

———. [Nandini.] "New Vrindaban Topic of Major News Articles." *ISKCON World Review* 7 (July 1987): 3.

———. [Nandini.] "Palace of Gold: Dubbed a 'Photographer's Dream.'" *ISKCON World Review* 6 (June 1986): 3.

———. [Nandini]. "Psychological Study: What Makes a Hare Krishna Devotee Tick?" *ISKCON World Review* 6 (September 1986): 7.

———. "Readers Rave over *Life* Cover." *ISKCON World Review* 1 (May 1981): 2.

———. [Nandini.] "Remembering Jayananda: Servant of Prabhupada." *ISKCON World Review* 3 (May 1984): 14.

———. [Nandini.] "Srila Bhaktipada Regaining Health in New Vrindaban." *ISKCON World Review* 5 (December 1985): 1.

———. [Nandini.] "Weiss's Psychological Study: Scientific Fact, Not Flattery." *ISKCON World Review* 6 (September 1986): 2.

———. [Nandini.] "West Virginia Jury Convicts Drescher." *ISKCON World Review* 6 (November 1986): 5.

Jayatirtha, ed. Translated by Jaya Sacinandana. *The Process of Deity Worship* (Arcana-paddhati). Los Angeles: Bhaktivedanta Book Trust, 1978.

Johnson, Hillary. "Children of a Harsh Bliss." *Life* (April 1980): 44–51.

Johnson, Janis. "Religious Beggars Criticized." *Washington Post,* January 1, 1975.

Kapoor, O. B. L. *The Philosophy and Religion of Sri Chaitanya.* New Delhi: Munshiram Manoharlal, 1977.

"Kary Will Harry Krishnas No More." *New York Daily News,* July 11, 1983.

Keating, Bern. *The Legend of the* Delta Queen. New Orleans: Delta Queen Steamboat Co., 1986.

Kenny, Mary. "New Stars Shine Bright." *London Daily Mail,* January 2, 1986.

King, Wayne. "Krishna Arms Caches Draw Police Scrutiny in California." *New York Times,* June 9, 1980.

———. "Religious Panhandlers Stirring Anger at Airports." *New York Times,* December 22, 1976.

Knott, Kim. *My Sweet Lord: The Hare Krishna Movement.* Wellingborough, U.K.: Aquarian Press, 1986.

Kozel, Ed. "Settlement Refutes Philadelphia Inquirer Statements: Hare Krishnas Deny Arsenal Possession." *Wheeling* [W.Va.] *News-Register,* January 5, 1979.

"Krishna Sect Denies Policy on Guns." *New York Times,* June 17, 1980.

Kroll, Robert. "Probes Undercut Krishna Image." *North East Bay* [Calif.] *Independent and Gazette,* September 15, 1979.

Kunti Dasi. "Clinton Meets Devotees at Washington Presentation." *ISKCON World Review* 14 (November–December 1995): 1.

Lindsey, Robert. "California Slaying Case Involves Ex-Mafia Figures and Krishnas." *New York Times,* November 2, 1977.

Lines, Charles. "Croome and Krishna." *Warwickshire and Worcestershire* [U.K.] *Life,* August 1982, 42–43.

Lunnen, Connie. "*Gurukula:* The Making of a Krishna Devotee, from Cradle to Grave." *Houston Chronicle Magazine,* January 20, 1974.

MacRobert, Alan. "The Krishna Question." *Boston Magazine* (December 1980): 172–74, 214–20.

Mankin, Eric. "Chanting for Dollars." *New West,* September 10, 1979, 89–94.

Maxwell, Evan. "Eleven Linked to Krishna Cult Indicted in Narcotics Case." *Los Angeles Times,* November 16, 1979.

———. "Mystics and Mobsters: Focus on a Curious Alliance." *Los Angeles Times,* December 18, 1977

Megan, Kathy. "Krishna and Community: A Quiet Truce of Separation." *Charleston* [W.Va.] *Gazette,* June 19, 1981.

Mukunda. "Associated Press Publishes FATE's 'Changing Bodies.'" *IPANL,* no. 2 (1978): 6.

———. "Government Donates Land for Temple." *IPANL,* no. 8 (1979): 8.

———. "Interview with Ravindra Svarupa: 'GBC Should Abandon Elitism.'" *ISKCON World Review* 7 (September 1987): 1.

———. "Krishna Constricts the *Life* Asura [Demon]." *IPANL* 3 (October 1980): 9–10.

———. "Satsvarupa Dasa Goswami Airs Views on ISKCON Guru Worship." *ISKCON World Review* 6 (December 1986): 3.

Mukunda, ed. *Who Are They?* Los Angeles: Bhaktivedanta Book Trust, 1982.

Muster, Bill. *World Travelers Almanac.* New York: Rand McNally, 1976.

Muster, Nori J. *The Story of the* Delta Queen: *A Legislative and Corporate History from the Files of Bill N. Muster and Richard C. Simonton.* Cincinnati: Cincinnati Historical Society, 1989.

Nandini [Nori J. Muster]. "*ISKCON World Review:* Story of a Hare Krishna Newspaper." Presented to North American Governing Body Commission, Dallas, September 28, 1988. Author's collection.

———. "Women in Krishna Consciousness: A Psychological Perspective." Presented at ISKCON Current Affairs Seminar, Towaco, N.J., June 1988. Author's collection.

Nordheimer, Jon. "Young Ascetics Honor Lord Krishna." *New York Times,* September 6, 1972.

"$125 Million Lawsuit Filed against Krishna Leader and Other Sect Officials." *Cult Awareness Network News,* September 1994.

Parker, Robert Miles. *L.A.* New York: Harcourt Brace Jovanovich, 1984.

Paskevich, Michael. "Bovan Case: Krishnas File Suit to Erase 'Link.'" *Orange County* [Calif.] *Daily Pilot,* December 1, 1977.

Pement, Eric. "Hare Krishna Starved My Soul." In *Escape from Darkness.* Edited by James R. Adair and Ted Miller. Wheaton: Victor Books, 1982.

Perry, Charles. "Hare Krishna Founder Dies." *Rolling Stone,* January 12, 1978.

Public Relations Center, Inc. *Public Relations Report for International Society for Krishna Consciousness.* Chicago: Public Relations Center, Inc., 1975.

"Pyramid House Talks" recording and transcript (December 3, 1980) at the Pyramid Center for Krishna Consciousness, Topanga, Calif.

Ramesvara. "Focusing on the Real Issue." *ISKCON Public Affairs Newsletter,* no. 8 (1979): 1–2.

————. "The Hard Rain of Karma." *Back to Godhead* 15 (October 1980): 21, 29–30.

————. "'There Cannot Be Peace.'" *Back to Godhead* 19 (July 1984): 24–27.

Ramesvara, and Subhananda. "On the Position of the Initiating Guru in the Western USA Zone." Position paper submitted to the GBC, July 1980. Author's collection.

Rasamanjari, and Amrita. "Conversation at Santa Monica Mall Between Ramesvara Swami, Rasamanjari and Amrita." May 7, 1986. Author's collection.

Ravindra Svarupa. "'Under My Order': Reflections on the Guru in ISKCON." June 1985. Author's collection.

Remensky, Carl. "Krishna Sect Splintering in Top Ranks." *Pittsburgh Post-Gazette,* December 5, 1985.

Rochford, E. Burke, Jr. "Factionalism, Group Defection, and Schism in the Hare Krishna Movement." *Journal for the Scientific Study of Religion* 28, no. 2 (1989): 162–79.

————. *Hare Krishna in America.* New Brunswick: Rutgers University Press, 1985.

Roszak, Theodore. *Unfinished Animal: The Aquarian Frontier and the Evolution of Consciousness.* London: Faber and Faber, 1976.

Rothchild, John, and Susan Berns Wolf. *The Children of the Counterculture.* Garden City: Doubleday, 1976.

Rouvales, Christina. "Krishna Chief Blames 'Crazy Man' for Attack." *Pittsburgh Post-Gazette,* December 5, 1985.

Ryon, Ruth. "Krishna Sect Deep into Real Estate." *Los Angeles Times,* November 26, 1978.

Satsvarupa. *Prabhupada: He Built a House in Which the Whole World Can Live.* Los Angeles: Bhaktivedanta Book Trust, 1983.

————. *Prabhupada Lilamrita.* Los Angeles: Bhaktivedanta Book Trust, 1979.

————. "Secretary to a Pure Devotee." *Back to Godhead,* no. 68 (1974): 24–28.

Schmemann, Serge. "Soviet Says Hare Krishna Cloaks C.I.A. Daggers." *New York Times,* July 31, 1983.

Schumach, Murray. "Judge Dismisses Charges in Hare Krishna 'Brainwashing' Case." *New York Times,* March 18, 1977.

Schumacher, Edward. "West Virginia Marvels at Indian Palace." *New York Times,* September 3, 1979.

Senesi, Ed. "Inside ISKCON." *Forward* 4, no. 1 (1981): 1, 8, 10–11.

————. "Inside ISKCON." *Forward* 4, no. 2 (1981): 3, 8, 14–15.

Shabad, Theodore. "Hare Krishna Chant Unsettles Soviets." *New York Times,* March 15, 1982.

Sheppard, R. Z. "Good Hustle, Bad Karma." *Time,* November 7, 1988.

Shinn, Larry D. *The Dark Lord: Images of the Hare Krishnas in America.* Philadelphia: Westminster Press, 1987.

Sigall, Edward. "A Crackpot School That Teaches Kids to Die." *Personality* [South Africa], February 7, 1975.

Smith, Don, and John Penney. "Possible St. Denis' Remains Are Discovered in Stream Bed Grave." *Wheeling* [W.Va.] *News-Register,* January 7, 1987.

Spane, Ivan. "Death of a Spiritual Master." *Yoga Journal,* May–June 1978.

"Split: Pop Chameleon Annie Lennox Gives up on Sects as She Sheds Hare Krishna Hubby." *People,* May 20, 1985, 66.

Subhananda. "A Pilgrimage Journal: Impressions of India." *Back to Godhead* 15 (March–April 1980): 11–13, 30.

———. *A Request to the Media: Please Don't Lump Us In.* Los Angeles: Bhaktivedanta Book Trust, 1978.

Suhotra. "Two Faces of Krishna: To Those Who Refuse to Love His Smiling, Gentle Form, Krishna Shows Another." *Back to Godhead* 16 (November 1981): 21–22.

Sulochan. *The Guru Business.* Prepublication chapters distributed by Devotee Access Services, Berkeley, 1985–86.

Suplee, Curt. "The Temple of Tomorrowland, Heirs of Detroit's Assembly Line, Investing in Hare Krishna." *Washington Post,* May 27, 1983.

"Swami's Troubles Tarnish Life at 'Palace of Gold.'" *Los Angeles Times,* May 7, 1994.

Trippett, Frank. "Troubled Karma for the Krishnas: The Murder of a Disgruntled Disciple Sparks a Grand Jury Probe." *Time,* September 1, 1986.

Urmila. "A Woman's Place Is in Krishna Consciousness." Presented the ISKCON Current Affairs Seminar, Towaco, N.J., June 1988.

"Vrindivan in the New World." *Illustrated Weekly of India,* April 27, 1980.

Warner, Dave. "W.Va. Krishnas Study of Contrasts: Controversy Surrounds Thousand-Acre Commune." *Pittsburgh Post-Gazette,* June 19, 1978.

Watts, Alan W. *The Joyous Cosmology.* Foreword by Timothy Leary and Richard Alpert. New York: Pantheon Books, 1962.

Wax, Judith. "Raise Your Hand if You're a Spirit Soul." *Harper's,* December 1974.

Weiss, Arnold S. "Mental Health and Personality Characteristics of Hare Krishna Devotees and Sympathizers as a Function of Acculturation into the Hare Krishna Movement." Presented at the California Professional School of Psychology, Los Angeles, July 1, 1985.

Welborn, Larry. "Kulik Tied Close to Krishna Boss." *Orange County Register,* November 10, 1977.

Index

Nori J. Muster grew up in Southern California and was graduated from the University of California, Santa Barbara, in 1978 with a degree in sociology. She met Hare Krishna devotees during her senior year of college and joined their temple the day after graduation. She worked in the public relations office of the International Society of Krishna Consciousness (ISKCON) until 1988, when she left the organization. She holds a master's degree in interdisciplinary studies from Western Oregon State College and is a freelance writer and an artist.

Larry D. Shinn is the president of Berea College, Berea, Kentucky, and the author or editor of six book-length works, among them *The Dark Lord: Cult Images and the Hare Krishnas in America.* He holds a Ph.D. in history from Princeton University, a B.D. from Drew Theological School, and a B.A. from Baldwin Wallace College.